The Civil Code of the People's Republic of China

Meng Wan · Feng Zhu · Benedict Amour ·
Hailong Tang

The Civil Code of the People's Republic of China

English Edition

Springer

Meng Wan
School of Law
Beijing Foreign Studies University
Beijing, China

Feng Zhu
Human Rights Research Center
of Shandong University
Qingdao, China

Benedict Amour
Seagon Intellectual Property Ltd.
Beijing, China

Hailong Tang
Seagon Intellectual Property Ltd.
Beijing, China

With Contribution by
Beidi Wan
University of the Arts London
London, UK

Hongyu Han
Legal Translation and Publication Center
Law Press China
Beijing, China

ISBN 978-981-19-2793-5 ISBN 978-981-19-2794-2 (eBook)
https://doi.org/10.1007/978-981-19-2794-2

Translation from the Chinese language edition:《中华人民共和国民法典》(大字条旨版) © Law Press China 2020. Published by Law Press China. All Rights Reserved.

This Springer imprint is published by the registered company Springer Nature Singapore Pte Ltd.
The registered company address is: 152 Beach Road, #21-01/04 Gateway East, Singapore 189721, Singapore

Acknowledgments

This translation is for reference only. In case of discrepancy between the English translation and the original Chinese text, the Chinese text shall prevail.

Table of Contents

Book Five Marriage and Family

Book Six Succession

Book Seven Tort Liability

Order of the President of the People's Republic of China

No.45

The Civil Code of the People's Republic of China, adopted at the Third Session of the Thirteenth National People's Congress of the People's Republic of China on May 28, 2020, is hereby promulgated and shall take effect as of January 1, 2021.

XI Jinping

President of the People's Republic of China

May 28, 2020

THE CIVIL CODE
OF
THE PEOPLE'S REPUBLIC OF CHINA

(Adopted at the Third Session of the Thirteenth National People's Congress on May 28, 2020)

Contents

Book One General Part

Chapter I General Provisions

Article 1 [Purposes of Codification][1]

This Code is hereby enacted per the Constitution of the People's Republic of China for the purposes of protecting legal rights and interests of civil law subject-persons, regulating civil law relations, preserving the social and economic order, serving the needs of developing socialism with Chinese characteristics, and advancing core socialist values[2].

Article 2 [Scope of Regulation]

This Civil Code regulates the personal and proprietary relationships as between civil law subject-persons who are [all] equal in status, to wit, natural persons, legal persons, and organizations without juridical personality.

Article 3 [Legal Protection of Civil Rights]

The personal rights, personality rights, proprietary rights, and other legal rights and interests of civil law subject-persons are protected by law, and no organization or individual may infringe them.

---

1 The contents in brackets herein are supplemented by translators.

2 The core socialist values: prosperity, democracy, civility and harmony are values that underpin the nation; freedom, equality, justice and rule of law are values that buttress the society; patriotism, dedication, good faith and amity are values that underlie individual conduct.

M. Wan et al., *The Civil Code of the People's Republic of China*,
https://doi.org/10.1007/978-981-19-2794-2_1

Article 4 [Principle of Equality]

All civil law subject-persons are of equal legal status while/in performing civil acts.

Article 5 [Principle of Free Will]

When performing civil acts, civil law subject-persons shall adhere to the principle of free will in creating, altering, or terminating civil law relations based on their own free volition.

Article 6 [Principle of Fairness]

Civil law subject-persons performing civil acts shall observe the principle of fairness, and reasonably clarify and define the rights and obligations of each party to such acts.

Article 7 [Principle of Good Faith]

When performing civil acts, civil law subject-persons shall adhere to the principle of good faith, practice honesty and fulfill their commitments.

Article 8 [Principle of Legality, Public Order and Sound Morals]

When performing civil acts, civil law subject-persons may not violate the law or offend against public order or sound morals.

Article 9 [Principle of Greening]

When performing civil acts, civil law subject-persons shall conduct themselves in a manner conducive to conservation of resources and protection of ecological environment.

Article 10 [Application of Norms]

Civil disputes are to be resolved per law; where the law makes no specific provisions, custom may apply if this does not offend against public order or sound morals.

Article 11 [Preferential Application of Lex Specialis]

Where other laws contain special provisions on civil relations, such laws shall prevail.

Article 12 [Territoriality]

The laws of the People's Republic of China apply to civil acts within the territory of the People's Republic of China. Where law provides otherwise, its provisions shall apply.

Chapter II Natural Persons

Section 1 Capacity to Enjoy Civil Rights and Engage in Civil Acts

Article 13 [Commencement and End of Natural Persons' Capacity for Civil Rights]

A natural person shall have the capacity to enjoy civil rights from the time of birth until the time of death and shall exercise such rights and assume civil obligations per law.

Article 14 [Equality of Natural Persons' Capacity for Civil Rights]

All natural persons have equal capacity for civil rights.

Article 15 [Criteria for Judging Time of Birth and Death of Natural Persons]

The time of birth and the time of death of a natural person shall be ascertained according to the time recorded on his/her birth certificate or death certificate or, in the absence thereof, per the time recorded in the natural person's household registration or other valid registration of identity. Where sufficient evidence is available to disprove the time recorded in such documents, the time such evidence proves shall serve as the criterion.

Article 16 [Special Protection of Fetal Interests]

Where the protection of a fetus' interests such as inheritance or receipt of gifts is involved, the fetus shall be deemed to have the capacity for civil rights. However, a stillborn fetus lacks such capacity *ab initio*.

Article 17 [Age Standard for Majority and Minority]

A natural person who has fully attained the age of eighteen is an adult. A natural person who has not fully attained the age of eighteen is a minor.

Article 18 [Persons with Full Capacity to Engage in Civil Juristic Acts]

An adult has full capacity to engage in civil juristic acts and may independently engage in them.

A minor aged sixteen or above who depends on the income from his/her own labor as a primary source of sustenance is deemed a person with full capacity to engage in civil juristic acts.

Article 19 [Minors with Limited Capacity to Engage in Civil Juristic Acts]

Minors aged eight or above have limited capacity to engage in civil juristic acts and may engage in them only through their legal agents or subject to their consent or ratification. However, such minors may independently engage in civil juristic acts that are purely beneficial to them or suitable to their age or intelligence.

Article 20 [Minors with No Capacity to Engage in Civil Juristic Acts]

Minors under the age of eight lack capacity to engage in civil juristic acts and may engage in civil juristic acts only through their legal agents.

Article 21 [Adults with No Capacity to Engage in Civil Juristic Acts]

Adults incapable of discerning [the consequences of] their acts lack capacity to engage in civil juristic acts and may only engage in civil juristic acts through their legal agents.

The preceding paragraph is applicable to minors aged eight or above who are incapable of discerning [the consequences of] their acts.

Article 22 [Adults with Limited Capacity to Engage in Civil Juristic Acts]

Adults incapable of fully discerning [the consequences of] their acts have limited capacity to engage in civil juristic acts and may engage in civil juristic acts only through their legal agents or subject to their consent or ratification, but such adults may independently engage in civil juristic acts that are solely beneficial to them or suited to their intelligence and mental health condition.

Article 23 [Legal Agents]

Guardians of persons who have no or limited capacity to engage in civil juristic acts are such persons' legal agents.

Article 24 [Determination of Persons Having No or Limited Capacity to Engage in Civil Juristic Acts and Restoration of Their Capacity to Engage in Civil Juristic Acts]

For adults who are incapable of fully discerning [the consequences of] their acts, any person having an interest in such [incapacitated] adults or a relevant organization may petition a people's court to declare such adults as persons lacking or with limited capacity to engage in civil juristic acts.

Where a people's court has designated such an adult as a person lacking or with limited capacity to engage in civil juristic acts, the people's court may, at the request of such person, another interested person or a relevant organization, declare such adult to recover either limited or full capacity to engage in civil juristic acts based on the recovery of his/her intelligence and mental soundness.

A relevant organization as referred to in this Article includes, *inter alia*, a residents' committee, a villagers' committee, a school, a medical institution, women's federation, disabled persons' federation, an organization legally established for seniors, or a bureau of civil affairs.

Article 25 [Domicile of Natural Persons]

The domicile of a natural person is his/her place of residence recorded in such person's household or other valid identification registration system; if a natural person's habitual residence is inconsistent with his/her [registered] domicile, the habitual residence shall be deemed the domicile.

Section 2 Guardianship

Article 26 [Legal Obligations as Between Parents and Children]

Parents bear the duty to raise, educate and protect their minor children.

Adult children bear the obligation to provide for, support and protect their parents.

Article 27 [Guardians of Minors]

The parents of minor children shall serve as their guardians.

Where the parents of a minor are deceased or lack the capacity to serve as his/her guardians, the following persons with such capacity shall assume the guardianship thereof in the sequence as follows:

1. The minor's paternal grandparents and maternal grandparents;

2. The minor's elder siblings; or

3. Another individual or organization willing to serve as the minor's guardian, subject to consent by the local residents' committee, villagers' committee, or bureau of civil affairs in the place where the minor is domiciled.

Article 28 [Guardians for Adults with No or Limited Capacity to Engage in Civil Juristic Acts]

Where an adult lacks or has limited capacity to engage in civil juristic acts, the following persons with the competence to do so shall serve as such incapacitated adult's guardian, in the sequence as follows:

1. The adult's spouse;
2. The adult's parent or child;
3. Any other near relative of the adult; or
4. Any other individual or organization willing to serve as the adult's guardian, subject to consent by the local residents' committee, villagers' committee or bureau of civil affairs in the place where the adult is domiciled.

Article 29 [Testamentary Guardians]

Parents who are guardians of a child may in their last will and testament appoint a person to serve as guardian for such child.

Article 30 [Guardianship by Agreement]

A guardian may be selected via an agreement between or among persons legally qualified to serve as guardians, but the true wishes of the ward are to be respected.

Article 31 [Resolution of Guardianship Disputes]

Where a dispute arises over the choice of a guardian, a guardian shall be appointed by the local residents' committee, villagers' committee, or bureau of civil affairs in the place where the ward is domiciled, and any party objecting to such appointment may apply to a people's court to appoint a guardian; interested parties may also directly petition a people's court to appoint a guardian.

When appointing a guardian, the residents' committee, villagers' committee, bureau of civil affairs or people's court shall respect the true wishes of the ward and appoint a guardian per the principle of best interests for the ward from among those persons who legally qualify.

Where a ward's personal, proprietary, and other legal rights and interests are not subject to any protection before a guardian is appointed per the first paragraph of this Article, the local residents' committee, villagers' committee or [other] relevant organization as provided in law or the bureau of civil affairs in the place where the ward is domiciled shall serve as interim guardian.

A guardian once appointed may not be substituted without authorization; if an appointed guardian is substituted without authorization, the responsibilities of such originally appointed guardian are not thereby released.

Article 32 [Public Guardian]

Where no person legally qualifies to serve as a guardian, the local bureau of civil affairs shall serve as the guardian, and the residents' committee or villagers' committee where the ward is domiciled, being capable of exercising guardianship, may also act as guardian.

Article 33 [Guardianship over Adults by Consultation]

Adults with current full capacity to engage in civil juristic acts may, in anticipation of future incapacity, and in consultation with such adults' near relatives or other individuals or organizations willing to serve as such adults' guardian, appoint guardian in writing for themselves who shall perform corresponding duties when such adults should become incapacitated in whole or in part from engaging in civil juristic acts.

Article 34 [Rights and Duties of Guardian and Interim Life Care Measures]

The duties of a guardian are to represent the ward in engaging in civil juristic acts and to safeguard such ward's personal and proprietary rights, and other lawful rights and interests.

Guardians' rights arising from the fulfillment of their duties as required by law are to be protected by law.

Guardians who fail to fulfill their duties or who harm legal rights or interests of their wards shall bear legal liability therefor.

When a guardian is temporarily unable to fulfill his/her duties due to the occurrence of a sudden emergency or other exigent situation, thereby leaving the ward in a situation devoid of life care, the local residents' committee, villagers' committee, or bureau of civil affairs in the place where the ward is domiciled shall arrange for necessary interim measures to provide such life care to the ward.

Article 35 [Principles and Requirements for Guardian's Fulfillment]

Guardians shall fulfill their duties based on the principle of best interests for the ward. Guardians may not dispose of their wards' property except to protect the interests of their wards.

When fulfilling their duties and making decisions relating to minors' interests, guardians of minors shall respect the latter's true wishes considered in the light of their age and intelligence.

When fulfilling their duties, guardians of adults shall respect the latter's true wishes to the greatest extent possible and ensure that these wards may engage in civil juristic acts suited to their intelligence and mental health condition and aid them in so doing. Guardians may not interfere in any matters which their wards are capable of independently handling.

Article 36 [Disqualification of Guardian]

Where a guardian engages in any of the following acts, a people's court shall, at the request of an interested individual or organization, disqualify the guardian, adopt necessary interim measures, and appoint a new guardian in the ward's best interests per law:

1. Engaging in any acts which severely harm the physical or mental health of the ward;

2. Neglecting to perform the duties of a guardian, or being unable to perform such duties, while refusing to delegate all or part of such duties to others, thereby leaving the ward in critical distress; or

3. Engaging in other acts which severely harm the ward's legal rights and interests.

An interested individual or organization as referred to in this Article includes any other person legally qualified to serve as a guardian, a residents' committee, villagers' committee, school, medical institution, women's federation, disabled persons' federation, child protection organization, organization legally formed for senior citizens, or bureau of civil affairs, etc.

Where the foregoing individual or organization other than the bureau of civil affairs, as referenced in the preceding paragraph, fails to promptly request a people's court to disqualify a guardian, the bureau of civil affairs shall make a request to the people's court.

Article 37 [Continuing Support Following Disqualification]

A parent, child, or spouse legally obligated to pay a ward child support, maintenance or alimony shall continue to perform such obligation(s) even after being disqualified to serve as a guardian by a people's court.

Article 38 [Restoration of Qualification as Guardian]

After the ward's parent or child has been disqualified as a guardian by a people's court for reasons other than the commission of an intentional crime against the ward, if such person demonstrates true repentance and reform, and applies to the people's court for reinstatement, the people's court may, in light of the actual circumstances and, per the precondition that the true wishes of the ward be respected, reinstate such person as guardian, and the guardianship between the ward and the guardian [subsequently] appointed by the people's court shall simultaneously terminate.

Article 39 [Circumstances for Termination of Guardianship]

A guardianship shall terminate under any of the following circumstances:

1. The ward has gained or recovered the full capacity to engage in civil juristic acts;
2. The guardian has lost the competence to serve as a guardian;
3. The ward or guardian dies; or
4. Under any other circumstance in which the people's court resolves to terminate the guardianship.

Where a ward still requires a guardian after the termination of such guardianship, a new guardian is to be appointed per law.

Section 3 Declaration of Missing Person and Declaration of Death

Article 40 [Conditions for Declaration of Missing Person]

Where a natural person's whereabouts have been unknown for two years, another person thereby affected may petition a people's court to declare such natural person a missing person.

Article 41 [Calculating Time of Whereabouts Becoming Unknown]

The period during which a natural person's whereabouts are unknown shall be calculated from the date when the natural person was last heard from. If a person goes missing in wartime, the time of his/her whereabouts becoming unknown shall be calculated from the date the war ends or from a date [otherwise] determined by a relevant authority.

Article 42 [Custodians of a Missing Person's Property]

A missing person's property shall be placed in the interim custody of his/her spouse, adult children, parents, or any other person willing to assume custody thereof.

Where a dispute arises over the interim custody of a missing person's property, or the persons listed in the preceding paragraph are unavailable for or incapacitated for such purpose, the property shall be placed in the interim custody of a person appointed by a people's court.

Article 43 [Duties of Custodian]

A custodian shall properly manage a missing person's property and safeguard his/her proprietary interests.

The taxes, debts, and other payment obligations due that are owed by a missing person shall be paid by the custodian from the missing person's property.

A custodian who causes loss of or damage to the property of a missing person intentionally or due to gross negligence shall be liable for compensation therefor.

Article 44 [Replacement of Custodian]

Where a custodian fails to fulfill the duties of a custodian, harms the proprietary rights or interests of the missing person, or becomes incapacitated, a person with an interest in the missing person may petition a people's court to replace such custodian.

A custodian with just cause may petition a people's court for his/her replacement.

Where a people's court replaces a custodian, the new custodian has the right to demand a prompt transfer of the relevant property with a property management report from the previous custodian.

Article 45 [Revocation of Declaration of a Person Missing]

Where a missing person reappears, a people's court shall, at the request of such person or an interested person thereof, revoke the missing person declaration.

A missing person who reappears has the right to demand that a custodian promptly return his/her property and provide a property custody report.

Article 46 [Conditions for Declaration of Presumed Death]

An interested person may petition a people's court to declare the presumed death of a natural person under either of the following circumstances:

1. The natural person's whereabouts have been unknown for four years; or

2. The natural person's whereabouts have been unknown for two years because of an accident.

The two-year requirement for a natural person to be declared dead does not apply if the person's whereabouts have become unknown because of an accident and a competent authority certifies that for such natural person to be still alive is impossible.

Article 47 [Preferred Declaration of Presumed Death]

Where an interested person petitions a people's court to declare the presumed death of a natural person, whereas another person affected petitions it to declare the person missing, the people's court shall declare the person dead if the conditions therefor as provided in this Code are met.

Article 48 [Presumed Date of Death]

In the event of a person declared dead, the date when a people's court renders judgment declaring his/her death shall be deemed the date for such person's [presumed] death; for a person declared dead because his/her whereabouts are unknown due to an accident, the date of the occurrence of the accident shall be deemed the date of death.

Article 49 [Effect of Civil Juristic Acts Performed During Presumed Death]

The declaration of the death of a natural person who has not [actually] died shall not influence the effectiveness of the civil juristic acts the person performed during the period in which such person was declared dead.

Article 50 [Revocation of Declaration of Presumed Death]

Where a person declared dead reappears, a people's court shall, on petition of the said person or an interested person, revoke the declaration of presumed death.

Article 51 [Effect of Presumption of Death and Revocation Thereof upon Marriage]

A marital relationship with a person declared dead ceases to exist from the date of the declaration of presumed death. If the declaration of death is revoked, the foregoing marital relationship shall automatically revive from the date of revocation of the declaration of presumed death, except where the spouse has remarried or asserts in writing to the marriage registry an unwillingness to revive the marriage.

Article 52 [Effect of Revocation of Presumed Death upon Adoption]

Where a child of a person declared dead has been legally adopted by others during the effective period of the declaration of presumed death, the person declared dead may not claim after revocation of the declaration of presumed death that the adoption is invalid on the grounds that the child was adopted without his/her consent.

Article 53 [Revocation of Presumed Death and Restitution of Property]

When a declaration of the presumed death of a person is revoked, the person has the right to demand that those civil law subject-persons who have obtained his/her property under Book VI of this Code restore the property or make proper compensation if the property is unable to be restored.

Where an interested person conceals the true circumstances and [thereby] causes a natural person to be declared dead so as to obtain the latter's property, the interested person shall, in addition to restoring the wrongfully taken property, compensate any loss thereby incurred.

Section 4 Individual Industrial and Commercial Households and Rural-Land Contractual Management Households

Article 54 [Definition of Individual Industrial and Commercial Household]

A natural person who operates an industrial or commercial business may register it per law as an individual industrial and commercial household. An individual industrial and commercial household may take a trade name.

Article 55 [Definition of Rural-Land Contractual Management Household]

Members of a rural economic collective who, per law, have been granted a contract to operate a parcel of rural land and who engage in the operation of the land on a household basis are rural-land contractual management households.

Article 56 [Rules for Payment of Debts]

The debts of an individual industrial and commercial household shall be paid from the property of the individual who operates the business or the family property if the business is operated by a family, or, if it is impossible to distinguish whether the business is operated by an individual or by his/her family, from the family property.

The debts of a rural-land contractual management household shall be paid from the property of the household that is operating on the contracted rural land, or from the portion of the property of the family members actually engaged in such operation.

Chapter III Legal Persons

Section 1 General Rules

Article 57 [Definition of Legal Person]

A legal person is an entity or organization that possesses the capacity to enjoy civil rights and to engage in civil juristic acts, and that independently enjoys civil rights and assumes civil obligations per law.

Article 58 [Legal Requirements for Formation of Legal Person]

A legal person shall be established per law.

A legal person shall have its own legal name, governance structure, domicile, and property or funds. The specific conditions and procedures for the establishment of a legal person shall be governed by [applicable] laws and administrative regulations.

Where laws or administrative regulations provide that the formation of a legal person is subject to the approval of a relevant authority, such provisions shall apply.

Article 59 [Commencement and End of Legal Person's Capacity]

A legal person's capacity to enjoy civil rights and to engage in civil juristic acts commences with its formation and ends with its termination.

Article 60 [Assumption of Civil Liability by Legal Person]

A legal person shall independently assume civil liability to the extent of all its property.

Article 61 [Definition of Legal Representative and Legal Consequences of His/Her Acts]

A person responsible for representing a legal person in performing civil acts per law or per the legal person's articles of association is its legal representative.

A legal person shall assume the legal consequences of the civil acts which the legal representative performs in the legal person's name.

No restraints on the legal representative's power to represent the legal person which are set forth in its articles of association or [otherwise] imposed by the governing body of the legal person may be asserted against a *bona fide* counterparty.

Article 62 [Assumption of Liability from Legal Representative's Tort]

Where the legal representative of a legal person inflicts harm on another person while performing his/her duties, the legal person shall bear the civil liability thereby incurred.

After assuming such civil liability, the legal person has the right to indemnification, per law or its articles of association, against its legal representative who is at fault.

Article 63 [Domicile of Legal Person]

The domicile of a legal person is the place where its principal administrative office is seated. If a legal person is required by law to be registered, the locus of its principal administrative office shall be registered as its domicile.

Article 64 [Registration of Changes with Legal Person]

Where any change occurs with respect to any item that has been registered during the term of the existence of a legal person, the legal person shall apply to the registry for corresponding modification of its registration per law.

Article 65 [Legal Consequences of Discrepancy Between Actual and Registered Circumstances of Legal Person]

The actual circumstances of a legal person which are inconsistent with those recorded upon register may not be asserted as a defense against a *bona fide* counterparty.

Article 66 [Publicizing Registered Information]

The registry shall, per law, publicize promptly a legal person's relevant registration information.

Article 67 [Rights and Obligations of Legal Person Following Merger and Division]

Where a legal person merges, the surviving legal person shall enjoy the rights and assume the obligations of such legal person.

Where a legal person divides, the rights of such legal person shall be enjoyed and its obligations assumed jointly and severally by the legal persons flowing from the division, unless its creditors and debtors agree otherwise.

Article 68 [Occasions for Termination of Legal Person]

A legal person shall terminate after it has completed liquidation and de-registration per law for any of the following reasons:

1. The legal person being dissolved;

2. The legal person being declared bankrupt; or

3. For any other reason as provided for in law.

Where laws or administrative regulations provide that the termination of a legal person is subject to approval by a relevant authority, such provisions shall apply.

Article 69 [Occasions for Dissolution of Legal Person]

A legal person shall be dissolved under any of the following circumstances:

1. The term set forth in its articles of association expires, or any other cause for dissolution provided for in the articles of association arises;

2. The legal person's governing body resolves to dissolve the legal person;

3. The legal person needs to be dissolved because of a merger or division;

4. The legal person's business license or registration certificate is revoked per law, or the legal person has been ordered to close or dissolve; or

5. Any other circumstance prescribed by law.

Article 70 [Post-Dissolution Liquidation of Legal Person]

Where a legal person is dissolved for reasons other than a merger or division, the persons with the duty to liquidate it shall promptly form a liquidation team to liquidate the legal person.

Members of the legal person's executive or decision-making body such as directors or councilors, shall be charged with the duty to liquidate the legal person. If laws or administrative regulations provide otherwise, such provisions shall apply.

Those charged with the duty to liquidate the legal person who fail to perform their duty in time and thereby inflict damage or loss on others shall assume civil liability therefor; a competent authority or an interested person may petition a people's court to appoint proper persons to form a liquidation team to liquidate the legal person.

Article 71 [Legal Basis for Liquidation]

The procedure for liquidating a legal person and the authority of a liquidation team shall be subject to the provisions of relevant laws, and, in the absence thereof, relevant provisions of corporate laws shall apply *mutatis mutandis*.

Article 72 [Legal Status amid Liquidation, Post-Liquidation Disposal of Property and Termination of Legal Person]

A legal person shall continue in existence during the period of its liquidation but may not engage in any acts unrelated thereto.

Any remaining post-liquidation assets of a legal person shall be distributed per its articles of association or a resolution passed by its governing body. If law provides otherwise, its provisions shall apply.

A legal person terminates when its liquidation and de-registration conclude; a legal person not required by law to be registered ceases to exist on completion of liquidation.

Article 73 [Bankruptcy of Legal Person]

A legal person declared bankrupt terminates on completion of its bankruptcy liquidation and de-registration per law.

Article 74 [Branches of Legal Person and Assumption of Liability]

A legal person may establish branches per law. If laws or administrative regulations provide that such a branch must be registered, such provisions shall apply.

Where a branch of a legal person engages in civil acts in its own name, the legal person shall bear any civil liability/debts thereby incurred, which may be paid first from the assets the branch manages but the legal person must supply deficiency, if any.

Article 75 [Consequences of Promotion of Legal Person]

The legal consequences of the civil acts a corporate promoter engages in to form a legal person shall be assumed by the legal person, or, if no legal person forms, by the promoter or promoters. In the event of two or more promoters, they shall enjoy joint creditor's rights and assume joint and several liability.

Where promoters engage in civil acts in their own name in forming a legal person and thereby incur civil liability, a third-party creditor may elect to demand that either the legal person or the promoter(s) assume such liability.

Section 2 For-Profit Legal Persons

Article 76 [Definition and Types of For-Profit Legal Persons]

A legal person formed for the purpose of earning profits and distributing them among its shareholders and other investors is a for-profit legal person.

For-profit legal persons include limited liability companies, joint-stock companies limited by shares, and other enterprise legal persons.

Article 77 [Formation of For-Profit Legal Person]

A for-profit legal person forms via its registration per law.

Article 78 [Business License of For-Profit Legal Person]

A legally formed for-profit legal person shall be issued a business license by a registry. The date of issue of the business license shall be the date on which the for-profit legal person forms.

Article 79 [Articles of Association of For-Profit Legal Person]

Articles of association shall be made per law for a for-profit legal person to be established.

Article 80 [Governing Body of For-Profit Legal Person]

A for-profit legal person shall create a governing body.

The governing body shall exercise the authority to amend the legal person's articles of association, elect or replace members of its executive and supervisory bodies, and perform other responsibilities as the articles of association confer.

Article 81 [Executive Body of For-Profit Legal Person]

A for-profit legal person shall constitute an executive body.

The executive body shall have the authority to convene meetings of the governing body, determine the legal person's business and investment plans, decide the establishment of an internal management structure, and perform other functions and powers as provided in the legal person's articles of association.

Where the executive body of a legal person is the board of directors or the executive director, the chairman of the board of directors, executive director, or manager, shall be the legal representative, as the articles of association provide. If no board of directors is constituted or no executive director is appointed, the person charged with principal responsibilities per the legal person's articles of association shall be the legal person's executive body and legal representative. .

Article 82 [Supervisory Body of For-Profit Legal Person]

Where a for-profit legal person creates an oversight body such as a board of supervisors or a supervisor, this oversight body shall have, per law, the authority to inspect the legal person's financial affairs and oversee the acts of members of its executive body and senior managers in performing their duties, and exercise any other authority as provided in the legal person's articles of association.

Article 83 [Liabilities of Investors for Abuse of Rights]

Investors in a for-profit legal person may not abuse their investor rights to harm the interests of the legal person or those of other investors. Civil liability shall be imposed per law for abuse of such investor rights which harms the legal person or other investors.

Investors in a for-profit legal person may not abuse the legal person's independent position and their own limited liability to harm the interests of the legal person's creditors. Investors who abuse the legal person's independent position or their own limited liability to evade debts and thereby seriously harm the interests of the legal person's creditors shall be jointly and severally liable for the legal person's [corresponding] debts.

Article 84 [Restrictions on Improper Use of Affiliated Relationship]

Controlling investors, actual controllers, directors, supervisors, and senior management officers of a for-profit legal person may not impair the legal person's interests by taking advantage of any affiliated relationship and shall compensate any loss the legal person thereby incurs.

Article 85 [Invalidation of Resolutions]

Where the procedure(s) for convening a meeting of the legal person's governing or executive body to pass a resolution, or the voting method for such resolution, violates laws, administrative regulations, or the legal person's articles of association, or the content of such resolution contravenes the legal person's articles of association, an investor in such for-profit legal person may petition a people's court to invalidate such resolution. However, any civil law relations already formed between the legal person and a *bona fide* counterparty based on such resolution shall remain unaffected thereby.

Article 86 [General Obligations of For-Profit Legal Person]

A for-profit legal person shall, while engaging in its operating activities, observe business ethics, ensure the security of transactions, subject itself to governmental and public supervision and assume its social responsibilities.

Section 3 Non-Profit Legal Persons

Article 87 [Definition and Types of Non-Profit Legal Persons]

A non-profit legal person is one formed for the purpose of the public weal or other non-profit purpose, and which does not distribute any profits to its donors, promoters, or members.

Non-profit legal persons include, *inter alia*, public institutions, social organizations, foundations, and social service institutions.

Article 88 [Formation of Public-Institution Legal Person]

When meeting the requirements of a legal person and created to serve the needs of economic and social development and provide public interest services, a public institution forms into a public-institution legal person when it registers per law; if it is not required by law to undergo legal person registration, it qualifies as a public-institution legal person as of the date on which it forms.

Article 89 [Structure of Public-Institution Legal Person and Legal Representative Thereof]

Where a public-institution legal person creates a council, the council shall be its decision-making body, except where law provides otherwise. The legal representative of a public-institution legal person shall be determined per the provisions of laws and administrative regulations or the legal person's articles of association.

Article 90 [Formation of Social Organization Legal Person]

A social organization based upon the common will of its members for a public weal aim or for a non-profit aim such as furthering the common interests of its members, shall attain the status of a social organization legal person if it meets the requirements for a legal person and is legally registered as such. If not required by law to undergo legal person registration, it shall attain the status of a social organization legal person as of the date of its formation.

Article 91 [Constitution and Structure of Social Organization Legal Person]

Articles of association shall be made per law for a social organization legal person to be established.

A social organization legal person shall constitute a governing body such as a members' assembly or a congress of its members' representatives.

A social organization legal person shall set up an executive body such as a council. The chairman of the council, the president of the organization, or an individual with similar authority shall serve as the legal representative of the legal person per its articles of association.

Article 92 [Formation of Endowment Legal Person]

When meeting the requirements of a legal person, a foundation or a social services institution or a similar institution endowed with donated property for the purpose of furthering the public weal qualifies as an endowment legal person as of the date it registers as such.

When meeting the requirements of a legal person, a site legally established to hold religious activities may apply to register as a legal person and qualifies as an endowment legal person as of the date it registers as such. Laws and administrative regulations on religious sites shall apply thereto.

Article 93 [Constitution and Structure of Endowment Legal Person]

Articles of association shall be formulated per law to form an endowment legal person.

An endowment legal person shall set up a decision-making body such as a council or other form of democratic management body, and an executive body. The chairman of the council or a person with similar authority shall serve as its legal representative per its articles of association.

An endowment legal person shall set up a supervisory body such as a board of supervisors.

Article 94 [Rights of Donors]

Endowment donors have the right to inquire into and offer comments and suggestions on the use and management of the property they have donated to an endowment legal person, and the latter shall respond promptly and truthfully.

Where a decision is made by the decision-making body, executive body or the legal representative of an endowment legal person, and the procedure for making the decision contravenes laws, administrative regulations, or the legal person's articles of association, or the content of the decision violates the articles of association, a donor or any other interested person or the competent authority may petition a people's court to invalidate such decision, but any civil juristic relationship already formed between the endowment legal person and a *bona fide* counterparty based on such a decision shall be unaffected thereby.

Article 95 [Disposal of Remaining Assets upon Termination of Non-Profit Legal Person]

Where a non-profit legal person formed with the aim of [furthering] the public weal terminates, it may not distribute its remaining assets to its donors, founders, or members. The remaining assets shall continue to be used for the purpose of furthering the public weal based on the articles of association or a resolution adopted by its governing body; if it is not possible to dispose of such residual assets per the articles of association or a resolution by the governing body, a competent authority shall take charge of the transfer of the assets to another legal person with the same or a similar purpose and publish a notice to such effect to the public.

Section 4 Special Legal Persons

Article 96 [Types of Special Legal Persons]

As referenced in this Section, state agency legal persons, rural economic collective legal persons, urban and rural cooperative economic organization legal persons, and primary-level self-governing organization legal persons are special legal persons.

Article 97 [Formation of State Agency Legal Person]

An independently-funded state agency or a statutory agency that assumes administrative functions qualifies as a state agency legal person from the date on which it forms and may engage in the civil acts necessary for the performance of its functions.

Article 98 [Post-Termination Rights and Obligations of State Agency Legal Person]

A state agency legal person terminates when the state agency is closed, and its civil rights shall be enjoyed and its obligations assumed by the succeeding state agency legal person; in the absence of a succeeding state agency, these rights shall be enjoyed, and obligations assumed by the state agency legal person that has made the decision to close it.

Article 99 [Rural Economic Collective Legal Person]

A rural economic collective shall acquire the qualification as a legal person per law.

Any provision of laws or administrative regulations on rural economic collectives shall apply thereto.

Article 100 [Urban and Rural Cooperative Legal Person]

An urban or rural economic cooperative qualifies as a legal person per law.

Any laws or administrative regulations providing for urban and rural economic cooperatives shall apply thereto.

Article 101 [Primary-Level Self-Governing Organization Legal Person]

Urban residents' committees or villagers' committees, as primary-level self-governing organizations, acquire the status of legal persons and may engage in civil acts necessary for the performance of their functions.

Where no village economic collective has formed, a villagers' committee may, per law, perform the functions of a village economic collective.

Chapter IV Unincorporated Entities

Article 102 [Definition and Types of Unincorporated Entities]

An unincorporated entity is one which does not qualify as a legal person, but which may [nonetheless] engage in civil acts in its own name per law.

Entities without juridical personality include, *inter alia*, sole proprietorships, partnerships, and professional service firms that do not qualify as legal persons.

Article 103 [Procedures for Formation of Unincorporated Entities]

Entities without juridical personality shall register per provisions of law.

Any laws or administrative regulations providing that the formation of an unincorporated entity is subject to approval by a competent authority, shall govern.

Article 104 [Assumption of Liability by Unincorporated Entity]

Where an unincorporated entity becomes insolvent, its investors or founders shall assume unlimited liability for the debts of the entity, unless law provides otherwise.

Article 105 [Representative of Unincorporated Entity]

An unincorporated entity may designate one or more persons to represent it in engaging in civil acts.

Article 106 [Occasions for Dissolution of Unincorporated Entity]

An unincorporated entity shall be dissolved under any of the following circumstances:

1. The term prescribed in its articles of association expires or any other ground for dissolution as set forth in its articles of association arises;

2. Its investors or founders decide to dissolve it; or

3. Dissolution is required under any other circumstances as provided by law.

Article 107 [Liquidation of Unincorporated Entity]

Upon dissolution, an unincorporated entity shall be liquidated per law.

Article 108 [Mutatis Mutandis Application]

In addition to the provisions in this Chapter, those in Section 1 of Chapter III of this Book shall also apply to unincorporated entities *mutatis mutandis*.

Chapter V Civil Rights

Article 109 [Protection of Personal Liberty and Dignity]

The personal liberty and dignity of a natural person is protected by law.

Article 110 [Personal and Personality Rights of Civil Law Subject-Persons]

A natural person enjoys such rights as the right to life, right to bodily integrity, right to health, right to a name, right to likeness, right to reputation, right to honor, right to privacy, and right to freedom of marriage.

A legal person or an unincorporated entity enjoys the right to an entity name, right to reputation, and right to honor.

Article 111 [Legal Protection of Personal Information]

A natural person's personal information shall be protected by law. Any organization or individual that needs to access another person's personal information shall do so per law and guarantee the safety of such information, and may not illegally collect, use, process, or transmit such information, nor illegally trade, provide, or disclose such information

Article 112 [Protection of Personal Rights Related to Marriage and Family]

The personal rights of a natural person issuing from a marital or familial relationship are protected by law.

Article 113 [Equal Protection of Proprietary Rights]

The proprietary rights of civil law subject-persons are protected by law on an equal basis.

Article 114 [Definition and Types of Real Rights]

Civil law subject-persons enjoy real rights per law.

Real rights are the rights enjoyed by a right holder per law to directly and exclusively control a specific thing, which comprise ownership, usufruct, and security interest in collateral.

Article 115 [Subject Matter of Real Rights]

Things comprise immovables and movables. Where the law provides that a right shall be treated as a subject matter of property over which a real right lies, its provisions shall apply.

Article 116 [Principle of Statutory Jus in Rem[1]]

The types and contents of real rights are defined and limited by law.

Article 117 [Expropriation and Requisition]

Fair and reasonable compensation shall be paid where either immovable or movable property is expropriated or requisitioned in the public interest and per the scope of authority and procedure therefor prescribed by law.

Article 118 [Definition of Rights in Personam]

Civil law subject-persons enjoy rights *in personam* per law.

A right *in personam* is the right of an obligee to demand that a specific obligor engage in an act or refrain from an act based on a contract, tort, *negotiorum gestio*, unjust enrichment or otherwise by operation of law.

Article 119 [Binding Force of Contract]

A contract formed per law is legally binding on the parties thereto.

Article 120 [Assumption of Tort Liability]

Where a person's civil rights and interests are harmed by a tortious act, the injured person has the right to demand that the tortfeasor assume tort liability therefor.

---

1 I.e. *Numerus Clausus*.

Article 121 [Negotiorum Gestio[1]]

A person who, without a statutory or contractual obligation, manages another person's affairs to prevent the latter from suffering loss of interests, has the right to demand that the person who receives benefit therefrom reimburse the necessary expenses thus incurred.

Article 122 [Unjust Enrichment]

Where a person obtains an unjust enrichment without a legal cause, the person suffering a loss thereby is entitled to demand restitution thereof.

Article 123 [Definition of Intellectual Property Rights]

Civil law subject-persons enjoy intellectual property rights per law.

Intellectual property rights are the exclusive rights right holders enjoy per law in the following subject matters:

1. Works;
2. Inventions, new utility models, or designs;
3. Trademarks;
4. Geographic indications;
5. Trade secrets;
6. Layout designs of integrated circuits;
7. New plant varieties; and
8. Other subject matter as provided by law.

Article 124 [Right to Succession]

A natural person has the right to succession per law.

Private property a natural person legally owns may be inherited per law.

---

1 I.e. Management of Affair Without Mandate or Obligation.

Article 125 [Investment Rights]

Civil law subject-persons enjoy equity rights and other investment rights per law.

Article 126 [Other Civil Law Rights]

Civil law subject-persons enjoy other civil rights and interests per law.

Article 127 [Protection of Data and Virtual Assets]

Where laws particularly provide for the protection of data and virtual online assets, their provisions shall apply.

Article 128 [Special Protection of Civil Rights]

Where laws particularly provide for the protection of civil rights of minors, the elderly, the disabled, women, or consumers, their provisions shall apply.

Article 129 [Means of Acquiring Civil Rights]

Civil rights may be acquired via civil juristic acts, *de facto* acts, events provided by law, or other means prescribed by law.

Article 130 [Enjoyment of Civil Rights per Free Will and Law]

Civil law subject-persons shall exercise civil rights based on their own free will per law and free from interference.

Article 131 [Consistency of Rights and Obligations]

While exercising their civil rights, civil law subject-persons shall perform their obligations prescribed by law or as agreed with other parties.

Article 132 [No Abuse of Civil Rights]

No civil law subject-persons may abuse the civil rights and harm the interests of the State or those of the public, or lawful rights and interests of others.

Chapter VI Civil Juristic Acts

Section 1 General Rules

Article 133 [Definition of Civil Juristic Act]

A civil juristic act is one via which a civil law subject-person creates, alters, or terminates a civil law relationship via an expression of intent.

Article 134 [Consummation of Civil Juristic Act]

A civil juristic act may be consummated through a meeting of the minds of two or more parties, or by one party's unilateral expression of intent.

Where a legal person or an unincorporated entity adopts a resolution per the official discussion method and voting procedure prescribed by law or in its articles of association, such a resolution is a consummated civil juristic act.

Article 135 [Forms of Civil Juristic Acts]

A civil juristic act may be effectuated in writing or orally or in any other form; where a specific form is required by laws or administrative regulations, or agreed to by the parties, the act shall be executed in such form.

Article 136 [Time of Civil Juristic Act Becoming Effective]

Unless otherwise provided by law or agreed to by the parties, a civil juristic act takes effect at the time of its consummation.

An actor who engages in a civil juristic act may not alter or revoke the act unjustifiably, except doing so in compliance with law or with the counterparty's consent.

Section 2 Expression of Intent

Article 137 [Time of Expression of Intent Becoming Effective Against Counterparty]

An expression of intent in an oral communication takes effect from the time the person to whom the intent is expressed becomes aware of its content.

An expression of intent in a form other than an oral communication takes effect from the time it reaches the counterparty. Where such an expression of intent is made in non-oral form using an electronic data message format and the counterparty has designated a specific data-receiving system, it takes effect from the time the data message enters the system; if no data-receiving system is specifically designated, it takes effect from the time the counterparty knows or ought to have known that the data message has entered his/her system. Where the parties agree otherwise on the effective time of the expression of intent in the form of an electronic data message, their agreement shall apply.

Article 138 [Time of Unilateral Expression of Intent Becoming Effective]

Where an expression of intent is not made to any specific counterparty, it takes effect upon completion of the expression. If law provides otherwise, its provisions shall apply.

Article 139 [Time of Expression of Intent via Public Notice Becoming Effective]

An expression of intent made via a public notice takes effect at the time the public notice is announced.

Article 140 [Modes of Making Expression of Intent]

An actor engaging in a juristic act may make an expression of intent either expressly or tacitly.

Silence shall be deemed an expression of intent only when law so provides, the parties so agree, or the parties' trade usage so allows.

Article 141 [Withdrawal of Expression of Intent]

An actor may withdraw an expression of intent. The notice of withdrawal of the expression of intent must reach the counterparty before or at the same time as the expression of intent.

Article 142 [Interpretation of Expression of Intent]

The meaning of an expression of intent made to a counterparty shall be determined through its interpretation based on the words and sentences used, by reference to the relevant clauses, the nature and purpose of the civil juristic act, custom, and the principle of good faith.

Where an expression of intent is not made to any specific person, its interpretation shall not be based solely on the words and sentences used, but together with other relevant clauses, the nature and purpose of the civil juristic act, custom, and the principle of good faith so that the true intent of the actor may be ascertained.

Section 3 Effect of Civil Juristic Acts

Article 143 [Conditions for Validity of Civil Juristic Act]

A civil juristic act is valid when the following conditions are fulfilled:

1. The actor possesses the corresponding capacity to engage in civil juristic acts;

2. The intent expressed is true; and

3. The act neither violates any mandatory provisions of laws or administrative regulations nor offends against public order or sound morals.

Article 144 [Effect of Civil Juristic Act by Person Lacking Capacity to Engage in Civil Juristic Acts]

A civil juristic act performed by a person without capacity to engage in civil juristic acts is void.

Article 145 [Effect of Civil Juristic Act by Person with Limited Capacity to Engage in Civil Juristic Acts]

A civil juristic act performed by a person with limited capacity to engage in civil juristic acts which is purely beneficial to the person or is suitable to his/her age, intelligence and mental health, is valid; any other civil juristic act performed by such person is valid only if consent thereto or ratification thereof is obtained from his/her legal agent.

An involved counterparty may demand that the legal agent ratify such act within 30 days from receipt of a notification thereof. Silence by the legal agent shall be deemed a refusal to ratify. Before ratification, a *bona fide* counterparty has the right to revoke the act. The revocation shall be made by notice.

Article 146 [Effect of Fictitious Expression of Intent and Concealed Act]

A civil juristic act performed by an actor and his/her counterparty based on a fictitious expression of intent is void.

The validity of a civil juristic act concealed by a fictitious expression of intent shall be determined per relevant laws.

Article 147 [Effect of Civil Juristic Act Based on Material Misunderstanding]

Where a civil juristic act performed is based on a material misunderstanding, the actor(s) shall have the right to petition a people's court or arbitration tribunal to rescind such act.

Article 148 [Effect of Civil Juristic Act Induced by Fraud]

Where one party induces a counterparty by fraudulent means to engage in a civil juristic act against the latter's true intent, the defrauded party has the right to petition a people's court or arbitration tribunal to rescind such act.

Article 149 [Effect of Civil Juristic Act Induced by Third Party's Fraud]

Where a party knows or ought to have known that a civil juristic act by a counterparty is based on a third party's fraudulent act and is contrary to the counterparty's actual intent, the defrauded counterparty shall have the right to petition a people's court or arbitration tribunal to rescind such act.

Article 150 [Effect of Civil Juristic Act Performed Under Duress]

Where a party, against true intent, engages in a civil juristic act due to coersion by a counterparty or third party, the party coerced shall have the right to petition a people's court or arbitration tribunal to rescind such act.

Article 151 [Effect of Manifestly Unfair Civil Juristic Act]

Where one party takes advantage of a counterparty that is in a state of crisis or lacking in judgment, resulting in a manifestly unfair civil juristic act, the party thus harmed shall have the right to petition a people's court or arbitration tribunal to rescind such act.

Article 152 [Extinguishment of Right to Rescission]

A party's right to rescission of a civil juristic act becomes extinguished under any of the following circumstances:

1. The party has failed to exercise the right to rescission within one year from the date when s/he knew or ought to have known of the cause therefor, or the party who performed an act based on a material misunderstanding has failed to exercise the right to rescission within 90 days from the date when s/he knew or ought to have known of the cause for rescission;

2. The party acting under coercion has failed to exercise the right to rescission within one year from the date when the coercion ceased; or

3. The party who became aware of the cause for rescission has waived the right to rescission expressly or through his/her own conduct.

The right to rescission is extinguished if the party fails to exercise it within five years from the date when the civil juristic act was performed.

Article 153 [Effect of Civil Juristic Act Counter to Mandatory Norms and Sound Morals]

A civil juristic act in violation of the mandatory provisions of laws or administrative regulations is void, except where such mandatory provisions do not nullify such act.

A civil juristic act that offends against the public order or sound morals is void.

Article 154 [Effect of Civil Juristic Act Performed via Malicious Collusion]

A civil juristic act is void if it is engaged in via malicious collusion between the actor and a counterparty thereof and harms lawful rights and interests of a third party.

Article 155 [Void and Rescinded Civil Juristic Acts Null and Void ab Initio]

A void or rescinded civil juristic act has no legal force or binding effect *ab initio*.

Article 156 [Partial Invalidity of Civil Juristic Act]

Where invalidation of a part of a civil juristic act does not affect the validity of the remaining part, the remaining part of the act shall continue to be valid.

Article 157 [Legal Consequences of Civil Juristic Act Being Void, Rescinded or Invalidated]

When a civil juristic act is void, rescinded, or is [otherwise] declared to have no legal force, the property thus obtained by an actor based on the act shall be returned, or compensation be made based on the appraised value of the property if it is impossible or unnecessary to return the property. The party at fault shall make compensation to the counterparty for the loss thus incurred, or, if both parties are at fault, liability for the loss shall be assumed by the parties proportionally thereto. Laws providing otherwise shall govern, however.

Section 4 A Civil Juristic Act Subject to Condition or Term

Article 158 [Civil Juristic Act Subject to Condition]

A condition may be attached to a civil juristic act unless the nature of such act forecloses such attachment. A civil juristic act subject to a condition precedent takes effect when the condition is fulfilled. A civil juristic act subject to a condition subsequent becomes invalid when the condition is fulfilled.

Article 159 [Fictitious Fulfillment and Non-Fulfillment of Condition]

Where a condition is attached to a civil juristic act, if a party, for the sake of its own interests, improperly obstructs the fulfillment of the condition, the condition shall be deemed to have been fulfilled; if a party improperly facilitates the fulfillment of the condition, the condition shall be deemed not to have been fulfilled.

Article 160 [Civil Juristic Act Subject to Term]

A time limit may be attached to a civil juristic act, unless the nature of the act forecloses such attachment. A civil juristic act subject to a time of commencement of validity takes effect when the time arrives. A civil juristic act subject to a time of termination of validity ceases to be effective when the time arrives.

Chapter VII Agency

Section 1 General Rules

Article 161 [Scope of Agency]

Civil law subject-persons may engage in civil juristic acts through their agents.

A civil juristic act shall not be engaged in through an agent if the act must be engaged in by the principal personally per law, as agreed by the parties, or based on the nature of the act.

Article 162 [Effect of Agency]

A civil juristic act undertaken by an agent in the principal's name within the agent's scope of authority is binding upon the principal.

Article 163 [Types of Agency]

Agency consists of agency created by contract and agency created by law.

An agent under an agency contract shall perform per the principal's authorization. An agent by operation of law shall act per law.

Article 164 [Legal Consequences of Agent's Improper Act]

An agent who does not perform or fully perform his/her duty and thereby inflicts harm or loss on the principal shall assume civil liability therefor.

Where an agent maliciously colludes with a third party and thereby harms the principal's legal rights and interests, the agent and the third party shall be jointly and severally liable therefor.

Section 2 Agency Created by Contract

Article 165 [Letter of Authorization[1]]

In an agency created by contract, where authority is conferred in writing, the letter of authorization shall clearly state the name of the agent, the tasks delegated, and the scope and duration of the authority, and it must be signed or stamped by the principal.

Article 166 [Co-Agency[2]]

Where two or more agents are authorized to handle the same task for a principal, the agents shall jointly exercise their agency unless the parties agree otherwise.

Article 167 [Agency for Illegal Task and Its Legal Consequences]

Where an agent knows or ought to have known that an authorized task is illegal but still proceeds with it as authorized, or, if a principal knows or ought to have known that an act of the agent violates law but raises no objection thereto, the principal and the agent shall be jointly and severally liable therefor.

Article 168 [Prohibition of Self-Dealing or Dual Agency and Exceptions]

An agent may not, in the principal's name, engage in a civil juristic act with himself/herself, unless consent thereto or ratification thereof is obtained from the principal.

An agent shall not, in the name of one of his/her principals, engage in a civil juristic act with another of his/her principals s/he concurrently represents, unless consent thereto or ratification thereof is obtained from both principals.

---

1 I.e. Power of Attorney.

2 I.e. Joint Agency, or Combined Agency.

Article 169 [Sub-Agency]

Where an agent needs to sub-delegate his/her authority to a third party, consent thereto or ratification thereof shall be obtained from the principal.

Where the principal consents to or ratifies the sub-delegation of agency to a third party, the principal may directly instruct the third party to undertake the authorized task, and the agent shall be liable only for the selection of such third party and the instructions the agent gives thereto.

Where principal does not consent to or ratify the sub-delegation of agency to a third party, the agent shall be liable for the acts of the third party except where the agent sub-delegates the authority to a third party in an emergency to protect the principal's interests.

Article 170 [Agency Derived from Employment[1]]

A civil juristic act a person engages in for the fulfillment of the responsibilities assigned by a legal person or an unincorporated entity within the scope of authority and in the name of the legal person or the unincorporated entity shall be binding upon such legal person or unincorporated entity.

Restrictions a legal person or an unincorporated entity imposes on the scope of functions and authority of a person who performs the duties assigned by such legal person or unincorporated entity shall not be asserted against a *bona fide* counterparty.

Article 171 [Agency Without or Beyond Authority]

An act engaged in by an actor that lacks authority or exceeds authority, or engaged in by such person after the authority is terminated, shall be ineffective as against a principal who does not ratify it.

A counterparty may urge a principal to ratify such an act within 30 days

---

1 I.e. Employee as Agent.

after receipt of the notification thereof. Silence by the principal shall be deemed a refusal to ratify. A *bona fide* counterparty shall have the right to revoke such act via notice before its ratification.

Where the foregoing act is unratified, a *bona fide* counterparty shall have the right to demand that the actor fulfill the obligations or compensate the loss thereby incurred, but the amount of compensation may not exceed the amount of the benefit the counterparty would have received had the principal ratified the act.

Where a counterparty knows or ought to have known that such actor lacks authority, the counterparty and the actor shall be liable therefor in proportion to their respective fault.

Article 172 [Apparent Agency[1]]

An act performed by an actor without agency authority, beyond his/her authority, or after termination of authority, shall be effective as against the principal if the counterparty has grounds to believe that such actor has agency authority.

Section 3 Termination of Agency

Article 173 [Occasions for Termination of Agency Created by Contract]

An agency created by contract shall terminate under any of the following circumstances:

1. The term of the agency expires, or the authorized tasks have been completed;
2. The principal revokes the authorization, or the agent resigns;
3. The agent loses capacity to engage in civil juristic acts;
4. The agent or the principal dies; or

---

1 I.e. Agency by Estoppel, or Ostensible Agency.

5. The legal person or unincorporated entity, as the agent or the principal, terminates.

Article 174 [Exceptions to Termination of Agency Created by Contract]

An act engaged in by an agent under an agency contract after the principal dies shall remain valid under any of the following circumstances:

1. The agent did not know and could not have known of the principal's death;

2. The act is ratified by the principal's heir(s);

3. The letter of authorization clearly states that the agency ceases only on completion of the authorized tasks; or

4. The agent had started the act before the principal died and continued with it in the interests of the principal's heir(s).

The preceding paragraph shall apply *mutatis mutandis* where a legal person or an unincorporated entity principal terminates.

Article 175 [Occasions for Termination of Legal Agency/Agency Created by Law]

A legal agency shall terminate under any of the following circumstances:

1. The principal obtains or recovers full capacity to engage in civil juristic acts;

2. The agent loses the capacity to engage in civil juristic acts;

3. The agent or the principal dies; or

4. Any other circumstance as provided by law.

Chapter VIII Civil Liability

Article 176 [Civil Obligation and Civil Liability]

Civil law subject-persons shall perform their civil obligations and assume their civil liability per law or their agreements.

Article 177 [Several Liability]

Where two or more persons assume several liability per law, each shall be liable in proportion to their respective contribution to any harm thus caused if their respective contribution can be ascertained, or in equal proportions if their respective percentage of liability is unable to be ascertained.

Article 178 [Joint and Several Liability]

Where two or more persons bear joint and several liability per law, the obligee has the right to demand that some, or all of the said persons be liable.

Persons subject to joint and several liability shall each be liable in proportion to their respective contribution to any harm thus caused, or in equal shares if their respective percentage of liability is unable to be ascertained. A co-obligor who has paid more than his/her fair share shall be entitled to recover the excess from the other co-obligor(s).

Joint and several liability shall be either imposed by law or arranged by the parties.

Article 179 [Forms of Civil Liability]

The primary forms of civil liability include:

1. Cessation of harm;
2. Removal of obstruction/Abatement of nuisance;
3. Elimination of danger;
4. Specific restitution of property;
5. Restoration;
6. Repair, reworking or replacement;
7. Continuing performance;
8. Compensatory damages;
9. Payment of liquidated damages;
10. Elimination of negative effects and restoration of reputation; and

11. Formal apology.

Where laws provide for an award of punitive damages, their provisions shall apply.

The forms of civil liability this Article provides for can apply either singly or cumulatively.

Article 180 [Force Majeure]

Persons unable to perform their civil obligations due to *force majeure* events shall be relieved of civil liability therefor. If law provides otherwise, its provisions shall apply.

Force majeure refers to objective circumstances that are unforeseeable, inevitable, and insurmountable.

Article 181 [Justifiable Defense]

No civil liability shall lie in cases of justifiable defense.

A justifiable defender shall bear appropriate civil liability where his/her act of justifiable defense exceeding the limits of necessity inflicts undue harm.

Article 182 [Avoidance of Perils in Emergency]

Where avoidance of peril in an emergency results in harm to others, the one who causes the peril shall assume civil liability therefor.

Where a peril stems from natural forces, one who inflicts harm on others in seeking to avoid such peril shall be relieved of civil liability therefor but may pay proper compensation.

Where measures adopted to avoid a peril in an emergency are improper or exceed the limits of necessity and thereby inflict undue harm on others, the person avoiding the peril shall assume appropriate civil liability therefor.

Article 183 [Liability and Compensation Related to Protection of Another's Rights and Interests]

Where a person suffers loss or harm in protecting another's civil law rights and interests, the tortfeasor shall assume civil liability therefor, though the beneficiary may also make appropriate compensation. If there is no tortfeasor or the tortfeasor flees or is incapable of assuming civil liability, the beneficiary shall make suitable compensation on demand of the person harmed.

Article 184 [Emergency Rescuer Free from Civil Liability[1]]

One who volunteers to rescues another in an emergency and thereby inflicts injury on the latter shall be relieved of civil liability therefor.

Article 185 [Civil Liability for Infringements Against Heroes and Martyrs]

One who infringes the name, likeness, reputation, or honor of a hero or martyr and thereby harms the social and public interest shall bear civil liability therefor.

Article 186 [Concurrent Liability in Tort and Contract]

Where one party's breach of a contract inflicts harm on another person's personal or proprietary rights and interests, the latter may elect to demand that the former be liable for either breach of contract or commission of tort.

Article 187 [Preferential Satisfaction of Civil Liability]

Where civil law subject-persons are subject to concurrent civil, administrative, and criminal liability based on the same act, the imposition of administrative or criminal liability shall not affect the assumption of civil liability. If such persons' assets do not suffice for all their legal liabilities, the civil liability shall be satisfied first.

---

1 I.e. Good Samaritan Law.

Chapter IX Limitation of Actions

Article 188 [Regular Limitation Period and Maximum Period for Protection of Rights]

The limitation period for a person to petition a people's court for protection of civil rights is three years, unless law provides otherwise.

Unless law provides otherwise, the limitation period shall commence on the date when the obligee knows or ought to have known of his/her right having been harmed and the identity of the obligor. However, no protection for a right is to be granted by a people's court if 20 years have elapsed since the date of the occurrence of harm, except that the people's court may, on petition by the obligee, extend the limitation period under special circumstances.

Article 189 [Limitation Period for Debts Paid in Installments]

Where parties agree on the performance of a debt obligation in installments, the period of limitations shall be calculated from the date the last installment is due.

Article 190 [Limitation Period for Claims Against Legal Agents]

The period of limitations for a person without or with limited capacity to engage in civil juristic acts to bring a claim against his/her legal agent shall be calculated from the date when the legal agency terminates.

Article 191 [Limitation Period for Damages Claim Arising from Sexual Abuse of Minors]

The period of limitations within which for a minor to bring a sexual abuse damages claim shall be calculated from the date when the minor attains the age of eighteen.

Article 192 [Legal Effect of Expiration of Limitation Period]

An obligor may assert the expiration of the limitation period as an [affirmative] defense for his/her non-performance of an obligation.

An obligor who agrees to perform a previous obligation after the limitation period expires may not subsequently assert the expiration of the limitation period as a defense, and an obligor who has voluntarily performed such a previous obligation may not subsequently demand restitution.

Article 193 [Citation of Limitation Period]

A people's court may not apply the provisions for limitation periods *sua sponte*.

Article 194 [Occasions for Tolling of Limitation Period]

The limitation period is tolled where within the last six months of the limitation period an obligee is unable to exercise a right of claim due to the presence of one of the following obstacles:

1. A *force majeure* [event];

2. An obligee without capacity or with limited capacity to engage in civil juristic acts has no legal agent or the legal agent dies or loses the capacity to engage in civil juristic acts or the right to representation;

3. No heir or executor of an estate has been determined upon the commencement of succession;

4. The obligee is controlled by the obligor or another person; or

5. Other obstacles which render the obligee unable to exercise the right to claim.

The limitation period shall expire six months from the date on which the grounds for tolling the period of limitations cease to exist.

Article 195 [Occasions for Interruption of Limitation Period]

A limitation period shall be interrupted under any of the following circumstances, and the limitation period shall run anew from the time of the interruption or the time when the subject proceeding concludes:

1. The obligee demands that the obligor perform the obligation;

2. The obligor agrees to perform the obligation;

3. The obligee files a lawsuit or arbitration proceeding against the obligor; or

4. Another circumstance arises that has the same effect as the obligee filing a lawsuit or arbitration proceeding.

Article 196 [Where Limitation Period Does Not Apply]

The limitation period does not apply to the following claims:

1. A claim for cessation of harm, removal of obstruction/abatement of nuisance, or elimination of a danger;

2. A claim for restitution of property lodged by a person who has a real right in immovable property or registered movable property;

3. A claim for payment of child support, maintenance, or alimony; or

4. Other claims to which the limitation period is inapplicable per law.

Article 197 [Limitation Period as Statutory and Its Waiver as Void]

The time period, methods of calculation, and the grounds for tolling and interruption of the limitation period are provided for in law, and any arrangements parties agree otherwise to are void.

A party's advance waiver of interests flowing from the limitation period is void.

Article 198 [Limitation Period for Arbitration]

Where laws provide for a limitation period for arbitration, their provisions shall apply; in the absence of such provisions, those on the limitation period for litigation set forth therein shall apply.

Article 199 [Peremption]

The time period for the exercise of the right to revocation or rescission and the right to cancellation or termination, among others, as provided for by law or agreed to by the parties, shall start from the date when the right holder knows or ought to have known of the existence of the said rights, and the provisions on the tolling, interruption and extension of the limitation period shall not apply, unless law provides otherwise. On expiration of the period, the right to revocation and the right to rescission or cancellation, among others, shall be extinguished.

Chapter X Calculating Time Period

Article 200 [Units of Calculation for Time Period]

Time periods as referred to in this Code are calculated by year, month, day and hour based on the Gregorian calendar.

Article 201 [Commencement of Time Periods]

Where a time period is calculated by year, month and day, the day on which the time period begins shall not be counted and the period shall run from the following day.

Where a time period is calculated by hour, the period shall begin to run from the time as provided in law or in the parties' agreement.

Article 202 [Expiration of Period]

Where a time period is calculated by year and month, the corresponding date of the due month shall be the last day of the time period; in the absence of such a date, the last day of that month shall be the last day of the time period.

Article 203 [Last Day Extension and Closing Hour of Last Day]

Where the last day of a time period falls on a legal holiday, the day after the holiday shall be deemed the last day of the period.

The last day of a time period ends at 24:00; if business hours apply, the last day shall end at the time of the close of business.

Article 204 [Time Period Subject to Law or Agreement]

The calculation of a time period shall be governed by the provisions of this Code unless law or the parties' agreement provides otherwise.

Book Two Real Rights

Part One General Provisions

Chapter I General Rules

Article 205 [Regulatory Scope of This Book]

This Book regulates the civil law relations flowing from the ownership and use of property.

Article 206 [Basic Socialist Economic System and Socialist Market Economy]

The State upholds and improves the basic economic system which keeps public ownership as the mainstay of the economy and allows diverse forms of ownership to develop side by side, implements a system in which distribution according to work is dominant and a variety of modes of distribution coexist, and practices a socialist market economy.

The State consolidates and develops the public sector economy while encouraging, supporting, and guiding the development of the non-public sector economy.

The State practices a socialist market economy and guarantees the equal legal status and development rights of all market participants.

Article 207 [Equal Protection of Real Rights]

The real rights of the State, collectives, private individuals, and other right holders enjoy equal protection under law and no organization or individual may infringe them.

M. Wan et al., *The Civil Code of the People's Republic of China*,
https://doi.org/10.1007/978-981-19-2794-2_2

Article 208 [Publication of Real Rights]

The creation, modification, transfer or extinction of a real right in immovable property shall be subject to registration per law. The creation and transfer of a real right in movable property shall be subject to delivery per law.

Chapter II Creation, Modification, Transfer, and Extinction of Real Rights

Section 1 Registration of Immovable Property

Article 209 [Effect of Registration of Real Right in Immovable Property]

The creation, modification, transfer or extinction of a real right in immovable property shall become effective on its registration per law and shall have no legal effect in the absence thereof, unless law provides otherwise.

Registration of title is not required for natural resources that are the property of the State per law.

Article 210 [Registry and Unified Registration of Immovable Property]

The registration of immovable property shall be administered by the registry at the situs where the immovable property resides.

The State implements a unified registration system for immovable property. The scope, registry, and measures for the unified registration shall be prescribed by laws and administrative regulations.

Article 211 [Information Required for Immovable Property Registration]

When applying for registration of immovable property, an applicant shall, considering the different items to be registered, provide necessary materials such as proof of title to the immovable property, along with its metes and bounds and area.

Article 212 [Duties of Registry]

A registry shall perform the following functions:

1. Examining the proof of title and other necessary materials an applicant provides;

2. Inquiring of the applicant as to relevant items for registration;

3. Registering the relevant items truthfully and promptly; and

4. Performing other functions per the provisions of laws and administrative regulations.

Where further proof is required for the relevant information of the immovable property to be registered, the registry may require the applicant to submit supplementary materials and may conduct on-site inspections, if necessary.

Article 213 [Acts Not Allowed for Registry]

A registry may not engage in any of the following acts:

1. Requiring an appraisal of immovable property;

2. Carrying out repeated registrations in the guise of annual inspections; or

3. Engaging in any other acts that exceed the scope of its registration functions.

Article 214 [Time for Change of Real Property Right to Take Effect]

The creation, modification, transfer or extinction of a real right in immovable property that is required by law to be registered takes effect at the time of its recording in an immovable property register.

Article 215 [Separation of Contractual Effect from Change of Real Rights]

A contract parties conclude for the creation, modification, transfer, or extinction of a real right takes effect on its formation, unless law or the parties' agreement provides otherwise, and the validity of such a contract shall remain unaffected by the non-registration of the real right.

Article 216 [Effect of Register and Its Maintenance]

A register of immovable property shall be the basis for determining the ownership and content of the real rights therein.

A register of immovable property shall be maintained by a registry.

Article 217 [Register Versus Certificate of Title with Respect to Immovable Property]

A certificate of title to immovable property is evidence of a right holder's entitlement to the immovable property. The items recorded in the certificate of title to immovable property must be consistent with those recorded in the register of immovable property; in case of any discrepancy between the two, those recorded in the register of immovable property shall prevail, unless evidence establishes a clear error therein.

Article 218 [Inquiring About and Copying Registered Information of Immovable Property]

A right holder or an interested person may apply to inquire about and copy the information registered for immovable property and the registry shall provide such information.

Article 219 [Proper Use of Registered Information]

An interested person shall not disclose or illegally use registered information regarding a right holder's immovable property.

Article 220 [Rectification of Registration and Registration of Demurrer]

A right holder or an interested person who believes that an item is incorrectly recorded in the register of immovable property may apply for rectification of the registration. Where the right holder recorded in the immovable property register consents in writing to such rectification, or where evidence proves an error in the register, the registry shall rectify it.

Where the right holder recorded in an immovable property register disagrees with such rectification, an interested person may apply for registration of a demurrer. If the registry registers the demurrer but the applicant does not bring a lawsuit within 15 days from the date thereof, the registration of the demurrer becomes ineffective. Where a demurrer is improperly registered and the right holder incurs damage or loss as a result, the right holder may demand that the applicant pay compensation therefor.

Article 221 [Forenotice Registration]

Where parties conclude an agreement for the sale of a home or for any other real right in immovable property, they may apply for a forenotice registration with a registry per their agreement to ensure the future realization of the real right. If, after the forenotice registration the immovable property is disposed of without the consent of the right holder registered in the forenotice, the disposition shall be ineffective in terms of the real right.

Where, after the forenotice is registered, the obligee's right is extinguished, or no application for registration of the real right in immovable property is made within 90 days from the date on which the said real right becomes registrable, the forenotice registration shall become ineffective.

Article 222 [Compensation for Errors in Registration]

A party that submits false materials in an application for registration and thereby inflicts damage or loss on another shall be liable for compensation therefor.

Where damage or loss accrues to another person due to an error in registration, the registry shall be liable for compensation therefor. After paying such compensation, the registry shall have the right to indemnification against the person causing such error.

Article 223 [Registration Fees]

A fee for the registration of immovable property shall be levied on a per-item basis and may not be charged in proportion to its area, size, or purchase price.

Section 2 Delivery of Movable Property

Article 224 [Effect of Delivery of Movable Property]

The creation or transfer of a real right in movable property shall take effect on delivery unless law provides otherwise.

Article 225 [Effect of Registration of Special Movable Property]

The unregistered creation, modification, transfer or extinction of real right in watercraft, aircraft and motor vehicles shall be ineffective against a *bona fide* third party.

Article 226 [Summary Delivery[1]]

Where a right holder already possesses movable property before a real right in it is created or transferred, the real right in such movable property takes effect at the time when a [corresponding] civil juristic act takes effect.

Article 227 [Assignment of Claim to Possession]

Where a third party possesses movable property before a real right in such movable property is created or transferred, the person obligated to deliver the movable property may transfer the right to its return against the third party in lieu of delivery.

1 I.e. *Traditio Brevi Manu*, or Delivery with the Short Hand.

Article 228 [Constructive Transfer[1]]

Where, upon transfer of a real right in movable property, the parties agree that the transferor shall continue in possession of the movable property, the real right in the movable property shall take effect when such agreement comes into force.

Section 3 Other Rules

Article 229 [Change of Real Right via Legal Document or Eminent Domain]

Where a real right is created, altered, transferred, or extinguished by a legal document issued by a people's court or arbitration tribunal, or based on eminent domain by a people's government, the creation, modification, transfer or extinction of the real right becomes effective when the legal document or expropriation decision takes effect.

Article 230 [Acquisition of Real Right via Succession]

Where a real right is acquired through succession, the real right as inherited takes effect when succession commences.

Article 231 [Change of Real Right Due to de Facto Act]

Where a real right is created or extinguished by a *de facto* act such as the lawful construction or demolition of a house, the creation or extinction of the real right takes effect when the *de facto* act is consummated.

Article 232 [Disposal of Real Right in Immovable Property Acquired by Means Other Than Civil Juristic Act]

Where a real right in immovable property as acquired in accordance with

---

1 I.e. Constructive Possession, or Besitzkonstitut.

provisions in this Section is required per provisions of law to be registered, the disposal of such real right, if unregistered, shall be ineffective.

Chapter III Protection of Real Rights

Article 233 [Means of Resolution of Real Rights Disputes]

Where a real right is infringed, the right holder may solve the dispute through such avenues as settlement, mediation, arbitration and litigation.

Article 234 [Right to Petition for Confirmation of Real Rights]

Where a dispute arises over the ownership or content of a real right, an interested person may demand confirmation of such right.

Article 235 [Claim for Return of Property]

Where a person not entitled to do so possesses immovable or movable property, the right holder may demand return thereof.

Article 236 [Claim for Removal of Obstruction]

Where an obstruction or a potential obstruction lies against a real right, the right holder may demand removal of the obstruction or elimination of a danger.

Article 237 [Claim for Restitution]

Where immovable or movable property is destroyed or damaged, the right holder may, per law, demand its repair, reworking, replacement, or restoration to its original condition.

Article 238 [Claim for Damages]

Where an infringement of a real right inflicts damage or loss, the right holder may demand that the infringer pay damages or assume other civil liability per law.

Article 239 [Individual and Cumulative Use of Protection Methods]

The methods of real right protection set forth in this Chapter may apply either individually or cumulatively based on the circumstances of the infringement of a right.

Part Two Ownership

Chapter IV General Rules

Article 240 [Definition of Ownership]

Owners are entitled to possess, use, benefit from, and dispose of their immovable or movable property per law.

Article 241 [Jura In Re Aliana Created by Owner[1]]

Owners of immovable or movable property are entitled to create usufructs and security interests in their immovable or movable property. Usufructuaries or security interest holders may not harm the rights and interests of the owners when exercising their rights.

Article 242 [Exclusive Ownership by the State]

No organization or individual may acquire title to the immovable and movable property whose ownership is, as prescribed by law, exclusive to the State.

Article 243 [Eminent Domain]

Collectively-owned land and the houses and other immovable property of an organization or individual may be expropriated in the public interest within the scope of authority and pursuant to the procedures therefor provided by law.

Where collectively-owned land is expropriated, land compensation,

1 I.e. A Right over Another Person's Property Created by Owner.

resettlement subsidies and compensation for rural villagers' dwellings and other ground attachments as well as growing crops shall be paid in full and without delay per law, and the social security premiums of farmers whose land has been expropriated shall be arranged, their livings secured, and their legal rights and interests safeguarded.

Where dwellings or other immovable property of organizations or individuals is expropriated, compensation shall be paid therefor per law to safeguard lawful rights and interests of those affected. Housing conditions shall also be guaranteed for individuals whose dwellings are expropriated.

No organization or individual may engage in such acts as embezzling, misappropriating, covertly distributing, withholding, or delaying payment of such funds as the compensation fees for expropriation.

Article 244 [Protection of Arable Land]

The State extends special protection to arable land, strictly restricts the conversion of agricultural land into that used for construction and controls the overall volume of the land used for construction. Collectively-owned land may not be expropriated in a manner that exceeds [an authority's] mandate or violates the procedures therefor provided in law.

Article 245 [Requisition]

To respond to an emergency such as provision of disaster relief or epidemic prevention and control, immovable or movable property of an organization or individual may be requisitioned within the scope of authority and pursuant to the procedures therefor provided in law. Requisitioned immovable or movable property shall be returned to the said organization or individual after such use. Compensation shall be paid for such requisition and for the destruction, damage or loss of the property after such use.

Chapter V State Ownership, Collective Ownership and Private Ownership

Article 246 [Scope of State Property, Nature of State Ownership and Exercise of Right of State Ownership]

Where law prescribes that property is owned by the State, such property belongs to the State, namely, to the people as a whole.

The right of ownership over State-owned property shall be exercised by the State Council on behalf of the State. If law provides otherwise, its provisions shall apply.

Article 247 [State Ownership of Minerals, Waters and Sea Areas]

Mineral deposits, waters, and sea areas are owned by the State.

Article 248 [State Ownership of Uninhabited Islands]

Uninhabited islands are owned by the State, and the State Council exercises the right of ownership over them on its behalf.

Article 249 [Scope of State-Owned Land]

Urban land is owned by the State. The land in rural and urban suburbs that belongs to the State per law is the property of the State.

Article 250 [State Ownership of Natural Resources]

Natural resources, such as forests, mountains and other elevations, grasslands, uncultivated land, and tidal flats, other than those owned by collectives per law, belong to the State.

Article 251 [State Ownership of Wild Animal and Plant Resources]

Wild animal and plant resources that belong to the State per law are the property of the State.

Article 252 [State Ownership of Radio-Frequency Spectrum Resources]

Radio-frequency spectrum resources belong to the State.

Article 253 [Ownership of Cultural Relics]

Cultural relics that belong to the State per law are the property of the State.

Article 254 [State Ownership of National Defense Assets and Infrastructure]

National defense assets belong to the State.

Infrastructures such as railways, roads, electric power facilities, telecommunications facilities, and oil and gas pipelines that belong to the State per law are the property of the State.

Article 255 [Real Rights of State Agencies]

A State agency has the right to possess and use the immovable and movable property directly under its control and to dispose of such property per law and relevant State Council regulations.

Article 256 [Real Rights of Public Institutions Established by State]

A public institution established by the State has the right to possess and use the immovable and movable property directly under its control, and to benefit from and dispose of such property per law and relevant State Council regulations.

Article 257 [The Investor System of State-Funded Enterprises]

For enterprises the State invests in, the State Council and the local people's governments shall, on behalf of the State, perform an investor's duties and enjoy an investor's rights and interests per law and administrative regulations.

Article 258 [Protection of State Property]

State-owned property is protected by law, and no organization or individual may misappropriate, loot, covertly distribute, withhold, or destroy such property.

Article 259 [Legal Liability with Respect to State Property Management]

Institutions and their staff charged with management and supervision of State-owned property shall improve their management and supervision thereof per law, strive to preserve and increase the value of such property, and prevent any loss thereof; they shall bear legal liability per law if losses occur to State-owned property from their abuse of office or dereliction of duty.

In the course of such procedures as enterprise restructuring, merger or division, or affiliated transactions, anyone who, in violation of regulations on State-owned property management, causes loss to State-owned property by transferring it at a low price, conspiring to covertly divide it, creating security interests in it without authorization, or other [such] means, shall bear legal liability therefor per law.

Article 260 [Scope of Property Owned by Collectives]

Collectively-owned immovable and movable property includes:

1. Land, forests, mountains and other elevations, grasslands, uncultivated land, and tidal flats that are owned by collectives per law;

2. Buildings, production facilities, and farmland water conservancy facilities owned by collectives;

3. Educational, scientific, cultural, public health, sports, and other facilities owned by collectives; and

4. Any other immovable and movable property owned by collectives.

Article 261 [Rural Collective Ownership with Major Issues to Be Decided Collectively]

The immovable and movable property of a rural collective shall be owned by its members collectively.

The following matters shall be decided by the collective's members per statutory procedures:

1. Land contracting plans, and the subcontracting of land to any organization or individual outside the collective;

2. Adjustment of contracted land among individual land contractual management right holders;

3. Methods of use and distribution of such funds as land compensation fees;

4. Such matters as ownership changes in collectively funded enterprises; and

5. Other matters as provided by law.

Article 262 [Exercise of Right of Collective Ownership of Immovable Property]

The right of ownership of collectively-owned land, forests, mountains and other elevations, grasslands, uncultivated land, and tidal flats shall be exercised per the following provisions:

1. Where they belong to the rural collective of a village, the right of ownership shall be exercised by the collective economic organization of the village or the villagers' committee on behalf of the collective per law;

2. Where they are owned by two or more rural collectives within a village, the right of ownership shall be exercised by their respective collective economic organizations or villagers' groups on behalf of the collectives per law; and

3. Where they belong collectively to the rural collective of a rural township, the right of ownership shall be exercised by the economic organizations of the township on behalf of the collective.

Article 263 [Exercise of Right of Urban Township Collective Ownership]

An urban township collective that owns immovable and movable property has the right to possess, use, benefit from, and dispose of such property per law and administrative regulations.

Article 264 [Right of Members of Collective to Know About Collective Property]

Rural collective economic organizations, villagers' committees, and villagers' groups shall make public the status of the collectively-owned property to the members of the collectives per laws, administrative regulations, and their articles of association, and local covenants. Members of these collectives have the right to examine and make copies of relevant materials.

Article 265 [Protection of Collective Property and Protection of Rural Collective Member's Lawful Rights and Interests]

Property a collective owns is protected by law, and no organization or individual may misappropriate, loot, covertly distribute, or destroy such property.

Where a decision made by a rural collective economic organization, a villagers' committee, or a person in charge thereof harms legal rights and interests of a member of the collective, the injured member may petition a people's court to invalidate such decision.

Article 266 [Scope of Private Property]

A private individual shall have the right to own his/her lawful income, houses, daily use articles, production tools, raw materials, and other immovable and movable property.

Article 267 [Protection of Lawfully-Owned Private Property]

Property a private individual lawfully owns is protected by law, and organizations or individuals are prohibited from misappropriating, looting, or destroying such property.

Article 268 [Companies and Enterprises Funded by State, Collective and Private Individual]

The State, collectives, and private individuals may form limited liability companies, joint stock companies limited by shares, or other enterprises via capital contributions per law. Where the immovable or movable property of the State, collectives, and private individuals is invested in an enterprise, the investors shall, per their agreement or in proportion to their investment, enjoy the right to receive returns on assets, participate in major decisions, and select business managers, and shall meanwhile be obligated to perform their duties.

Article 269 [Property of a Legal Person]

A for-profit legal person shall have the right to possess, use, benefit from, and dispose of its immovable and movable property per laws, administrative regulations, and its articles of association.

The provisions of relevant laws, administrative regulations, and articles of association shall apply to the rights of a legal person other than a for-profit legal person as to its immovable and movable property.

Article 270 [Protection of Property Owned by Social Organization Legal Person and Endowment Legal Person]

Immovable and movable property legally owned by a social organization legal person, or an endowment legal person is protected by law.

Chapter VI Condominium Ownership

Article 271 [Condominium Ownership]

An owner has the title to an exclusive portion of a building, such as a dwelling or premises used to operate a business, and the right to co-own and jointly manage common areas outside of such exclusive portions.

Article 272 [Owner's Rights and Obligations with Respect to Exclusive Portions]

An owner shall have the right to possess, use, benefit from, and dispose of his/her exclusive portion. The owner may not endanger the safety of the building or harm legal rights and interests of other owners when exercising such right.

Article 273 [Owner's Rights and Obligations with Respect to Common Areas]

An owner enjoys rights and assumes obligations with respect to common areas outside his/her exclusive portion and may not refuse to perform such obligations on the grounds of waiver of the [corresponding] right.

Where an owner transfers a portion used as a dwelling or used for commercial operations, the right to co-own and jointly manage common areas shall transfer therewith.

Article 274 [Ownership of Roads and Green Spaces, etc. Within Building Zone]

Roads within a building zone are co-owned by all owners, except for those that form part of an urban public road system. Green spaces within the building zone are co-owned by all owners, except for those that form part of urban public green spaces and those clearly belonging to private individuals. Other public places, public facilities, and premises used for property management service within the building zone are co-owned by all owners.

Article 275 [Ownership of Parking Spaces and Garages]

The ownership of parking spaces and garages planned for parking vehicles within the building zone shall be agreed on by the parties by way of sale, collateral gift, lease, or via any other means.

Parking spaces for parking vehicles that occupy roads or other areas jointly belonging to all owners are co-owned by all owners.

Article 276 [Prioritized Needs of Owners for Parking Spaces and Garages]

Parking spaces and garages planned for parking vehicles within the building zone shall first serve the needs of owners.

Article 277 [Establishment, Guidance and Assistance of Owners' Self-Governing Body]

Owners may form an owners' assembly and elect the members of an owners' committee. The specific conditions and procedures for the formation of the owners' assembly and the owners' committee shall conform to applicable laws and regulations.

The relevant departments of the local people's government and the residents' committee shall provide guidance to and assist in the formation of the owners' assembly and the election of the members of the owners' committee.

Article 278 [Matters Subject to Joint Decision by Owners and Relevant Voting Procedures]

The following matters shall be jointly decided by owners:

1. Making and amending the owners' assembly's procedural rules;
2. Making and amending the management covenants;
3. Electing or replacing members of the owners' committee;
4. Selecting and dismissing a property management service firm or other manager;
5. Using maintenance funds for buildings and their ancillary facilities;
6. Raising maintenance funds for buildings and their ancillary facilities;
7. Altering or rebuilding buildings and their ancillary facilities;

8. Changing the intended use of common areas or using them to engage in business activities; and

9. Other major matters relating to co-ownership and the right of co-management.

The quorum for matters subject to unit owners' joint decision shall be two-thirds or more of total owners representing two-thirds or more of total exclusive area. Decisions on matters set forth in Subparagraphs 6 through 8 shall be subject to the consent of three-quarters or more of participating owners representing three-quarters or more of the participating exclusive area. Decisions on other matters set forth in the preceding paragraph shall be subject to the consent of more than half of the participating owners representing more than half of the participating exclusive area.

Article 279 [Restrictions on Owner's Conversion of Unit Use]

No owner may turn a dwelling into premises used for commercial operations in violation of laws, regulations, or management covenants. An owner who intends to turn a dwelling into premises used for commercial operations shall, in addition to abiding by laws, regulations, and the management covenants, obtain unanimous consent thereto from all interested owners.

Article 280 [Effect of Decisions by Owners' Assembly and Owners' Committee]

Decisions of the owners' assembly or the owners' committee are legally binding on owners.

Where a decision made by the owners' assembly or the owners' committee harms lawful rights and interests of an owner, the owner thus afflicted may petition a people's court to invalidate it.

Article 281 [Ownership and Use of Maintenance Funds for Buildings and Ancillary Facilities]

The maintenance funds for buildings and their ancillary facilities are co-owned by owners. The funds may, upon joint decision by the owners, be used for the maintenance, renewal, and renovation of common areas, such as elevators, roofs, exterior walls, and wheelchair accessible facilities. Information on raising and using the maintenance funds for buildings and their ancillary facilities shall be publicized on a regular basis.

Where a building and its ancillary facilities must be maintained in an emergency, the owners' assembly or the owners' committee may, per law, apply for the use of the maintenance funds for the buildings and their ancillary facilities.

Article 282 [Income Derived from Common Areas]

Income derived from common areas that is received by a developer, property services firm, or other manager is co-owned by all owners after deduction of reasonable costs.

Article 283 [Expenses on and Income from Buildings and Ancillary Facilities]

Where an agreement on matters such as sharing of expenses on and distribution of income from a building and its ancillary facilities exists, such matters shall be determined per the agreement; if no such agreement exists or the agreement is ambiguous, such matters shall be determined based on the proportion of the area of each owner's exclusive portion to the total exclusive area.

Article 284 [Managing Body for Buildings and Ancillary Facilities]

Owners may either manage the buildings and the ancillary facilities on their own or retain a property services firm or other manager for such a purpose.

Owners have the right per law to replace a property services firm or other manager the developer has retained.

Article 285 [Relationship Between Owners and Property Services Firm or Other Manager]

A property services firm or other manager shall, as mandated by the owners, manage the buildings and their ancillary facilities within a building zone per the provisions of Book Three of this Code relating to property services contracts, subject itself to the supervision of the owners, and respond to owners' inquiries about property services promptly.

The property services firm or other manager must carry out emergency measures and other management measures imposed by the government per law and actively cooperate in the performance of relevant work.

Article 286 [Owner's Relevant Obligations and Responsibilities]

Owners shall abide by laws, regulations, and management covenants and their relevant acts shall satisfy the requirements of resource efficiency and ecological environment protection. Owners shall cooperate per law in the emergency and other management measures imposed by the government per law which are carried out by the property services firm or other manager.

As regards any acts that harm the legal rights and interests of others, such as improperly disposing of garbage, discharging pollutants or emitting noise, feeding and keeping animals, or constructing structures in violation of rules and regulations, encroaching on passageways, or refusing to pay property management fees, the owners' assembly or the owners' committee shall have the right to demand per law, regulations and management covenants that the actor cease such infringements, abate nuisances, eliminate dangers, restore to original condition, and compensate any losses.

Where an owner or an actor refuses to perform relevant obligations, a party affected thereby may submit a report to, or lodge a complaint with the competent administrative department, which shall handle the case per law.

Article 287 [Protection of Owner's Lawful Rights and Interests]

An owner shall have the right to demand that the developer, the property services firm or other manager or other owners assume civil liability for any of their acts that harm such owner's lawful rights and interests.

Chapter VII Neighboring Relations

Article 288 [Principles for Neighboring Relations]

Neighboring persons entitled to rights in immovable property shall properly deal with neighborly relations in adherence to the principles of benefiting production, convenience of daily lives, solidarity and mutual assistance, and fairness and reasonableness.

Article 289 [Norms for Neighboring Relations]

Where laws and regulations provide for neighborhood relationships, their provisions shall apply. Local customs may apply if no such provisions exist.

Article 290 [Neighboring Relations Regarding Use of Water and Drainage]

A holder of a real right in immovable property shall provide to a neighboring right holder the necessary convenience for the use of water and/or drainage.

The right to use of naturally flowing water shall be reasonably shared among neighboring right holders in immovable property. Persons discharging water shall follow the natural water flow.

Article 291 [Neighboring Relations Regarding Passage]

A holder of real right in immovable property shall provide necessary convenience to other neighboring right holders who must use his/her land for passage and other access.

Article 292 [Use of Neighboring Land or Structure]

Where a holder of real right in immovable property must use neighboring land or structure to construct or maintain a building or lay electrical wires, cables, or pipelines for water, heating, gas, or the like, the right holder of the neighboring land or structure shall provide the necessary convenience.

Article 293 [Neighboring Relations Regarding Ventilation, Lighting and Access to Sunlight]

The construction of a building may not violate the State's applicable construction standards or obstruct the ventilation, lighting, or access to sunlight of neighboring buildings.

Article 294 [Harm Caused by Imponderabilia[1] from Neighboring Right Holders]

A holder of real right in immovable property may not, in violation of regulations of the State, discard solid waste or emit harmful substances such as atmospheric pollutants, water pollutants, soil pollutants, noise, light radiation and electromagnetic radiation.

Article 295 [Maintaining Security of Neighboring Immovable Property]

A holder of real right in immovable property may not endanger the safety of neighbouring immovable property when engaged in such work as excavation

---

1 I.e. Imponderables.

of land, construction of buildings, laying of pipes and installation of equipment.

Article 296 [Avoiding Damage to Neighboring Immovable Property While Using It]

A holder of real right in immovable property who uses neighboring immovable property for the purpose of use of water, drainage, passage, laying of pipes, etc., shall spare no effort to avoid causing damage to the right holder thereof.

Chapter VIII Co-Ownership

Article 297 [Co-Ownership and Its Types]

Immovable or movable property may be co-owned by two or more organizations or individuals. Co-ownership consists of proportionate co-ownership and joint co-ownership.

Article 298 [Proportionate Co-Ownership]

Proportionate co-owners own co-owned immovable or movable property based on their respective shares.

Article 299 [Joint Co-Ownership]

Joint co-owners jointly own co-owned immovable or movable property.

Article 300 [Right of Co-Owners to Management of Co-Owned Property]

Co-owners shall manage co-owned immovable or movable property per their agreement. In the absence of an agreement or if the agreement is ambiguous, each co-owner is entitled and obligated to manage it.

Article 301 [Disposal, Major Repair, Change of Nature or Intended Use with Respect to Co-Owned Property]

Unless agreed otherwise by co-owners, any disposal of co-owned immovable or movable property, or any major repair thereof, or change of the nature or intended use of the co-owned immovable or movable property shall be subject to the consent of proportionate co-owners whose portions account for two-thirds or more of the total portions, or to the consent of all joint co-owners.

Article 302 [Sharing of Management Expenses Concerning Co-Owned Property]

The management costs of and other burdens on a co-owned property shall be borne per the agreement among co-owners if such an agreement exists; in the absence of an agreement or if the agreement is ambiguous, these costs and burdens shall be borne by proportionate co-owners proportionally, and by joint co-owners jointly.

Article 303 [Partition of Co-Owned Property]

Where co-owners agree not to partition co-owned immovable or movable property so as to maintain co-ownership, their agreement shall apply. However, a co-owner may demand partition if there is a compelling reason therefor. In the absence of an agreement or if the agreement is ambiguous, a proportionate co-owner may demand partition at any time as a matter of right, whereas a joint co-owner may demand partition when the basis for the co-ownership ceases to exist or a compelling reason for partition exists. Compensation shall be made if partition causes damage to other co-owners.

Article 304 [Ways of Partitioning Co-Owned Property]

Co-owners may determine the means of partition of their co-owned property by consultation. Where they fail to reach an agreement, and if the co-owned immovable or movable property is divisible and its value is undiminished by division, partition in kind shall be conducted; where it is difficult to divide the co-owned property or if its value would be lessened by division, partition shall be conducted by dividing the proceeds obtained from taking of it based on its appraised value or from auction or sale of it.

Where the part of immovable or movable property acquired by one co-owner after partition is defective, the other co-owners shall share his/her losses.

Article 305 [Right to Dispose of Portions and Preferential Right to Purchase]

A proportionate co-owner may transfer the portion s/he owns in the co-owned immovable or movable property. The other co-owners have the erential right to the purchase of such portion on equal terms.

Article 306 [Enjoyment of Preferential Right to Purchase]

Where a proportionate co-owner transfers the portion s/he owns in the co-owned immovable or movable property, s/he shall notify the other co-owners of the conditions of transfer promptly. The other co-owners shall exercise their preferential right to purchase within a reasonable period.

Where two or more co-owners assert their right of priority to purchase, they shall determine through consultation the proportion of the portion each will purchase; if no agreement is thereby reached, they shall exercise their preferential right to purchase in proportion to their respective portions at the time of transfer.

Article 307 [External and Internal Relations of Co-Owners in Terms of Claims and Obligations Derived from Co-Ownership]

Co-owners shall enjoy joint claims and assume joint and several obligations derived from the co-owned immovable or movable property with respect to external relationships unless law provides otherwise or where a third party is aware that the co-owners are not in a relationship of joint claims or joint and several obligations. Unless co-owners agree otherwise, proportionate co-owners shall enjoy claims and assume obligations in proportion to their respective portions, while joint co-owners shall enjoy joint claims and assume joint obligations with respect to internal relationships. A proportionate co-owner who has performed an obligation exceeding his/her portion shall have the right to pursue a claim for contribution against other co-owners.

Article 308 [Presumption of Proportionate Co-Ownership]

In the absence of an agreement among co-owners or if the agreement is ambiguous as to whether the co-owned immovable or movable property is subject to proportionate co-ownership or to joint co-ownership, the immovable or movable property shall be deemed to be subject to proportionate co-ownership, unless co-owners are in such a relationship as a familial one.

Article 309 [Determination of Portions of Proportionate Co-Owners]

The portions of proportionate co-owners in immovable or movable property shall be determined based on their capital contributions in the absence of an agreement [to such effect] or if the agreement is ambiguous. If determining the amount of respective capital contributions is impossible, each proportionate co-owner shall be presumed to have an equal portion.

Article 310 [Mutatis Mutandis Application of This Chapter to Joint Usufruct and Joint Security Interest]

Where two or more organizations or individuals are jointly entitled to a usufruct or a security interest, the relevant provisions of this Chapter shall apply *mutatis mutandis*.

Chapter IX Special Provisions on Acquisition of Title

Article 311 [Bona Fide Acquisition]

Where a person with no right to dispose of immovable or movable property transfers such property to another, the rightful owner has the right to recover it; unless law provides otherwise, however, the transferee shall acquire title to such immovable or movable property if the following conditions are met:

1. The transferee is a *bona fide* buyer when the immovable or movable property is transferred;

2. The transfer is for a reasonable price; and

3. The immovable or movable property transferred has been registered as required by law or has been delivered to the transferee when no registration is required.

Where a transferee acquires title to immovable or movable property per the provisions of the preceding paragraph, the original owner shall have the right to claim damages against the person who disposed of the property without right.

Where a *bona fide* party acquires a real right other than title, the provisions of the preceding two paragraphs shall apply *mutatis mutandis*.

Article 312 [Bona Fide Acquisition of Lost Property]

An owner or any other right holder has the right to recover lost property. Where the lost property is possessed by another via a transfer, the owner or other right holder has the right to claim damages against a person who has disposed of the lost property without right, or, within two years from the date on which the owner or other right holder knows of or ought to have known of the transferee, to demand that the transferee return the property. However, where the transferee has acquired the lost property at auction or from a qualified business operator, the right holder shall, at the time of demand for the return of the property, reimburse the costs the transferee has incurred. After payment of the costs to the transferee, the owner or other right holder has the right to recover the costs from the person who disposed of the property without right.

Article 313 [Extinguishment of Original Rights Attached to Movable Property Acquired Bona Fide]

After a *bona fide* transferee acquires movable property, the original rights attached thereto are extinguished unless the *bona fide* transferee knew or ought to have known of such rights at the time of the transfer.

Article 314 [Return of Lost Property]

When lost property is found, it shall be returned to its right holder. The finder must promptly notify the right holder or deliver it to a relevant authority such as a public security department.

Article 315 [Treatment of Lost Property by Relevant Authority]

Where a competent authority receives lost property and knows the identity of the right holder, the authority shall promptly tell the right holder to retrieve the lost property; if the authority is unaware of the right holder's identity, it shall promptly issue a lost-and-found notice.

Article 316 [Obligation of Finder and Relevant Authority to Safeguard Lost Property]

A finder shall safeguard a lost article before it is delivered to a competent authority, and the authority shall safeguard it pending its retrieval. Civil liability shall arise where the lost property is destroyed, damaged or lost due to intentional act or gross negligence.

Article 317 [Obligation of Right Holder to Retrieve Lost Property]

The right holder of lost property shall, at the time of retrieving it, pay to the finder or the relevant department all necessary expenses incurred, such as those for its safekeeping.

Where a right holder has offered a reward for finding lost property, s/he shall perform the reward obligations as promised when retrieving the lost property.

Where a finder appropriates lost property to his/her own use, s/he is neither entitled to demand reimbursement of costs such as the costs of safekeeping , nor entitled to demand that the right holder perform an obligation as promised.

Article 318 [Escheatment of Uncollected Lost Property upon Expiration of Publication Period]

Where no one claims lost property within one year from the date a lost-and-found notice is posted, the lost property shall escheat to the State.

Article 319 [Drifting, Buried and Hidden Things Found or Discovered]

Where a drifting thing is found or, one buried underground or hidden is discovered, the provisions relating to the finding of lost property shall apply *mutatis mutandis*, unless law provides otherwise.

Article 320 [Transfer of Ownership of Accessory Thing]

Where a main thing is transferred, its accessory thing(s) shall also be transferred unless the parties agree otherwise.

Article 321 [Ownership of Natural Fruits and Civil Fruits]

Unless parties agree otherwise, the natural fruits of a thing shall be acquired by the owner of the thing, or by a usufructuary if both an owner and a usufructuary of the thing exist.

The civil fruits of a thing shall be acquired as agreed by parties if a corresponding agreement exists, or, in the absence of an agreement or if the agreement is ambiguous, per trade usage.

Article 322 [Ownership of Property Acquired via Accession]

A thing created by processing, merger or mixing shall be owned as agreed if an agreement exists, or per law in the absence of an agreement or if the agreement is ambiguous. In the absence of any provisions in law, its ownership shall be determined per the principles of making full use of a thing and protecting a party without fault. Where one party's fault or determination of ownership causes damage to a counterparty, the party at fault shall pay damages or compensation to the injured one.

Part Three Usufructs

Chapter X General Rules

Article 323 [Definition of Usufruct]

A usufructuary has the right, per law, to possess, use, and benefit from immovable or movable property owned by another person.

Article 324 [Usufruct over Natural Resources Owned by State and Collectives]

Organizations and individuals may, per law, possess, use, and benefit from natural resources the State owns, natural resources owned by the State and used by collectives, and natural resources owned by collectives per law.

Article 325 [Use of Natural Resources]

The State implements a system of paid use of natural resources, except where law provides otherwise.

Article 326 [Exercise of Usufructuary Rights]

Usufructuaries shall, when exercising their rights, observe the provisions of laws for the protection, rational development and exploitation of resources and the protection of the ecological environment. An owner may not interfere with a usufructuary's exercise of rights.

Article 327 [Right of Usufructuary to Compensation for Expropriation and Requisition]

Where a usufruct is extinguished or its exercise adversely affected by expropriation or requisition of immovable or movable property, the usufructuary shall have the right to compensation per the provisions of Articles 243 and 245 of this Code.

Article 328 [Legal Protection of Right to Use of Sea Areas]

The right to use of sea areas acquired per law is protected by law.

Article 329 [Legal Protection of Right to Prospect for Minerals, etc.]

The rights, acquired per law, to prospect for and mine minerals, to draw water, and to use waters and tidal flats for aquaculture or fishing shall receive protection under law.

Chapter XI Right to Contractual Land Management

Article 330 [Two-Tier Management System and Contractual Land Management]

Rural collective economic organizations shall adopt a two-tier management system, with household land contracting and operating as the basis, integrated with collective management.

A system of contractual land management is adopted per law for cultivated land, forestland, grassland and other land used for agricultural purpose, which are owned by farmers collectively or owned by the State but used by farmers collectively.

Article 331 [Definition of Right to Contractual Land Management]

A holder of the right to contractual land management has the right, per law, to possess, use, and benefit from the cultivated land, forestland and grassland s/he contracts and manages, and to engage in agricultural production such as crop and plant cultivation, forestry, and animal husbandry .

Article 332 [Time Period for Contracting of Land]

The term of a contract for cultivated land is 30 years. The term of a contract for grassland ranges from 30 to 50 years. The term of a contract for forestland ranges from 30 to 70 years.

On expiration of the contract term as provided in the preceding paragraph, a holder of the right to contractual land management shall continue with the contract per the provisions of laws on rural land contracting.

Article 333 [Creation and Registration of Right to Contractual Land Management]

The right to contractual land management is created when the contract on the right to contractual land management takes effect.

A registry shall issue a certificate, such as a certificate of the right to contractual land management or a certificate of the right to forestry, to a holder of the right to contractual land management and maintain a register for this purpose to record and confirm such rights.

Article 334 [Swap or Transfer of Right to Contractual Land Management]

Holders of rights to contractual land management are entitled to exchange or transfer such rights per law. The contracted land may not be used for non-agricultural construction without legal approval therefor.

Article 335 [Registration of Swap or Transfer of Right to Contractual Land Management]

Where the right to contractual land management is exchanged or transferred, the parties may apply to a registry for registration thereof; in the absence of registration, such exchange or transfer shall not be asserted against a *bona fide* third party.

Article 336 [Adjustment of Contracted Land]

Within the term of the contractual land management, the party providing the contracted land shall not adjust the contracted land.

Where special circumstances such as severe damage to the contracted land stemming from natural disasters render a suitable adjustment of the contracted cultivated land and grassland necessary, such adjustment shall be made per the provisions of laws on rural land contracting.

Article 337 [Withdrawal of Contracted Land]

Within the term of the contractual land management, the party providing the contracted land may not take back the contracted land, except where law provides otherwise.

Article 338 [Compensation for Expropriation of Contracted Land]

Where contracted land is expropriated, an interested holder of the right to contractual land management has the right to corresponding compensation per the provisions of Article 243 of this Code.

Article 339 [Transfer of Right to Land Management]

A holder of the right to contractual land management may decide on his/her own initiative per law to transfer the right to land management to others via leasing, contributing it as capital or other means per law.

Article 340 [Definition of Right to Land Management]

Within the time period as agreed in a contract, a holder of the right to land management has the right to occupy the rural land, to engage in agricultural production and operation on his/her own, and to benefit therefrom.

Article 341 [Creation and Registration of Right to Land Management]

A right to land management which is transferred for a term of five years or longer is created when the contract for the transfer takes effect. Parties may apply to a registry for registration of the right to land management; in the absence of registration, such right shall not be asserted against a *bona fide* third party.

Article 342 [Transfer of Right to Management of Land Contracted via Other Means]

Where rural land is contracted by such means as bidding, auction, or public negotiation, for which a certificate of title is obtained via registration per law, the right to manage such land may, per law, be transferred via leasing, contributing it as capital, mortgaging, or other means.

Article 343 [Mutatis Mutandis Application to Contractual Management of State-Owned Agricultural Land]

Where contractual management is adopted for State-owned agricultural land, the relevant provisions of this Book shall apply *mutatis mutandis*.

Chapter XII Right to Use of Land for Construction

Article 344 [Definition of Right to Use of Land for Construction]

A holder of the right to use of State-owned land zoned for construction is entitled per law to possess, use, and benefit from a parcel of such land and use it to construct buildings, structures, and ancillary facilities.

Article 345 [Creation of Multi-Tier Right to Use of Land for Construction]

The right to use of land for construction may be created separately on the surface of the parcel or above or below it.

Article 346 [Principles for Creation of Right to Use of Land for Construction]

The right to use of land for construction shall be created in conformity with the requirements for resource efficiency and ecological environment protection as well as the provisions of laws and administrative regulations on planned use of land, and the creation of such right may not harm usufructs already established therein.

Article 347 [Modes of Creating Right to Use of Land for Construction]

The right to use of land for construction may be created via transfer or gratuitous grant.

Tendering, auctioning or other means of public bidding shall be adopted in transferring a parcel of land used for business, such as for industrial, commercial, tourism, recreational, and commercial residential purposes, or where two or more prospective users compete for the right to use of the same parcel of land.

The creation of a right to use of land for construction via gratuitous grant is rigourously controlled.

Article 348 [Contract for Transfer of Right to Use of Land for Construction]

Where the right to use of land for construction is created through tendering, auctioning, agreement, or other means of transfer, the parties shall execute a contract in writing for the transfer of the right to use of land for construction.

A contract for the transfer of the right to use of land for construction generally contains the following terms:

1. Name and address of each party;

2. Metes and bounds and area of the parcel;

3. Space to be occupied by buildings and structures and their ancillary facilities;

4. Planned use and zoning conditions for the parcel;

5. Term of the right to use of land for construction;

6. Transfer fees and other fees and mode of their payment; and

7. Means of dispute resolution.

Article 349 [Registration of Right to Use of Land for Construction]

To create a right to use of land for construction, an application shall be filed with a registry for registration of such right. The right to use of land for construction is created upon registration. The registry shall issue a certificate of title to the right holder.

Article 350 [Regulation of Purpose of Use of Land]

A holder of the right to use of land for construction shall reasonably use the land and may not alter its planned use. Where necessity compels a change to the planned use, approval must be obtained from a relevant administrative agency per law.

Article 351 [Right Holder's Obligation to Pay Transfer Fees, etc.]

A holder of the right to use of land for construction shall pay transfer fees and other fees per law and contract.

Article 352 [Ownership of Buildings, etc. Constructed by Holder of Right

to Use of Land for Construction]

The buildings, structures, and ancillary facilities thereof constructed by a holder of the right to use of land for construction shall belong to such right holder, unless evidence proves to the contrary.

Article 353 [Channels for Circulation of Right to Use of Land for Construction]

Holders of the right to use of land for construction are entitled to transfer, exchange, contribute as capital, give away as gift, or mortgage such right, unless law provides otherwise.

Article 354 [Format and Period for Contract Disposing of Right to Use of Land for Construction]

Where the right to use of land for construction is transferred, exchanged, contributed as capital, given in gift, or mortgaged, the parties shall execute a corresponding contract in writing. The time period of the use shall be decided by the parties, but shall not exceed the remaining term of the right to use of land for construction.

Article 355 [Registration of Change Following Circulation of Construction Land Use Right]

Where the right to use of land for construction is transferred, exchanged, contributed as capital, or given in gift, an application for registration of the change shall be filed with a registry.

Article 356 [Buildings and Other Fixtures Transferring with Construction Land Use Right in Circulation]

Where the right to use of land for construction is transferred, exchanged, contributed as capital, or given in gift, the buildings, structures and ancillary facilities thereof affixed to the land shall transfer with it.

Article 357 [Construction Land Use Right Transferring with Buildings and Other Fixtures and Facilities in Circulation]

Where a building or structure, and ancillary facilities thereof are transferred, exchanged, contributed as capital, or given in gift, the right to use of land for construction for the parcel of land occupied by the building, structure, and ancillary facilities affixed thereto shall transfer with them.

Article 358 [Premature Withdrawal of Construction Land Use Right and Compensation Therefor]

Where a parcel of land for construction needs to be taken back in the public interest before the expiration of the right to its use, compensation shall be paid for the houses and other immovable property on the land per the provisions of Article 243 of this Code, and a corresponding portion of the transfer fees shall also be refunded.

Article 359 [Renewal of Right to Use of Land for Construction]

The right to of land for construction of residential buildings shall automatically renew on the expiration of its term. The payment, reduction, or exemption of renewal fees shall be administered per the provisions of laws and administrative regulations.

The renewal of the right to use of land for construction for non-residential buildings, on expiration of its term, shall be administered per the provisions of applicable laws. The ownership of the buildings and other immovable property on such parcel of land shall be determined by reference to a corresponding agreement, or, in the absence of such agreement or if the agreement is ambiguous, per the provisions of laws and administrative regulations.

Article 360 [Deregistration of Construction Land Use Right]

Where the right to use of land for construction is extinguished, the transferor of the right shall deregister the right promptly. The registry shall then recall the certificate of title thereof.

Article 361 [Laws Applicable to Collective Land Used for Construction]

The use of collectively-owned land for construction shall be administered per the provisions of laws on land administration.

Chapter XIII Right to Use of Homesite

Article 362 [Definition of Right to Use of Homesite]

A holder of the right to use of a homesite has the right to occupy and use the parcel of land owned by the collective, and to use such parcel to build a dwelling and ancillary facilities per law.

Article 363 [Norms Applicable to Acquisition, Exercise and Transfer of Right to Use of Homesite]

Relevant laws and State regulations on land administration shall apply to the acquisition, exercise, and transfer of the right to use of a homesite.

Article 364 [Destruction of Homesite and Acquisition of Replacement]

Where a homesite is destroyed due to such causes as natural disasters, the corresponding right to use of homesite is extinguished. Villagers who have lost their homesites shall have replacements per law.

Article 365 [Registration of Change and Deregistration of Homesite Use Right]

Where a registered right to use of a homesite is transferred or extinguished, registration of the change or deregistration of the right shall be made without delay.

Chapter XIV Right of Habitation

Article 366 [Definition of Right of Habitation]

A holder of the right of habitation has the usufruct of possessing and using another person's dwelling as agreed in the contract to meet his/her habitation needs.

Article 367 [Contract of Habitation Right]

To create a right of habitation, the parties shall execute a contract on such right in writing.

A contract for a right of habitation generally contains the following terms:

1. Name and address of each party;
2. Location of the dwelling;
3. Conditions of and requirements for the habitation;
4. Duration of the right of habitation; and
5. Means of dispute resolution.

Article 368 [Creation of Habitation Right]

A right of habitation shall be created gratis unless the parties agree otherwise. To create a right of habitation, an application for the registration of the right shall be filed with a registry. The right of habitation is created upon registration.

Article 369 [Transfer and Inheritance of Habitation Right and Lease of Underlying Dwelling]

A right of habitation may not be transferred or inherited. The dwelling in which a right of habitation is created may not be leased unless the parties agree otherwise.

Article 370 [Extinguishment of Habitation Right]

A right of habitation is extinguished when its term expires, or if the person entitled to the right dies. Where a right of habitation is extinguished, deregistration of the right shall be made without delay.

Article 371 [Mutatis Mutandis Application of this Chapter to Creation of Habitation Right via Wills]

Where a right of habitation is created by a will, the relevant provisions of this Chapter shall apply *mutatis mutandis*.

Chapter XV Easements

Article 372 [Definition of Easement]

A holder of the right to an easement has the right to use the immovable property of another person as agreed in a contract to increase the benefits of his/her own immovable property.

The immovable property of another person as referred to in the preceding paragraph is the servient estate[1], and the immovable property of the person entitled to the easement is the dominant estate[2].

Article 373 [Contract of Easement]

To create an easement, the parties shall execute an easement contract in writing.

An easement contract generally contains the following terms:

1. Name and address of each party;

2. Location of the servient estate and the dominant estate;

3. Purposes and methods of using the servient estate;

---

1 I.e. Servient Tenement, or Burdened Land.

2 I.e. Dominant Tenement, or Benefited Land.

4. Duration of the easement;

5. Fees and their mode of payment; and

6. Means of dispute resolution.

Article 374 [Creation and Registration of Easement]

An easement is created at the time an easement contract takes effect. Where the parties require registration, an application may be filed with a registry for the registration of the easement; an easement may not be asserted against a *bona fide* third party in the absence of registration.

Article 375 [Servient Owner's Obligations[1]]

The owner of a servient estate shall allow the holder of an easement to use the servient estate as agreed in their contract and may not interfere with the exercise of such right by the easement holder.

Article 376 [Dominant Owner's Obligations[2]]

An easement holder shall use the servient estate per the purposes and methods as agreed in the contract and minimize restrictions on the real right of the owner of the servient estate.

Article 377 [Duration of Easement]

The duration of an easement shall be subject to the parties' agreement but may not exceed the remaining term of a usufruct such as the right to contractual land management or the right to use of land for construction.

Article 378 [Succession of Easement]

Where an owner of land entitled to or burdened with an easement creates a usufruct such as a right to contractual land management or a right to use of a

---

1 I.e. Easement Giver's Obligations, or Grantor's Obligations.

2 I.e. Easement Holder's Obligations, Easement Receiver's Obligations, or Grantee's Obligations.

homesite on the land thereof, the usufructuary shall continue to be entitled to or burdened with such easement.

Article 379 [Restrictions of Prior Usufructs on Easements]

Where a usufruct such as a right to contractual land management, a right to use of land for construction or a right to use of a homesite exists on a parcel of land, the owner of the land may not create an easement on it without the usufructuary's consent.

Article 380 [Transfer of Easement]

An easement may not be separately transferred. When a right to contractual land management, a right to use of land for construction or a similar right is transferred, the attached easement shall transfer along with it, unless agreed otherwise in the contract.

Article 381 [Mortgage of Easement]

An easement may not be separately mortgaged. Where a right to contractual land management, a right to use of land for construction or a similar right is mortgaged, the attached easement shall also transfer upon enforcement of the mortgage.

Article 382 [Inseparability of Easement from Dominant Estate and Rights Thereupon]

Where a dominant estate or a right to contractual land management or right to use of land for construction created thereupon is transferred in part and the part transferred involves an easement, the transferee is likewise entitled to enjoyment of such easement.

Article 383 [Inseparability of Easement from Servient Estate and Rights Thereupon]

Where a servient estate or such rights created thereupon as the right to contractual land management and to use of land for construction are transferred in part, and the part transferred is subject to an easement, the transferee will be legally bound by such easement.

Article 384 [Legal Reasons for Servient Owner to Unilaterally Cancel Easement Contract]

Where any of the following circumstances applies with respect to the holder of an easement, the servient owner has the right to cancel the easement contract and the easement is extinguished accordingly:

1. S/he abuses the right to the easement in violation of the provisions of laws or the contract; or

2. In the case of paid use of the servient estate, s/he does not pay fees due within the period as provided in the agreement and still fails to pay within a reasonable grace period after being urged twice for such payment.

Article 385 [Procedures for Change, Transfer or Extinguishment of Registered Easement]

Where a registered easement is altered, transferred, or extinguished, the registration of the change or the deregistration thereof shall be made without delay.

Part Four Security Interests

Chapter XVI General Rules

Article 386 [Definition of Security Interest]

Where an obligor does not perform due obligations, or any event occurs which triggers the enforcement of a security interest as agreed by the parties, the holder of the security interest shall enjoy a preferential claim on collateral per law, unless law provides otherwise.

Article 387 [Application Scope of Security Interest and Counter-Guarantee]

Where obligees desire to secure their claims in civil acts such as lending, buying and selling, they may create a security interest therefor per the provisions of this Code and other laws.

Where a third party provides security to an obligee for an obligor, the obligor may be required to provide a counter-guarantee. The provisions of this Code and other laws shall apply to counter-guarantees.

Article 388 [Security Contract]

A security interest shall be created by execution of a security contract per the provisions of this Code and other laws. Security contracts include those for mortgages, pledges, and other contracts with a security function. A security contract is an accessorial contract subordinate to a principal contract defining principal claims and obligations. If a principal contract is void, its security contract(s) is/are also void, unless law provides otherwise.

Where a security contract is voided, if the obligor, the grantor, and the obligee are at fault, they shall assume respective civil liability in proportion thereto.

Article 389 [Coverage of Security Interest]

The scope covered by a security interest includes the principal claim and interest thereof, liquidated and compensatory damages, and cost incurred in keeping the collateral and enforcing the security interest.

Article 390 [Extension of Security Interest to Proceeds or Substitutes of Collateral and Substitutes or Proceeds Being Placed in Escrow]

Where collateral is destroyed, damaged, or lost, or is expropriated during the existence of the security interest, the holder of the security interest enjoys priority to the insurance proceeds, damages or compensation received as a result thereof. If the term of performance of the secured claim has not yet expired, the insurance proceeds, damages or compensation may also be placed in escrow.

Article 391 [Legal Consequences of Transfer of Secured Obligations Without Grantor's Consent]

Where a third party grants security and an obligee allows an obligor to transfer all or part of the secured obligation(s) without such third party's written consent, the grantor shall be no longer liable to secure that portion of the obligation(s) so transferred.

Article 392 [Rules for Enforcement of Guarantee with Concurrence of Guaranty and Security Interest]

Where both collateral and a guaranty secure an obligee's claim and the obligor does not perform his/her obligations when due, or any [other] event occurs which, per the parties' agreement, triggers enforcement of a security interest , the obligee may enforce the claim per the agreement reached between and among the parties. In the absence of such agreement or if the agreement is ambiguous, where the obligor has pledged the collateral, the obligee shall first enforce the claim against the collateral and, where a third party has pledged the collateral, the obligee may elect to enforce the claim against the collateral or hold the guarantor liable. After the third party who provides guarantee[1] has assumed such liability, s/he shall have the right of recovery against the obligor.

---

1 Guarantee is used throughout the translation in a broad sense to include both security interest and guaranty.

Article 393 [Occasions for Extinguishment of Security Interest]

A security interest is extinguished under any of the following circumstances:

1. The principal claim is extinguished;
2. The security interest is enforced;
3. The obligee renounces the security interest; or
4. Any other circumstance in which a security interest is extinguished per law.

Chapter XVII Mortgages

Section 1 General Mortgages

Article 394 [Definition of Mortgage]

Where, to secure the performance of an obligation, an obligor or a third party mortgages property to an obligee without parting with possession thereof, the obligee shall have a preferential claim on such property if the obligor does not perform his/her obligations when due or any [other] event occurs which, per the parties' agreement, triggers enforcement of the mortgage .

The obligor or the third party as specified in the preceding paragraph is the mortgagor, the obligee is the mortgagee, and the property provided to secure the claim is the mortgaged property.

Article 395 [Scope of Mortgageable Property]

The following property, which an obligor or a third party has the right to dispose of, may be mortgaged:

1. Buildings and other fixtures attached to the land;
2. Right to use of land for construction;
3. Right to use of sea areas;
4. Production equipment, raw materials, goods in process and finished

products;

5. Buildings and watercraft under construction and aircraft being built;

6. Means of transport; and

7. Other property not forbidden by laws or administrative regulations to be mortgaged.

A mortgagor may cumulatively mortgage the property enumerated in the preceding paragraph.

Article 396 [Floating Mortgage/Charge]

An enterprise, an individual industrial and commercial household or an agricultural production operator may create a floating mortgage/charge over its production equipment, raw materials, and semi-finished and finished products that it currently owns or will acquire in future and, if the obligor does not perform his/her obligations when due or any [other] event occurs which triggers enforcement of the security interest in such mortgaged/charged property per the parties' agreement, the obligee enjoys a preferential claim on the mortgaged/charged movable property as ascertained and fixed when the floating mortgage/charge crystallizes into a fixed mortgage/charge and attaches to such movable property.

Article 397 [Concurrent Mortgage of Right to Use of Land for Construction and Buildings Attached Thereto]

Where a building is mortgaged, the right to use of land for construction in the area occupied by the building shall also be mortgaged. Where a right to use of land for construction is mortgaged, any building on the land shall likewise be mortgaged.

Where a mortgagor does not mortgage the building and the land use right together as provided in the preceding paragraph, the one not mortgaged shall be deemed to be mortgaged with the other at the same time.

Article 398 [Restrictions on Mortgage of Construction Land Use Right Held by Township and Village Enterprises]

A right to use of land for construction held by a township or village enterprise may not be separately mortgaged. Where a factory building or any other building of a township or village enterprise is mortgaged, the right to use of land for construction in the area occupied by the building shall be likewise mortgaged.

Article 399 [Scope of Property Prohibited from Mortgage]

The following property may not be mortgaged:

1. Land ownership;

2. Right to use of land owned by a collective, such as homesites, and [barren] land and elevations retained for household usufruct, unless permitted by law;

3. Educational and medical and health facilities, and other public weal facilities of non-profit legal persons established for public weal purposes, such as schools, kindergartens, and medical institutions;

4. Property whose ownership or right of use is undefined or disputed;

5. Property that has been frozen, sequestrated, or placed under supervision per law; and

6. Other property that may not be mortgaged under provisions of laws or administrative regulations.

Article 400 [Contract for Mortgage]

To create a mortgage, the parties shall execute a mortgage contract in writing.

A mortgage contract generally contains the following terms:

1. Type and amount of the secured claim;

2. Time period during which the obligor shall perform the obligation;

3. Such items as name and amount of the mortgaged property; and

4. Scope of the claim secured or security interest.

Article 401 [Pass to Mortgagee of Title to Mortgaged Property in Case of Default by Obligor]

Where, before the due date of performance of an obligation, the mortgagee reaches an agreement with the mortgagor per which the ownership of the mortgaged property is to pass to the obligee if the obligor fails to perform an obligation when due, the mortgagee shall only enjoy preferential payment from the mortgaged property per law.

Article 402 [Registration of Immovable Property Mortgage]

To create a mortgage on property as specified in Subparagraphs 1 through 3 of the first paragraph of Article 395 of this Code, or on a building under construction as specified in Subparagraph 5 of the same paragraph, the mortgage shall be registered. The mortgage shall be created upon registration.

Article 403 [Effect of Registration of Chattel Mortgage]

A chattel mortgage shall be created when the mortgage contract takes effect; in the absence of registration, such mortgage may not be asserted against a *bona fide* third party.

Article 404 [Without Recourse to Bona Fide Transferee of Mortgaged Chattel]

A chattel mortgage may not be asserted against a buyer who has paid a reasonable purchase price and acquired the mortgaged chattel in the ordinary course of business.

Article 405 [Mortgage Versus Lease]

Where property is leased to another who takes possession of it before the creation of the mortgage, such lease shall remain unaffected by the mortgage subsequently created upon such property.

Article 406 [Disposition of Mortgaged Property]

A mortgagor may transfer the mortgaged property to another during the term of the mortgage. If the parties agree otherwise, their agreement shall apply. The mortgage shall remain unaffected by such transfer.

A mortgagor who transfers the mortgaged property shall notify the mortgagee thereof in due time. If the mortgagee can demonstrate that the transfer of the mortgaged property may jeopardize the mortgage, the mortgagee may demand that the mortgagor use the proceeds thereof to pay off the obligation before it is due or place such proceeds in escrow. The portion of the proceeds from the transfer that exceeds the amount of the obligation shall belong to the mortgagor, while shortfall, if any, shall be covered by the obligor.

Article 407 [Inseparability of Mortgage from Secured Claim]

A mortgage may not be transferred independently of the secured claim or be used as security for another claim. Where a claim is transferred, the mortgage securing the claim shall transfer along with it, except where law or the parties' agreement provides otherwise.

Article 408 [Protection and Maintenance of Mortgage]

Where a mortgagor's acts serve to reduce the value of mortgaged property, the mortgagee has the right to demand that the mortgagor desist from such acts. Where the value of the mortgaged property is reduced, the mortgagee has the right to demand that the mortgagor restore its value or provide additional security to make up for the reduced value. Where the mortgagor neither restores the original value of the mortgaged property nor provides additional security therefor, the mortgagee has the right to demand that the obligor pay off the debt in advance.

Article 409 [Disposition of Mortgage and Its Priority Ranking]

A mortgagee may waive the right to a mortgage or a ranking among mortgagees. A mortgagee and a mortgagor may agree to alter such terms as the ranking and the amount of the secured claim. However, any such alteration to the mortgage shall not adversely affect other mortgagees without their written consent.

Where an obligor creates a mortgage on self-owned property and the mortgagee waives the mortgage or ranking, or alters the mortgage right, the other guarantors or security grantors shall be relieved of their guarantee liability to the extent of such mortgagee's preferential rights and interests forfeited thereby, except where the other guarantors or security grantors undertake to remain committed to the original guaranty or security.

Article 410 [Enforcement of Mortgage]

Where an obligor fails to perform obligations when due or an event occurs which triggers enforcement of a mortgage as agreed by the parties , the mortgagee may, in agreement with the mortgagor, enjoy the preferential right to take the mortgaged property in payment based on its appraised value or to take the proceeds from auction or sale of the mortgaged property for satisfaction of the obligation.When such an agreement jeopardizes the interests of any other obligee, such other obligee may petition a people's court to invalidate it.

Where a mortgagee and a mortgagor fail to agree on the methods for enforcing a mortgage, the mortgagee may petition a people's court to have the mortgaged property auctioned off or sold.

Taking of the mortgaged property in payment based on appraised value or sale of the mortgaged property shall be based on its market price.

Article 411 [Ascertainment of Property Subject to Floating Mortgage/ Charge]

Where a floating mortgage/charge is created per the provisions of Article

396 of this Code, the mortgaged/charged property shall be ascertained when any one of the following situations arises:

1. The claim is unsatisfied when the term for performance of the obligation expires;

2. The mortgagor/chargor is declared bankrupt or dissolved;

3. An event occurs which triggers the enforcement of the mortgage/charge as agreed; or

4. Any other circumstance that seriously affects the satisfaction of the claim.

Article 412 [Effect of Mortgage on Fruits of Mortgaged Property]

Where an obligor fails to perform obligations due or an event occurs that triggers enforcement of the mortgage per the parties' agreement and, as a result, the mortgaged property is sequestrated by a people's court per law, the mortgagee is entitled to collect the natural fruits or civil fruits accrued from the mortgaged property from the date of the sequestration, except where the mortgagee fails to notify the person who is obligated to pay such civil fruits.

The fruits as specified in the preceding paragraph shall first be used to offset the costs of their collection.

Article 413 [Disposition of Proceeds from Mortgaged Property]

Where the appraised value of a mortgaged property or the proceeds from its auction or sale exceed the amount of the claim, the excess shall revert to the mortgagor, while shortfall, if any, shall be covered by the obligor.

Article 414 [Order of Priority for Satisfaction of Claims with Respect to Multiple Mortgages]

Where the same property is mortgaged to two or more obligees, the proceeds from its auction or sale shall be applied to satisfaction of claims per the following provisions:

1. Where the mortgages have all been registered, satisfaction shall be based on chronological order of registration;

2. A registered mortgage shall precede an unregistered one; and

3. Where none of the mortgages are registered, related claims shall be satisfied on a *pro rata* basis.

The preceding paragraph may [also] apply *mutatis mutandis* to the order of satisfaction for other registrable security interests.

Article 415 [Order of Priority for Satisfaction of Claims with Concurrence of Mortgage and Pledge]

Where both a mortgage and a pledge are created on the same property, the satisfaction of claims with proceeds from auction or sale of the property shall be based on the chronological sequence of mortgage registration and delivery of the property.

Article 416 [Priority of Chattel Mortgage for Securing Payment of Purchase Price]

Where the principal claim a chattel mortgage secures is the purchase price of the mortgaged property, and the mortgage is registered within 10 days after delivery of the subject matter, the mortgagee shall outrank all the other security interest holders of the buyer of the mortgaged property, except for a lienholder with security interest thereon.

Article 417 [Effect of Mortgage on Newly-Added Buildings]

After a right to use of land for construction is mortgaged, no newly-added buildings on the parcel shall constitute a part of the mortgaged property. When a mortgage on the right to use of land for construction is enforced, newly-added buildings on such land shall transfer along with the right to use of land for construction, but the mortgagee has no preferential claim on the proceeds from disposition of such newly-added buildings.

Article 418 [Effect of Enforcement of Mortgaged Right to Use of Land Owned by a Collective]

Where a right to use of land owned by a collective is mortgaged per law and subsequently enforced, the nature of the ownership of the land and the purpose of its use may not be altered without undergoing the procedures legally prescribed therefor.

Article 419 [Duration of Mortgage]

A mortgagee shall exercise a mortgage right within the limitation period for the principal claim(s) secured; failure to do so will lead to denial of protection by a people's court.

Section 2 Revolving Mortgage

Article 420 [Definition of Revolving Mortgage]

Where an obligor or a third party provides collateral for a series of revolving claims which will arise within a specified period of time, if the obligor fails to perform an obligation when it falls due or an event occurs that triggers enforcement of the mortgage per the parties' agreement, the mortgagee shall have a preferential claim on the mortgaged property up to the ceiling of the balance of claims as specified in the mortgage contract.

A claim that exists before the creation of the revolving mortgage for the revolving claims may, on consent of the parties, be included in the claims secured by such mortgage.

Article 421 [Transfer of Claims Under Revolving Mortgage]

Before the obligee's balance of claims secured by the mortgage for the revolving claim(s) is finalized, if part of the claim(s) is/are transferred, the mortgage shall not also be transferred, unless the parties agree otherwise.

Article 422 [Alteration of Terms and Conditions of Contract for Revolving Mortgage]

Before the balance of claims secured by a revolving mortgage for the revolving claims crystallizes, the mortgagee and the mortgagor may agree to alter the period for the crystallization of the balance of claims, the scope of the claims, and the ceiling of the balance of claims secured, provided such alterations do not adversely affect other mortgagees.

Article 423 [Crystallization of Balance of Claims Under Revolving Mortgage]

A mortgagee's balance of claims crystallizes under one of the following circumstances:

1. The period agreed for the crystallization of the balance of claims expires;

2. In the absence of an agreement on the period for the balance crystallization or if the agreement is ambiguous, the mortgagee or the mortgagor demands crystallization of the claim balance after the lapse of two years from the date of the creation of the revolving mortgage;

3. It will be impossible for a new claim to arise;

4. The mortgagee knows or ought to have known that the mortgaged property has been frozen or sequestrated;

5. The obligor or the mortgagor is declared bankrupt or dissolved; or

6. Any other circumstance under which the balance of claims crystallizes per law.

Article 424 [Applicable Laws for Revolving Mortgages]

In addition to the provisions of this Section, the relevant provisions of Section 1 of this Chapter shall apply *mutatis mutandis* to revolving mortgage.

Chapter XVIII Pledges

Section 1 Pledge Over Movable Property

Article 425 [Definition of Pledge over Movable Property]

Where an obligor or a third party pledges movable property and delivers it into a creditor's possession to secure the performance of an obligation, if the obligor does not perform the obligation when due or an event occurs that triggers enforcement of the pledge per the parties' agreement, the obligee shall have a preferential right of satisfaction from such movable property.

The obligor or third party as specified in the preceding paragraph is the pledgor, the obligee is the pledgee, and the movable property delivered is the pledged property.

Article 426 [Scope of Movable Property Prohibited from Pledge]

Movable property whose transfer is prohibited by laws or administrative regulations may not be pledged .

Article 427 [Contract of Pledge]

Parties shall execute a pledge contract in writing to create a pledge.

A pledge contract generally contains the following terms:

1. The type and amount of the secured claim;
2. The term within which for the obligor to perform the obligation;
3. Such items as the name and quantity of the pledged property;
4. The scope of the security interest; and
5. The time and mode of delivery of the pledged property.

Article 428 [Pass to Pledgee of Title to Pledged Movable Property in Case of Default by Obligor]

Where, before the expiration of the period for performance of an obligation, the pledgee and the pledgor agree that title to the pledged property shall pass to the obligee if the obligor does not perform such obligation when due, the pledgee shall only enjoy a preferential right of satisfaction from the pledged property per law.

Article 429 [Commencement of Pledge]

A pledge is created on delivery of the pledged property by the pledgor.

Article 430 [Collection of Fruits and Their First Use to Cover Their Collection Costs]

A pledgee shall have the right to collect the fruits accruing from a pledged property unless agreed otherwise in the contract.

The fruits as specified in the preceding paragraph shall first be used to offset the costs of their collection.

Article 431 [Liability of Pledgee for Use and Disposition of Pledged Property Without Consent of Pledgor]

A pledgee who, during the validity of the pledge, uses or disposes of the pledged property without the pledgor's consent and thereby causes damage to the pledgor, shall be liable for compensation therefor.

Article 432 [Pledgee's Obligation to Keep Pledged Property and Liability for Compensation]

A pledgee is obligated to properly keep pledged property and shall be liable for compensation where it is destroyed, damaged, or lost due to improper custody.

Where the pledgee's acts are likely to cause damage to or destruction or loss of the pledged property, the pledgor may demand that the pledgee place the pledged property in escrow or demand that the pledgee accept performance of the obligation before due and return the pledged property.

Article 433 [Protection and Maintenance of Pledge]

Where through no fault of the pledgee, the pledged property is likely to suffer damage or significant diminution in value sufficient to prejudice the pledgee's right, the pledgee shall have the right to demand that the pledgor provide additional security; if the pledgor does not do so, the pledgee may have the pledged property sold at auction or at sale and may, by agreement with the pledgor, apply the proceeds from the auction or sale to satisfy the obligation before it is due or place such proceeds in escrow.

Article 434 [Sub-Pledge by Pledgee Without Pledgor's Consent]

A pledgee who, during the validity of the pledge, sub-pledges pledged property to a third party without the consent of the pledgor and thereby causes destruction, damage, or loss of the pledged property, shall be liable for compensation therefor.

Article 435 [Waiver of Pledge]

A pledgee may waive the pledge. When an obligor creates a pledge over self-owned property and the pledgee waives the pledge, the other guarantors or security grantors shall be relieved of their guarantee liability to the extent of such pledgee's preferential rights and interests forfeited thereby, unless the other guarantors or security grantors undertake to remain committed to the original guaranty or security.

Article 436 [Return of Pledged Property and Realization of Pledge]

A pledgee shall return pledged property after the obligor has performed the obligation or the pledgor has satisfied the secured claim before it is due.

Where an obligor does not perform an obligation or an event occurs triggering enforcement of the pledge per the parties' agreement, the pledgee may, in agreement with the pledger and based on the appraised value, take the pledged property in satisfaction of the claim, or have a preferential right of satisfaction from the proceeds of auction or sale of the pledged property.

The appraisal-based taking or sale of the pledged property shall be based on its market price.

Article 437 [Enforcement of Pledge Without Delay]

A pledgor may demand that the pledgee enforce the pledge in due time after expiration of the period for the performance of the obligation; if the pledgee does not do so, the pledgor may petition a people's court to have the pledged property sold at auction or at sale.

Where a pledgor demands that the pledgee enforce the pledge without delay, and the pledgor sustains damage or loss due to the pledgee's neglect to do so, the pledgee shall be liable for compensation therefor.

Article 438 [Disposition of Proceeds from Pledged Property]

Where pledged property is taken in payment by the pledgee based on its appraised value or sold at auction or sale, if the appraised value or the proceeds from auction or sale exceed the amount of the debt claim, the excess shall revert to the pledgor, while shortfall, if any, shall be covered by the obligor.

Article 439 [Revolving Pledge]

A pledgor and a pledgee may agree to create a revolving pledge.

In addition to the relevant provisions of this Section, those of Section 2 of Chapter 17 of this Book shall apply *mutatis mutandis* to revolving pledges.

Section 2 Pledge Over Rights

Article 440 [Scope of Pledgeable Rights]

The following rights, which an obligor or a third party has the right to dispose of, may be pledged:

1. Bills of exchange, promissory notes, and cheques;

2. Bonds and certificates of deposit;

3. Warehouse receipts and bills of lading;

4. Negotiable fund shares and equity shares;

5. Assignable proprietary rights in such intellectual property rights as the rights to exclusive use of registered trademarks, patents, and copyrights;

6. Existing and after-acquired accounts receivables; and

7. Other proprietary rights that may be pledged per the provisions of laws and administrative regulations.

Article 441 [Creation of Pledge over Securities]

A pledge over a bill of exchange, promissory note, cheque, bond, certificate of deposit, warehouse receipt, or bill of lading is created when the certificate evidencing the underlying right is delivered to the pledgee, or, in the absence of such a certificate, when the pledge is registered. If law provides otherwise, its provisions shall apply.

Article 442 [Special Methods for Realization of Pledge over Securities]

Where the maturity date for payment or goods delivery against a pledged bill of exchange, promissory note, cheque, bond, certificate of deposit, warehouse receipt, or bill of lading precedes the due date of the secured principal claim, the pledgee may redeem the instrument or take delivery of the goods and, in agreement with the pledgor, apply the money or the goods for satisfaction of the debt before due or place the money or goods in escrow.

Article 443 [Creation of Pledge over Fund Shares or Equity Shares and Restriction on Transfer Thereof]

A pledge over fund shares or equity shares is created upon the registration of such pledge.

The fund shares or equity shares may not be transferred after their pledge unless the pledgor and the pledgee agree otherwise via negotiation.The proceeds obtained by the pledgor from the transfer of the pledged fund shares or equity shares shall be used for satisfaction of the secured debt before it is due or be placed in escrow.

Article 444 [Creation of Pledge over Proprietary Rights in Intellectual Property and Restrictions on Transfer Thereof]

A pledge over a proprietary right in such intellectual property rights as the right to exclusive use of a registered trademark, patent right, or copyright, is created upon registration.

Where a proprietary right in intellectual property rights is pledged, the pledgor may not assign it or license it to another person, unless the pledgor and the pledgee agree otherwise via negotiation. The proceeds obtained by the pledgor from the assignment or licensing of the pledged proprietary right in intellectual property shall be used for satisfaction of the secured debt before it is due or be placed in escrow.

Article 445 [Creation of Pledge over Accounts Receivables and Restrictions on Transfer Thereof]

A pledge over an account receivable is created on its registration.

An account receivable, after being pledged, may not be transferred except where the pledgor and the pledgee agree otherwise via negotiation. The proceeds obtained by the pledgor from the transfer of an account receivable shall be used for satisfaction of the secured debt before it is due or be placed in escrow.

Article 446 [Laws Applicable to Pledge over Rights]

In addition to the provisions of this Section, the relevant provisions of Section 1 of this Chapter shall apply *mutatis mutandis* to pledge over rights.

Chapter XIX Liens

Article 447 [Definition of Lien]

Where an obligor does not perform an obligation when due, the obligee may retain the obligor's chattel(s) which is/are already in the legitimate possession of the obligee and shall have a preferential claim on such chattel(s).

The obligee as specified in the preceding paragraph is the lien holder or lienor and the chattel(s) in possession for this purpose is/are the property under a lien.

Article 448 [Relationship Between Chattel(s) Retained and Underlying Claim]

Chattel(s) retained under a lien by the obligee shall be in the same legal relationship as the underlying claim, except as between enterprises.

Article 449 [Restrictions on Scope of Lien]

Chattels not subject to lien per law or parties' agreement may not be so retained.

Article 450 [Special Provisions for Divisible Property Retained]

Where property retained under a lien is subject to partition, the value of the part or portion thereof retained shall correspond to the amount of the debt.

Article 451 [Lienor's Obligation to Keep Retained Property with Due Care]

A lienor is obligated to keep the retained property with due care and shall be liable for its destruction, damage or loss due to improper custody.

Article 452 [Lienor's Right to Collect Fruits]

A lienor shall have the right to collect the fruits accruing from the property retained under a lien.

The fruits as specified in the preceding paragraph shall first be used to offset the cost of their collection.

Article 453 [Time Period for Performance of Obligation by Lienee]

A lienor and an obligor/lienee shall agree on the time period for performance of the obligation after property is retained under a lien; in the absence of such agreement or if the agreement is ambiguous, the lienor shall grant the obligor/lienee a period of 60 or more days as the time period for performance, except for chattel(s) that is/are fresh, living, or perishable and therefore not easy to keep. Where an obligor/lienee fails to perform upon expiration of the period for performance, the lienor may, in agreement with the obligor/lienee, appraise and take the retained property in payment, or auction off or sell the retained property and enjoy preferential satisfaction from the proceeds therefrom.

The appraisal-based taking or sale of the retained property shall be based on its market price.

Article 454 [Obligor's Right to Demand Enforcement of Lien by Lienor]

An obligor may demand that a lienor enforce a lien after expiration of the term of performance of an obligation; if the lienor does not do so, the obligor may petition a people's court to have the retained property sold at auction or at sale.

Article 455 [Exercise of Lien]

After property retained under a lien is taken in payment by the lienor based on its appraised value or sold at auction or at sale, if its value or proceeds therefrom exceed the amount of the debt claim, the excess shall revert to the obligor, who shall cover shortfall, if any.

Article 456 [Order of Priority with Respect to Concurrence of Lien, Mortgage and Pledge]

Where a lien is created on a chattel over which a mortgage or pledge has already been created, the lienor shall have a preferential right to satisfaction.

Article 457 [Special Occasions for Extinguishment of Lien]

A lien is extinguished when the lienor loses possession of the retained property or accepts another form of security from the obligor.

Part Five Possession

Chapter XX Possession

Article 458 [Norms Applicable to Rightful Possession]

Where possession of immovable or movable property is based on a contractual relationship or the like, the use of such property, the benefits therefrom, and the liability for breach of contract and other such matters shall be subject to the provisions of the underlying contract; in the absence of such provisions in the contract or if they are ambiguous, the provisions of relevant laws shall apply.

Article 459 [Liability for Damage Caused by Wrongful Possession]

Where a possessor inflicts damage on immovable or movable property in his/her possession through its use, a *mala fide* possessor shall be liable for compensation therefor.

Article 460 [Right Holder's Demand for Return and Possessor's Right to Reimbursement for Costs]

Where immovable or movable property is in another's possession, the right holder of the property may demand return of the property and its fruits.

However, the right holder shall pay the necessary costs incurred by a *bona fide* possessor for the maintenance of the immovable or movable property.

Article 461 [Right Holder's Claim to Damages]

Where immovable or movable property in another person's possession is destroyed, damaged, or lost, and the right holder of the the property demands compensation, the possessor shall return to the right holder the insurance proceeds, damages or compensation arising from the destruction, damage or loss thereof; if the right holder is not fully compensated, a *mala fide* possessor shall cover the loss/shortfall.

Article 462 [Right to Protection of Possession]

Where immovable or movable property is wrongfully taken, its possessor is entitled to demand recovery. Where an obstruction is imposed against the possession, the possessor has the right to demand removal of the obstruction or elimination of a danger. Where harm is caused due to the wrongful taking or obstruction, the possessor shall have the right to claim damages therefor.

The possessor's right to demand recovery is extinguished if such right is not exercised within one year from the date of the wrongful taking.

Book Three Contracts

Part One General Provisions

Chapter I General Rules

Article 463 [Regulatory Scope of This Book]

This Book regulates the civil law relations arising from contracts.

Article 464 [Definition of Contract and Application of Laws to Agreements Involving Personal Relations]

A contract is an agreement for the formation, alteration, or termination of a civil law relationship between civil law subject-persons.

Agreements concerning marriage, adoption, guardianship, or similar personal relationship shall be subject to the provisions of applicable laws governing personal relationships; in the absence of such provisions, those of this Book may apply *mutatis mutandis* according to the nature of such agreements.

Article 465 [Effect of Contract Lawfully Formed]

A contract formed per law is protected by law.

A contract formed per law is legally binding only on the parties thereto unless law provides otherwise.

Article 466 [Interpretation of Terms and Conditions of Contract]

Where a dispute arises between or among parties as to the understanding of a contractual term, the meaning of the disputed term shall be determined based on the provisions of the first paragraph of Article 142 of this Code.

M. Wan et al., *The Civil Code of the People's Republic of China*,
https://doi.org/10.1007/978-981-19-2794-2_3

Where a contract is executed in two or more language versions, which are of equal effect per agreement, the words and sentences used in each text shall be presumed to convey the same meaning. Where the words and sentences used in each version are discrepant, they shall be construed by reference to related terms, and the nature and purpose(s) of the contract, and the principle of good faith and other factors.

Article 467 [Applications of Laws to Non-Typical Contracts and Contracts with Foreign Elements]

The General Provisions of this Book shall apply to any contract not expressly provided for in this Code or other laws, while those provisions for the most similar contract in this Book and other laws may be applied *mutatis mutandis*.

The laws of the People's Republic of China shall apply to the contracts of Chinese-foreign equity joint ventures, contracts of Chinese-foreign contractual joint ventures, and contracts of Chinese-foreign cooperation in the exploration and exploitation of natural resources, all of which are to be performed within the territory of the People's Republic of China.

Article 468 [Application of Laws to Non-Contractual Claim-Obligation Relations]

For claim-obligation relations not arising from a contract, the provisions of laws specifically governing such relations shall apply; in the absence of such provisions, the relevant provisions of the General Provisions of this Book shall apply, except where they may be inapplicable due to the nature of the claim-obligation relation.

Chapter II Conclusion of Contracts

Article 469 [Forms of Contract]

Parties may conclude a contract in writing, orally, or in other forms.

'In writing' refers to any form that represents or produces the content therein in a visible form; such as a written agreement, letter, telegram, telex, or facsimile.

A data message in such form as an electronic data exchange or email, which represents or produces the content therein in a visible form, and which is readily accessible for reference and use, shall be deemed to be "in writing".

Article 470 [Main Clauses of Contracts and Contract Templates]

The content of a contract is agreed to by the parties and generally includes the following terms:

1. Name or appellation and domicile of each party;
2. Subject matter;
3. Quantity;
4. Quality;
5. Price or remuneration;
6. Time period, place, and mode of performance;
7. Liability for breach; and
8. Means of dispute resolution.

The parties may conclude a contract by reference to the various types of contract templates.

Article 471 [Means of Concluding Contract]

The parties may conclude a contract by adopting an offer and acceptance method or other means.

Article 472 [Definition of Offer and Its Elements]

An offer is an expression of intent to conclude a contract with another person, and such expression of intent shall meet the following conditions:

1. Its content is specific and definite; and

2. It indicates clearly that the offeror shall be bound by such expression of intent once accepted by the offeree.

Article 473 [Invitation to Make Offer]

An invitation to make an offer is a manifestation that the person extending such invitation expects another person to make an offer to him/her. Auction announcements, bidding announcements, stock prospectuses, bond prospectuses, fund prospectuses, commercial advertisements, and promotions, and mailed price catalogs, are invitations to make an offer.

A commercial advertisement and promotion shall constitute an offer if the content meets the conditions therefor.

Article 474 [Time of Offer Becoming Effective]

The provisions of Article 137 of this Code shall apply to the time when an offer takes effect.

Article 475 [Withdrawal of Offer]

An offer may be withdrawn. The provisions of Article 141 of this Code shall apply thereto.

Article 476 [Where Offer May Not Be Revoked]

An offer may be revoked, except under any of the following circumstances:

1. By stating a fixed time for acceptance or otherwise, the offeror has expressly indicated that the offer is irrevocable; or

2. It was reasonable for the offeree to rely on the offer as being irrevocable

and the offeree has accordingly made reasonable preparations for the performance of the contract.

Article 477 [Revocation of Offer]

Where an expression of intent to revoke an offer is made orally, the content of such expression of intent must become known to the offeree before the offeree accepts the offer; where an expression of intent to revoke an offer is not made orally, it must reach the offeree before the offeree accepts the offer.

Article 478 [Lapse of Offer]

An offer lapses under any of the following circumstances:

1. The offer is rejected;

2. The offer is revoked per law;

3. The offeree does not accept it upon expiration of the time period therefor; or

4. The offeree materially alters the terms of the offer.

Article 479 [Definition of Acceptance]

An acceptance is an expression of intent by the offeree indicating assent to an offer.

Article 480 [Means of Making Acceptance]

An acceptance shall be made by way of a notice, except where an acceptance may be made by performing an act as a result of the practices the parties have established between themselves or of trade usage, or as indicated in the offer.

Article 481 [Time Limit for Acceptance]

An acceptance must reach the offeror within the time limit specified in the offer.

Where no time limit for acceptance is indicated in the offer, an acceptance shall reach the offeror per the following provisions:

1. Where an offer is made orally, acceptance thereof shall be made immediately; or

2. Where an offer is made by means other than orally, the acceptance shall reach the offeror within a reasonable time.

Article 482 [Calculation of Time Period for Acceptance of Offers Made via Letter or Telegram]

Where an offer is made via a telegram or a letter, the period of time for acceptance begins to run from the date shown on the letter or the day when the telegram is handed in for dispatch, or if no such date is shown on the letter, from the mailing date shown by its postmark.Where an offer is made by means of instantaneous communication such as telephone, facsimile, or email, the period of time for acceptance begins to run from the moment that the offer reaches the offeree.

Article 483 [Time When Contract Is Formed]

A contract forms at the time an acceptance takes effect, except where law or the parties' agreement provides otherwise.

Article 484 [Time When Acceptance Becomes Effective]

Where an acceptance is made via a notice, the provisions of Article 137 of this Code shall apply to the time when the acceptance takes effect.

Where an acceptance is made without notice, and, by virtue of the offer or as a result of practices established between the parties or of trade usage, the offeree may indicate assent by performing an act, the acceptance takes effect the moment the act is performed.

Article 485 [Withdrawal of Acceptance]

An acceptance may be withdrawn. The provisions of Article 141 of this Code shall apply thereto.

Article 486 [Late Acceptance]

Where an acceptance is sent by the offeree beyond the period of time for acceptance, or where the acceptance is sent within the period of time but is unable to reach the offeror in due time under normal circumstances, such an acceptance constitutes a new offer, unless the offeror notifies the offeree without delay that the acceptance is effective.

Article 487 [Late Acceptance Sent Within the Period of Time]

Where an acceptance was sent by the offeree within the period of time therefor, and the acceptance has been sent in such circumstances that if its transmission had been normal it would have reached the offeror in due time, but it reached the offeror beyond the period of time due to other causes, the late acceptance is effective as an acceptance unless, the offeror informs the offeree without delay that s/he considers the acceptance as having run beyond the period of time for acceptance and does not accept it.

Article 488 [Material Alteration of Offer by Acceptance]

The terms of an acceptance shall be consistent with those contained in the offer. Any material alteration the offeree proposes to the terms of the offer constitutes a new offer. An alteration relating, among other things, to the subject matter of the contract, the quantity, quality, price or remuneration, time of performance, place and manner of performance, liability for breach, or methods of dispute resolution constitutes a material modification of the terms of an offer.

Article 489 [Non-Material Alteration of Offer by Acceptance]

Where an acceptance containing additional or different terms which do not materially alter the terms of the offer, constitutes an effective acceptance and the terms of the contract are the terms of the acceptance, unless the offeror, without undue delay, objects to the discrepancy, or the offer clearly indicates no allowance of any alterations by the offeree.

Article 490 [Time When Written Contract Forms]

Where the parties execute a contract in the form of a written agreement, it forms when the parties all sign, stamp, or affix their fingerprints thereto. Before signing, stamping, or affixing their fingerprints thereto, where one party has already performed the principal obligation and the counterparty has accepted the performance, the contract forms at the time of such acceptance.

Where laws, administrative regulations or the parties' agreement requires a contract to adopt a written form and the parties do not do so, if one party has already performed the principal obligation and the other has accepted the performance, the contract forms at the time of such acceptance.

Article 491 [Time for Formation of Contract in Form of Letter or Data Message or Online Contract]

Where parties execute a contract in the form of a letter, data message, or similar manner, and require a confirmation letter to be signed, the contract forms upon the signing thereof.

Where information about goods or services published by a party via an information network such as the internet meets the conditions for an offer, unless the parties agree otherwise, the contract forms when the counterparty selects such product or service and successfully submits an order therefor.

Article 492 [Locus Contractus]

The place where an acceptance takes effect shall be the place of the formation of the contract.

Where a contract is executed in the form of a data message, the recipient's principal place of business shall be the place of the formation of the contract; in the absence of a principal place of business, the recipient's domicile shall be the place of the formation of the contract. Where the parties agree otherwise, such agreement shall prevail.

Article 493 [Locus of Formation of Written Contract]

Where the parties execute a contract in the form of a written contract, the place where the contract is ultimately signed, stamped, or where their fingerprints are affixed thereto shall be the place of the formation of the contract, unless they agree otherwise.

Article 494 [Contract Based on State Purchase Order or Mandatory Task, Compulsory Offer and Compulsory Acceptance]

Where the State issues a State purchase order or a mandatory task to meet such needs as emergency and disaster relief, pandemic prevention and control or similar matters, civil law subject-persons involved shall conclude corresponding contracts between them based on their rights and obligations as provided in applicable laws and administrative regulations.

A party with an obligation to make an offer per the provisions of laws and administrative regulations shall make a reasonable offer without delay.

A party with an obligation to make an acceptance per the provisions of laws and administrative regulations may not reject a reasonable request of a counterparty to conclude a contract.

Article 495 [Preliminary Contract]

A letter of subscription, purchase order or booking form in which the parties agree to conclude a contract within a stated period in the future constitutes a preliminary contract.

Where one party fails to perform the obligation to conclude a contract as agreed in a preliminary contract, the counterparty may demand that such party be liable for breach of the preliminary contract.

Article 496 [Standard Clauses]

A standard clause refers to one that one party prepares in advance for repeated use, and which is not negotiated with the counterparty when the contract is concluded.

When concluding a contract containing standard clauses, the party providing such standard clauses shall set forth the parties' rights and obligations therein pursuant to the principle of fairness and shall, in a reasonable manner, bring the counterparty's attention to the clauses that affect such counterparty's vital interests and concerns, such as the clause exempting or reducing the liability of the party providing the standard clause, and explain such clause on demand by the other party. Where the party providing a standard clause does not perform the foregoing obligation of bringing attention to or explaining it, which causes the counterparty to fail to notice or understand a clause that affects his/her vital interests and concerns, the counterparty may demand that such clause not form part of the contract.

Article 497 [Occasions for Invalidity of Standard Clause]

A standard clause is null and void under any of the following circumstances:

1. The existence of a situation under which the clause is null and void, as provided for in Section 3 of Chapter VI of Book One and Article 506 of this Code;

2. The party providing the standard clause unreasonably exempts his/her liability or reduces it, increases the liability of the counterparty, or

otherwise limits the major rights of the counterparty; or

3. The party providing the standard clause excludes the major rights of the counterparty.

Article 498 [Construction of Standard Clauses]

Where a dispute arises over the understanding of a standard clause, the clause shall be construed per its common understanding. In the case of two or more constructions of a standard clause, the clause shall be construed against the party providing the standard clause. Where a standard clause is inconsistent with a non-standard clause, the non-standard clause shall prevail.

Article 499 [Advertisement of Reward]

Where a person offering a reward via an announcement promises to pay a reward to anyone who completes a particular act, a person who has completed such act may demand the person to pay the reward.

Article 500 [Liability for Culpa in Contrahendo[1]]

Where a party, in the course of concluding a contract, commits an act that falls under one of the following situations and thereby causes losses to the other party, s/he shall be liable for compensation:

1. Negotiating in bad faith under the guise of concluding a contract;

2. Intentionally concealing material facts or providing false information regarding the conclusion of the contract; or

3. Engaging in any other act in violation of the principle of good faith.

Article 501 [Parties' Obligation of Confidentiality]

Parties may not disclose or unjustifiably use trade secrets or other confidential information obtained while concluding a contract, regardless of

---

1 I.e. Fault in Conclusion of a Contract.

whether the contract forms or not. A party that discloses or unjustifiably uses such trade secrets or information and thereby causes a loss to the counterparty shall be liable for compensation therefor.

Chapter III Effectiveness of Contracts

Article 502 [Time When Contract Takes Effect]

A contract formed per law takes effect on its formation unless law or the parties' agreement provides otherwise.

Where laws or administrative regulations provide that a contract shall be subject to approval and other procedures, such provisions shall apply. Where a failure to undergo approval or other procedures affects the effectiveness of a contract, it does not affect the effectiveness of the clause(s) therein concerning such obligations as filing for approval and other relevant clauses. Where the party obligated to complete an application for approval or other procedures fails to perform the obligation, the counterparty may demand that such party be liable for breach of such obligation.

Where laws or administrative regulations provide that alteration, assignment, or rescission or termination of a contract shall be subject to approval or other procedures, such provisions shall apply.

Article 503 [Ratification by Principal of Contract Concluded by Person Without Authority]

Where a person lacking the authority to do so concludes a contract in the name of a principal, and the principal has already started performing the contractual obligations or accepted the performance of the counterparty, such principal shall be deemed to have ratified the contract.

Article 504 [Effect of Contract Concluded by Person Beyond Authority]

Where the legal representative of a legal person or the person in charge of an unincorporated entity concludes a contract beyond the scope of his/her authority, such an act is effective, and the contract is binding on the legal person or the unincorporated entity, unless the counterparty knew or ought to have known that the legal representative or the person in charge acted beyond the scope of his/her authority.

Article 505 [Effect of Contract Concluded Beyond Party's Business Scope]

Where parties conclude a contract beyond their scope of business , the validity of the contract shall be determined according to the provisions in Section 3 of Chapter VI of Book One of this Code and relevant provisions of this Book, and the contract shall not be deemed invalid solely on the grounds that it is beyond their business scope.

Article 506 [Effect of Exemption Clause]

An exemption clause in a contract excluding or limiting liability for the following acts is void:

1. Causing physical injury to the counterparty; or
2. Causing losses to the counterparty's property intentionally or through gross negligence.

Article 507 [Effect of Dispute Resolution Clause]

Where a contract fails to take effect, or is void, rescinded or canceled, or terminated, the effect of a clause concerning means of dispute resolution shall remain unaffected thereby.

Article 508 [Laws Applicable to Effect of Contract]

For questions or situations concerning the validity of a contract on which this Book is silent, the relevant provisions in Chapter VI of Book One of this Code shall apply.

Chapter IV Performance of Contracts

Article 509 [Principles for Performance of Contracts]

Parties shall fully perform their respective contractual obligations per their agreement.

Parties shall adhere to the principle of good faith, and perform such obligations as giving notices, rendering assistance, and maintaining confidentiality based on the nature and purpose of the contract as well as trade usage.

Parties shall avoid wasting resources, polluting the environment, or damaging the ecology during performance of their contract.

Article 510 [Remedies for Absence or Ambiguity of Contract Terms]

After a contract takes effect, and if parties have not yet reached agreement on such terms as those addressing quality, price or remuneration, or the place of performance, or if the agreement is ambiguous, the parties may supplement their agreement [accordingly]; where the parties fail to reach a supplementary agreement, such terms shall be defined by reference to [other] relevant terms in their contract or to the practices established between the parties or to trade usage.

Article 511 [Performance of Contract with Ambiguous Terms]

Where an agreement between parties on the terms of their contract is ambiguous and such terms cannot be defined based on the provisions of the preceding article, the following provisions shall apply:

1. Where no quality requirements are clearly stated, the contract shall be performed per a mandatory national standard, or a recommended national standard in the absence of a mandatory one, or the standard

of the industry in the absence of a recommended national standard. In the absence of any national or industrial standards, the contract shall be performed in accordance with a general standard or a specific standard that accords with its purposes.

2. Where no price or remuneration is clearly stated, the contract shall be performed based on the market price in the place of performance at the time the contract is concluded. Where the government-set or government-guided price applies as mandated by law, the contract shall be performed based on such price.

3. Where no place of performance is clearly stated, the contract shall be performed at the place of the party receiving the funds when monetary payment is involved, or, where real estate is to be delivered, at the *situs* where the real estate is located. For other subject matters, the contract shall be performed at the place where the party performing the obligation is located.

4. Where no period for performance is clearly stated, an obligor may perform his/her obligations at any time, and the obligee may also demand that the obligor perform at any time. However, the counterparty shall be granted the time necessary to prepare;

5. Where no method of performance is clearly stated, the contract shall be performed in a way that favors accomplishing its purposes; and

6. Where no division of performance costs is clearly stated, the costs shall be borne by the party performing the obligation; where the performance costs rise due to causes attributable to the obligee, the obligee shall pay the increased portion of the costs.

Article 512 [Time of Delivery for Electronic Contracts]

Where the subject matter of an electronic contract executed via the internet or other information network involves the delivery of goods by courier services, the time of delivery is the time when the recipient acknowledges receipt of the goods. Where the subject matter of such electronic contract is the provision of services, the time for provision is the one stated in the generated electronic or physical certificate. In the absence of a time stated in such certificate or if the time stated therein is inconsistent with the actual time for provision of the services, the actual time for provision of the services shall prevail.

Where the subject matter of such electronic contract is delivered via online transmission, the time of delivery shall be the time when the subject matter of the contract enters the specific system designated by the counterparty and becomes available for searching and identifying.

Where the parties to such electronic contract agree otherwise on the mode and time for delivery of goods or provision of services, their agreement shall apply.

Article 513 [Government-Set and Government-Guided Prices]

Where a government-fixed or government-guided price applies, if such price is adjusted within the delivery period provided for in the contract, the contract price shall be the price as adjusted at the time of delivery.Where an overdue delivery of the subject matter occurs, the contract shall be performed based on the original price if the price has risen, or on the price as adjusted if the price has fallen.Where a delayed collection of the subject matter or a late payment of the price occurs, the contract shall be performed based on the adjusted price if the price has risen, or the original price if it has fallen.

Article 514 [Currency for Monetary Payment Obligations]

Where an obligation takes a monetary form, unless law or the parties' agreement provides otherwise, the obligee may demand that the obligor perform using the legal tender of the place of actual performance.

Article 515 [Enjoyment and Shifting of Right of Choice in Contract Containing Multiple Subject Matters]

Where a contract has multiple subject matters of which the obligor is demanded to perform only one, the obligor shall have the right of choice [from among them], unless law or the parties' agreement provides otherwise or the practices established between the parties or trade usage requires otherwise.

Where the party with the right of choice does not choose within the agreed period or on expiration of the period of performance, and still fails to choose within a reasonable period after being urged, the right of choice shall shift to the counterparty.

Article 516 [Exercise of Right of Choice]

A party shall promptly notify the counterparty when exercising the right of choice and the subject matter of the contract to be performed shall be finalized when such notice reaches the counterparty. The subject matter may not be changed after its finalization except with the counterparty's consent.

Where one of the subject matters available for choice becomes impossible to perform, the party with the right of choice may not choose such subject matter, except where such impossibility of performance has been induced by the counterparty.

Article 517 [Proportionate Debt-Claims and Obligations]

With two or more obligees, if the subject matter is divisible and each obligee has a right to the debt-claim in proportion to his/her own portion, such is a proportionate debt-claim; with two or more obligors, if the subject matter is divisible and each obligor assumes an obligation in proportion to his/her own portion, such is a proportionate obligation.

Where difficulty arises in determining portions among obligees with a proportionate debt-claim or obligors with a proportionate obligation, each shall be deemed to have an equal portion.

Article 518 [Joint and Several Debt-Claims and Obligations]

With two or more obligees, if any or all obligees may claim that the obligor(s) perform the obligation(s), their debt-claim is a joint and several one; with two or more obligors, if the obligee may demand that any or all the obligors perform the entire obligation, such is a joint and several obligation.

A joint and several debt-claim or a joint and several obligation shall be provided for in law or created by the parties.

Article 519 [Determination of Portions Between and Among Obligors with Joint and Several Obligation and Right of Recovery]

Where difficulty arises in determining the portion of obligation between and among obligors with joint and several obligation, each shall be deemed to have an equal portion.

An obligor who has performed a joint and several obligation that exceeds his/her respective portion shall have the right to pursue a claim for contribution against the other jointly and severally liable obligors to the extent of the outstanding portion of their respective obligation and shall accordingly enjoy the rights of an obligee. However, no harm may thereby accrue to the interests of obligee(s). Any defenses the other jointly and severally liable obligors have against the obligee may also be asserted against such pursuing obligor.

Where an obligor with joint and several obligation against whom a claim for contribution to the excess has been lodged, is unable to perform his/her contribution owed, the other jointly and severally liable obligors shall be liable for such obligor's contribution on a *pro rata* basis to a corresponding extent.

Article 520 [Spillover Effect of Joint and Several Obligations]

Where one of the obligors with joint and several obligation has performed his/her obligation, offset his/her obligation or placed the subject matter in escrow, the obligations of the other obligors towards the obligee shall be extinguished to a corresponding extent, and such obligor shall have the right to pursue a claim for contribution against the other obligors in accordance with the provisions of the preceding article.

Where an obligee remits the obligation of one of the obligors with joint and several obligation, the obligations of the other jointly and severally liable obligors towards the obligee are extinguished to the extent of such obligor's portion remitted.

Where one obligor's joint and several obligation and the obligee's debt-claim merge in the same person, such obligee's claim against the other jointly and severally liable obligors shall continue in force after deduction of the portion merged.

An obligor's delay in the acceptance of prestation by one of the jointly and severally liable obligors shall produce an effect which also operates in favor of all the other jointly and severally liable obligors.

Article 521 [Inter-Creditor Relations Among Creditors with Joint and Several Debt-Claims and Application of Law Thereto]

Where difficulty arises in defining the portion among obligees with joint debt-claims, each obligee shall be deemed to have an equal portion.

Joint creditors who have actually received performance of an obligation shall repay the other joint obligees on a *pro rata* basis.

The relevant provisions on joint and several obligations in this Chapter shall also apply *mutatis mutandis* to joint debt-claims.

Article 522 [Performance of Contract in Favor of Third Party]

Where an obligee and an obligor agree that the latter shall perform an obligation in favor of a third party, if the latter fails to do so or the performance fails to conform to the agreement, such obligor shall be liable for such breach to the obligee.

Where laws provide or the parties agree that a third party may directly demand that the obligor perform the obligation to such third party and the third party does not expressly reject this [arrangement] within a reasonable time, if the obligor does not perform the obligation to the third party or the performance does not conform to the agreement, the third party may demand that the obligor assume liability for default. Any defenses that the obligor has against the obligee may be asserted against such third party.

Article 523 [Performance of Contract by Third Party]

Where the parties agree that an obligation shall be performed by a third party to the obligee, if the third party does not perform the obligation or the performance does not conform to the agreement, the obligor shall be liable for breach to the obligee.

Article 524 [Rules for Performance of Contract by Third Party with Legitimate Interest in Performance Thereof]

Where an obligor fails to perform an obligation, and a third party has a legitimate interest in such obligation, the third party shall be entitled to perform it in favor of the obligee on behalf of the obligor, unless the obligation may only be performed by the obligor based on the nature of the obligation, or as agreed by the parties, or per law.

After the obligee accepts the performance of such obligation by the third party, his/her claim against the obligor shall be assigned to the third party, unless the obligor and the third party agree otherwise.

Article 525 [Defense of Simultaneous Performance]

Where parties have reciprocal obligations with no set order of performance thereof, the parties shall simultaneously perform their obligations. Any party shall have the right to refuse a counterparty's demand for performance before the counterparty performs. A party shall have the right to refuse a counterparty's demand for corresponding performance if the counterparty's performance does not conform to the agreement.

Article 526 [Exceptio Non Adimpleti Contractus[1]]

Where parties are under reciprocal debt obligations with a set order of performance, if the party obligated to perform the debt obligation first does not do so, the party to perform subsequently shall have the right to refuse a demand for performance from the first party. Where the performance of the first party does not conform to the agreement, the party to perform subsequently shall have the right to reject a demand by the first party for performance of the corresponding obligation.

Article 527 [Defense of Uncertain Performance[2]]

A party obligated to perform an obligation first may suspend his/her performance if conclusive evidence demonstrates that any of the following circumstances applies with respect to the counterparty:

1. The state of the counterparty's operations seriously deteriorates;

2. The counterparty transfers property or spirits money away to evade its debts;

3. The counterparty loses commercial creditworthiness; or

4. Any other circumstance under which the counterparty loses or is likely to lose its ability to perform the obligation.

---

1 I.e. The Exception of Non-Performance, or The Exception of a Non-Performed Contract.

2 I.e. Defense of Uncertainty, Demurrer of Anticipatory Breach, or Einrede der Unsicherheit.

A party that suspends performance without conclusive evidence shall be liable for breach.

Article 528 [Exercising Defense of Uncertain Performance]

A party who suspends performance per the provisions of the preceding article shall notify the counterparty thereof without delay. Performance shall resume if the counterparty provides suitable guarantee. Where one party suspends performance, and the counterparty neither recovers ability to perform the obligation nor provides suitable guarantee within a reasonable period, such counterparty shall be deemed to be, as demonstrated with his/her act, in an anticipatory breach of the principal obligation and the party that suspends the performance may terminate the contract and demand that the counterparty be liable for breach.

Article 529 [Obligor's Performance Rendered Difficult Due to Obligee's Failure to Give Notice]

Where an obligee's failure to notify the obligor of its division, merger or change of domicile renders the obligor's performance of the obligation difficult, the obligor may suspend performance or place the subject matter thereof in escrow.

Article 530 [Performance by Obligor in Advance]

An obligee may reject an obligor's premature performance of an obligation, except where such advance performance does no harm to the obligee's interests.

The obligor shall bear the burden of any additional costs incurred by the obligee stemming from the obligor's advance performance of the obligation.

Article 531 [Partial Performance by Obligor]

An obligee may reject an obligor's partial performance of an obligation, except where such partial performance does no harm to the obligee's interests.

The obligor shall bear the burden of any additional costs incurred by the obligee stemming from the obligor's partial performance.

Article 532 [Effect of Changes with Party upon Performance of Contract]

After a contract takes effect, no party may fail to perform its contractual obligations on the grounds of a change in either party's name or entity name, legal representative, person in charge, or contract administrator.

Article 533 [Fundamental Change of Circumstances]

After a contract forms, where there occurs a fundamental change of circumstances upon which conclusion of the contract is based, and such change is neither a mere commercial risk nor a foreseeable event at the time of conclusion of the contract, if continuing performance of the contract is obviously unfair to one party, the party thus adversely affected may re-negotiate with the counterparty; where a [corresponding new] agreement cannot be reached within a reasonable period, such party may petition a people's court or arbitration tribunal to alter or terminate the contract.

The people's court or arbitration tribunal shall, considering the actual circumstances of the case, alter or terminate the contract in compliance with the principle of fairness.

Article 534 [Contract Supervision]

Where parties exploit a contract to engage in an act that harms the State and public interest, the market regulatory authority and other competent administrative authorities shall be responsible for supervising and handling such acts per the provisions of laws and administrative regulations.

Chapter V Preservation of Contracts

Article 535 [Obligee's Right of Subrogation]

Where an obligor neglects to exercise his/her debt-claim or an accessorial right related thereto against a counterparty, and this adversely affects the obligee's debt-claim that is due, the obligee may petition a people's court to order subrogation of the obligee to exercise the obligor's right against the counterparty in the obligee's own name, unless such right belongs exclusively to the obligor personally.

The scope of the right of subrogation is limited to the obligee's debt-claim which is due. The obligor shall bear the necessary costs arising from the obligee's exercise of the right of subrogation.

The counterparty's defenses against the obligor may be asserted against the obligee.

Article 536 [Exercising Right of Subrogation Before Due Date of Claim]

Before the due date of the obligee's debt-claim, where a circumstance occurs under which the limitation period for the obligor's principal claim or an accessory right related thereto is set to expire, or the obligor does not file a claim in a bankruptcy proceeding in due time, and the satisfaction of the obligee's claim is thereby adversely affected, the obligee may, by subrogation, demand the obligor's counterparty to perform the obligation to the obligor, file the obligor's claim with the bankruptcy trustee, or perform other necessary acts.

Article 537 [Effect of Exercise of Subrogation Right]

Where a people's court rules in favour of the establishment of the right of subrogation, the counterparty of the obligor shall perform the obligation to the obligee. After the obligee accepts the performance, the corresponding rights and obligations between the obligee and the obligor as well as between the obligor and the counterparty shall terminate. Where the obligor's claim or an accessorial right related thereto against the counterparty becomes subject to preservation or enforcement procedures, or where the obligor becomes bankrupt, provisions of relevant laws shall apply.

Article 538 [Obligee's Right of Invalidation Against Obligor's Disposition of Interests for Nil Consideration]

Where an obligor disposes of his/her proprietary rights and interests gratis by waiving claims, giving up the security for claims, or transferring property for nil consideration, or maliciously extends the period of time for satisfaction of his/her overdue claim, and the satisfaction of the obligee's debt-claim is thereby adversely affected, the obligee may petition a people's court to invalidate the obligor's act.

Article 539 [Obligee's Right of Invalidation Against Obligor's Transactions at Unreasonable Price to the Prejudice of Obligee]

Where an obligor transfers his/her property at a manifestly unreasonably low price, purchases another's property at an obviously unreasonably high price, or provides guarantee for another's obligation, and the satisfaction of the obligee's claim is thereby adversely affected, the obligee may petition a people's court to invalidate the obligor's act if the counterparty of the obligor knows or ought to have known of such circumstance.

Article 540 [Scope of Right of Invalidation and Assumption of Necessary Costs]

The scope of the right of invalidation shall be limited to the obligee's debt-claim. The obligor shall assume the necessary costs for the obligee's exercise of the right of invalidation.

Article 541 [Peremption for Obligee's Right of Invalidation[1]]

The right of invalidation shall be exercised within one year from the date on which the obligee knows or ought to have known of the cause for the invalidation. The right of invalidation shall be extinguished where an obligee does not exercise such right within five years from the date on which the obligor's act occurs.

Article 542 [Effect of Exercising Right of Invalidation]

Where an act by an obligor adversely affecting the satisfaction of the obligee's claim is invalidated, such act shall lack legally binding force *ab initio*.

Chapter VI Alteration and Assignment of Contracts

Article 543 [Alteration of Contract by Agreement]

The parties may alter a contract by agreement based on consultation.

Article 544 [Presumption of No Alteration for Ambiguous Alteration]

Where the agreement on the terms intended to be altered of a contract is ambiguous, the contract is presumed to have not been altered.

Article 545 [Assignment of Debt-Claim]

An obligee may assign his/her debt-claim in whole or in part to a third party, except where any of the following circumstances occurs:

1. A claim is unassignable by virtue of its nature;
2. A claim is unassignable per the parties' agreement; or
3. A claim is unassignable per law.

Where the parties agree that a nonpecuniary claim may not be assigned, such agreement cannot be asserted against a *bona fide* third party. Where the

1 I.e. Preclusion Period, Preclusive Period, Ausschlussfristen, or *Délai de Péremption* for Obligee's Right of Invalidation.

parties agree that a pecuniary claim may not be assigned, such agreement cannot be asserted against a third party.

Article 546 [Notice of Claim Assignment]

Where an obligee assigns his/her claim but does not notify an obligor thereof, the assignment shall be ineffective against such obligor.

The notice of the assignment of a claim may not be revoked, except with the assignee's consent.

Article 547 [Concurrent Assignment of Accessorial Right Together with Claim]

Where an obligee assigns his/her claim, the assignee shall acquire the accessory right related thereto, except where the accessory right belongs exclusively to the obligee personally.

Failure to register the assignment of the accessory right or failure to change the possession thereof shall not affect the assignee's acquisition of such accessory right.

Article 548 [Obligor's Defense Against Assignee in Case of Claim Assignment]

After an obligor receives a notice of assignment of a claim, the obligor's defenses against the assignor may be asserted against the assignee.

Article 549 [Obligor's Right of Setoff Against Assignee in Case of Claim Assignment]

An obligor may claim a setoff against the assignee under any of the following circumstances:

1. When the obligor receives a notice of assignment of a claim, the obligor has a claim against the assignor that becomes due before or at the same time as the due date of the assigned claim; or

2. The obligor's claim and the assigned claim stem from the same contract.

Article 550 [Defrayment of Expenses Increased Due to Claim Assignment]

The increased portion of the performance costs due to the assignment of a claim shall be borne by the assignor.

Article 551 [Delegation of Obligation]

The obligor shall obtain consent from the obligee when delegating his/her obligation in whole or part to a third party.

The obligor or the third party may urge the obligee to consent within a reasonable period. Silence or inactivity on the part of the obligee shall be deemed non-consent.

Article 552 [Assumption of Obligation as Co-Obligor[1]]

Where a third party agrees with an obligor to assume an obligation and notifies the obligee thereof, or a third party indicates to the obligee his/her willingness to assume the obligation, if the obligee manifests no express refusal within a reasonable period, the obligee may demand that the third party assume a joint and several obligation along with the obligor to the extent of the obligation the third party expresses a willingness to assume as a co-obligor.

Article 553 [Delegatee's Defense in The Event of Delegation of Obligation]

Where an obligor delegates his/her obligation, the new obligor may assert any defenses of the original obligor against the obligee; where the original obligor has a claim against the obligee, the new obligor may not claim an offset against the obligee.

---

1 I.e. Debt Assumption Without Releasing Original Debtor, or Concurrent Assumption of Obligation.

Article 554 [Concurrent Delegation of Principal and Accessorial Obligations]

Where an obligor delegates his/her obligation, the new obligor shall assume an accessorial obligation related to the principal obligation, unless such accessorial obligation belongs exclusively to the original obligor personally.

Article 555 [Concurrence of Claim Assignment and Obligation Delegation]

A party may assign his/her rights and delegate his/her obligations concurrently under a contract to a third party with the consent of the counterparty.

Article 556 [Application of Laws to Concurrent Transfer of Claims and Obligations Under a Contract]

Where the rights and obligations under a contract are assigned and delegated simultaneously, the provisions on assignment of claims and delegation of obligations shall apply.

Chapter VII Termination of Contractual Rights and Obligations

Article 557 [Occasions for Termination of Claims and Obligations]

A claim or obligation shall terminate under any of the following circumstances:

1. The obligation has been performed;
2. Obligations offset each other;
3. The obligor has placed the subject matter in escrow per law;
4. The obligee has remitted the obligation;
5. The claim and obligation have merged onto the same person; or
6. Any other circumstance where the claim or obligation terminates per law or as agreed by the parties.

The relationship of rights and obligations under a contract shall terminate upon rescission or cancellation thereof.

Article 558 [Post Termination Obligations]

After the parties' claims and obligations are terminated, the parties shall, in compliance with the principle of good faith and based on trade usage, perform such obligations as giving notices, rendering assistance, maintaining confidentiality, and retrieving items used.

Article 559 [Extinguishment of Accessorial Right Attached to a Claim]

On termination of a claim and obligation, a right accessory to the claim shall also be extinguished, unless law or the parties' agreement provides otherwise.

Article 560 [Order of Satisfaction with Respect to Multiple Obligations[1]]

Where an obligor owes multiple obligations of the same kind to an obligee, and the obligor's prestation/payment does not suffice to satisfy all of these, while performing, the obligor shall designate which obligations are to be satisfied, unless the parties agree otherwise.

Where the obligor makes no such designation, an obligation that becomes due shall be performed first. Where several multiple obligations are due, the obligation not guaranteed or the one with the least guarantee shall be performed first. Where none of the obligations are guaranteed or the obligations are equally guaranteed, the obligation with which the obligor is most heavily burdened shall be performed first. Where the burdens are equal, the obligations shall be performed in the order of their due dates. Where the due dates are the same, the obligations shall be performed on a *pro rata* basis.

1 I.e. Debts of Same Kind.

Article 561 [Order of Performance with Respect to Concurrence of Cost, Interest and Principal Obligation/Debt]

In addition to performing the principal obligation, an obligor shall pay to the obligee interest and costs related to the satisfaction of the claim. Where the prestation/payment does not suffice to satisfy the whole obligation/debt, it shall be paid per the following sequence, unless the parties agree otherwise:

1. Relevant costs incurred in satisfaction of the claim;
2. Interest; and
3. The principal obligation/debt.

Article 562 [Rescission of Contract by Agreement]

The parties may rescind a contract through a consensus [reached] via negotiation.

The parties may agree on the causes for unilateral rescission of the contract by a party. Where a cause for rescission of the contract occurs, the party entitled to rescission may rescind the contract.

Article 563 [Cancellation of Contract per Law]

The parties may cancel a contract under any of the following circumstances:

1. The purpose of the contract is frustrated by *force majeure*;
2. Before expiration of the period for performance, one party expressly or via action(s) indicates that s/he will not perform the principal obligation;
3. One party delays his/her performance of the principal obligation and still does not perform it within a reasonable period after being urged;
4. One party delays his/her performance of the obligation or otherwise acts in breach of the contract, thereby rendering achievement of its purpose impossible; or
5. Any other circumstance as prescribed by law.

For a contract under which the obligor shall unceasingly perform an obligation for an indefinite period, either party thereto may terminate the contract at any time, subject to advance notice to the counterparty given within a reasonable time.

Article 564 [Time Period for Exercise of Right of Rescission or Cancellation]

Where a time period for exercising a right of rescission or cancellation is provided for in law or agreed by the parties, and the right is not exercised on expiration of the period, such right shall be extinguished.

Where no time period for exercising the right of rescission or cancellation is provided for in law or agreed by the parties, such right shall be extinguished if the party entitled to rescission or cancellation does not exercise such right within one year after s/he knows or ought to have known of the causes for rescission or cancellation, or within a reasonable period after being urged by the counterparty.

Article 565 [Procedure for Rescission or Cancellation of Contract]

Where one party demands rescission or cancellation of a contract per law, the counterparty shall be duly notified thereof. A contract is rescinded or canceled at the time the notice thereof reaches the counterparty, or, where the notice states that the contract shall be automatically rescinded or canceled if the obligor does not perform his/her obligation within a specified period, and the obligor fails to perform the obligation within such period, the contract shall be rescinded or canceled on the expiration of the period specified in the notice. Where the counterparty objects to the rescission or cancellation of the contract, either party may petition a people's court or arbitration tribunal to determine the validity of the rescission.

Where one party, without notifying the counterparty, petitions per law for rescission or cancellation of the contract by directly filing a lawsuit or applying for arbitration, and the people's court or arbitration tribunal rules favorably on such petition, the contract shall be rescinded or canceled when a duplicated copy of the complaint or the request for arbitration is served on the counterparty.

Article 566 [Effect of Contract Rescission or Cancellation]

Where a contract is rescinded or canceled and its obligations have not yet been performed, performance shall cease; if its obligations have been performed, the parties may, considering the performance status and the nature of the contract, demand restoration to the original status *quo ante* or other remedial measures to be taken, and shall have the right to demand compensation for losses.

Where a contract is canceled due to a breach, the party with the right to cancel the contract may demand that the breaching party be liable therefor, unless the parties agree otherwise.

After a principal contract is rescinded or canceled, a guarantor shall remain obligated to guarantee the obligor's civil liability unless the guaranty contract provides otherwise.

Article 567 [Force of Settlement and Liquidation Clauses of Contract Following Termination Thereof]

Termination of the relationship of rights and obligations under a contract does not negate the contract terms concerning settlement and liquidation.

Article 568 [Legal Setoff [1]]

Where parties owe mutual obligations and the subject matter of the obligations is of the same kind and quality, any party may offset his/her obligation against the obligation due of the counterparty, unless the obligation cannot be offset by virtue of its nature or per the parties' agreement or

1 I.e. Independent Setoff, or Statutory Setoff.

provisions of law.

A party who claims an offset shall give notice thereof to the counterparty. The notice becomes effective when it reaches the counterparty. No conditions or time limit may be tied to the offset.

Article 569 [Contractual Setoff]

Where the parties owe mutual obligations and the subject matter of the obligations is not of the same kind or quality, the obligations may also be offset by agreement between the parties via consultation.

Article 570 [Conditions for Placement of Subject Matter in Escrow with Competent Authority]

Where performance of an obligation becomes difficult under any of the following circumstances, an obligor may place the subject matter in escrow:

1. The obligee refuses to accept performance without just cause;
2. The obligee's whereabouts are unknown;
3. The obligee dies and his/her heirs or estate administrator is not yet identified, or the obligee loses his/her capacity to engage in civil juristic acts and his/her guardian is not yet designated; or
4. Any other circumstance as provided in law.

Where the subject matter is unsuitable for escrow or the costs thereof are too high, the obligor may sell the subject matter through auction or sale and place the proceeds in escrow per law.

Article 571 [Commencement of Escrow and Its Effect on Obligor]

An escrow is created when an obligor delivers to an escrow agency per law a subject matter or proceeds from its disposition at auction or sale.

Where an escrow has been created, the obligor is deemed to have delivered the subject matter to the extent of the escrow.

Article 572 [Notice of Escrow]

After a subject matter is placed in escrow, the obligor shall promptly notify the obligee or the obligee's heir(s), estate administrator, guardian, or property custodian.

Article 573 [Effect of Escrow upon Obligee]

After a subject matter is placed in escrow, the risk of destruction, damage, or loss thereof shall pass to the obligee. During escrow, the accrued fruits from the subject matter shall belong to the obligee. The costs thereby incurred shall be borne by the obligee.

Article 574 [Collection of Subject Matter from Escrow and Extinguishment of Right of Collection]

The obligee may collect a subject matter from escrow at any time, except that, where the obligee owes an obligation that is due to the obligor, the escrow agency shall, at the request of the obligor, reject the obligee's demand to collect it before the obligee performs such obligation or provides a guarantee therefor.

An obligee's right to collect the subject matter in escrow is extinguished if such right is not exercised within five years from the date the subject matter is placed in escrow, and such subject matter shall escheat to the State after the escrow agency's costs are deducted. Where, however, an obligee does not perform his/her obligation due and owed to the obligor, or where the obligee waives his/her right to collect the subject matter in escrow in writing to the escrow agency, the obligor shall be entitled to take back the subject matter after paying the escrow agency's costs.

Article 575 [Remission of Obligations]

Where an obligee remits part or whole of an obligor's obligations, the obligee's claims and debtor's obligations shall terminate in part or in whole accordingly, unless the obligor disapproves within a reasonable period.

Article 576 [Confusion or Merger of Claim and Obligation]

Where a claim and a reciprocal obligation merge onto the same person, the claim and obligation shall terminate unless a third party's interests are jeopardized thereby.

Chapter VIII Liability for Breach of Contract

Article 577 [Liability for Breach of Contract]

Where a party does not perform his/her contractual obligation or the performance does not conform to the agreement, s/he shall assume liability for breach of contract in such forms as continuing specific performance of his/her obligations, resort to [other] remedial measures, or compensation of losses.

Article 578 [Liability for Anticipatory Breach of Contract]

Where a party expressly states or indicates by his/her act that s/he will not perform his/her contractual obligation(s), the counterparty may demand that the former party be liable for [anticipatory] breach before expiration of the period for performance.

Article 579 [Specific Performance of Pecuniary Obligation]

Where a party fails to pay a price, remuneration, rent, or interest, or does not perform any other pecuniary obligation, the counterparty may demand such payment.

Article 580 [Specific Performance of Non-Pecuniary Obligation and Liability for Breach Thereof]

Where a party does not perform a non-pecuniary obligation or his/her performance does not conform to the agreement, the counterparty may demand specific performance thereof unless:

1. Such performance becomes impossible either *de jure* or *de facto*;

2. The subject matter of the obligation is unsuitable for compelling specific performance, or the costs of the performance are too high; or

3. The obligee fails to demand performance within a reasonable period.

Where one of the circumstances set forth in the preceding paragraph occurs and the purpose of the contract is thus frustrated, a people's court or arbitration tribunal may terminate the contractual relationship of rights and obligations on demand by a party, but the liability for breach shall remain unaffected thereby.

Article 581 [Substitute Performance of Contract by Third Party]

Where a party does not perform his/her obligation or his/her performance does not conform to the agreement, and the obligation may not be enforced on account of its nature, the counterparty may demand that such party bear the costs of a substitute performance by a third party.

Article 582 [Liability for Defective Performance]

Where a performance does not conform to an agreement, liability for breach shall be borne per the agreement between the parties thereto. Where an agreement does not include terms concerning liability for breach or the terms included are ambiguous, and if such terms are unable to be defined by reference to the provisions of Article 510 of this Code, the injured party may, by virtue of the nature of the subject matter and based on the amount of the loss, reasonably demand that the counterparty assume such liability for breach as repair, reworking, replacement, refund, or reduction in price or remuneration.

Article 583 [Liability for Damages Arising from Breach of Contract]

Where a party does not perform his/her contractual obligation(s) or his/

her performance does not conform to the agreement, and even after s/he has subsequently performed his/her obligation or has taken remedial measures, if the counterparty still sustains a loss, such breaching party shall pay damages therefor.

Article 584 [Scope of Damages]

Where a party does not perform his/her contractual obligation or his/her performance does not conform to the agreement, and the counterparty sustains a loss as a result, the amount of damages shall be equal to the loss suffered by the counterparty as a consequence of the breach, including the benefits expected to be obtained if the contract had been performed. However, such damages may not exceed the loss which the party in breach foresaw or ought to have foreseen at the time of the conclusion of the contract as a possible consequence of the breach of contract.

Article 585 [Liquidated Damages[1]]

The parties may agree that, upon breach by a party, a designated amount of liquidated damages shall be paid to the counterparty according to the circumstances of the breach, or the parties may agree on a method of calculating the damages arising therefrom.

Where liquidated damages as agreed are lower than the loss caused, a people's court or arbitration tribunal may increase the amount on demand of a party. Where the agreed liquidated damages are excessively higher than the loss caused, a people's court or arbitration tribunal may make suitable reduction on demand of a party.

Where the parties agree on liquidated damages for delayed performance, the party in breach shall continue to perform the obligation after paying such

---

1 I.e. Liquidated and Ascertained Damages (LADs).

liquidated damages.

Article 586 [Earnest Money as Security]

Parties may agree that one party shall pay earnest money to the counterparty to secure a claim. An earnest money contract forms on actual delivery of the earnest money.

The amount of the earnest money [payment] shall be agreed by the parties, except that it may not exceed 20% of the value of the subject matter of the principal contract, with any excess amount to not have the effect of earnest money. Where the actual amount of the earnest money delivered is more or less than the agreed amount, the agreed amount shall be deemed to have been altered.

Article 587 [Disciplinary Rules for Earnest Money]

After an obligor has performed his/her obligation, the earnest money shall constitute a part of the price or be refunded. Where the party paying the earnest money does not perform his/her obligation or does not perform it in conformity with the agreement, and the purpose of the contract is thus frustrated, s/he is not entitled to demand refund of the earnest money. Where a party receiving the earnest money does not perform his/her obligation or does not perform it in conformity with the agreement, with the purpose of the contract frustrated as a result, s/he shall refund twice the amount of the earnest money to the counterparty.

Article 588 [Concurrence of Liquidated Damages and Earnest Money]

Where parties agree on both liquidated damages and earnest money, if one party defaults, the counterparty may elect to resort to either the liquidated damages clause or the earnest money clause.

Where the earnest money does not suffice to compensate the loss caused by one party's breach, the counterparty may demand damages for the portion of the loss that exceeds the amount of the earnest money.

Article 589 [Refusal to Accept Performance and Delayed Acceptance of Performance]

Where an obligor performs his/her obligation per an agreement and the obligee refuses to accept the performance without just cause, the obligor may demand that the obligee compensate any additional costs thereby incurred.

The obligor need not pay interest for the period in which the obligee delays acceptance.

Article 590 [Force Majeure]

Where a party is unable to perform a contract due to *force majeure*, s/he shall be relieved of liability in whole or in part based on the effect of the *force majeure*, unless law provides otherwise. The party unable to perform a contract due to *force majeure* shall promptly give notice to the counterparty so as to mitigate the loss the counterparty might incur, and shall submit evidence of the *force majeure* event within a reasonable period.

Where the *force majeure* event occurs after a party has delayed performance, such party shall not be relieved of liability for breach.

Article 591 [The Rule of Mitigation]

After one party breaches, the counterparty shall take suitable measures to mitigate losses. Where losses are aggravated from failure to take suitable mitigating measures, no compensation may be claimed for the added losses.

The reasonable costs incurred by a party in mitigating his/her losses shall be borne by the breaching party.

Article 592 [Both Parties in Breach and Contributory Fault]

Where both parties are in breach, each shall bear corresponding liability therefor.

Where one party's breach causes loss to the counterparty, and the counterparty's fault contributes to the occurrence of such loss, the amount of compensation for such loss may be reduced accordingly.

Article 593 [Assumption of Liability for Breach of Contract Due to Causes Attributable to Third Party]

A party who breaches a contract due to causes attributable to a third party shall be liable for breach to the counterparty per law. The dispute between the breaching party and the third party shall be dealt with per the provisions of law or the parties' agreement.

Article 594 [Limitation Period for International Trade Contracts]

The limitation period for bringing a lawsuit or applying for arbitration over a dispute arising from a contract for the international sale of goods and a contract for the import and export of technology shall be four years.

Part Two Typical Contracts

Chapter IX Sales Contracts

Article 595 [Definition of Sales Contract]

A sales contract is a contract per which a seller transfers title to a subject matter to a buyer who pays a price therefor.

Article 596 [Terms and Conditions of Sales Contracts]

A sales contract generally contains terms specifying the name, quantity, quality, and price of the subject matter, the time period, place, and method of performance, the packaging, the standards and methods for inspection, the mode of settlement, the language used in the contract and the contract's effectiveness, among others.

Article 597 [Effect of Sale of Subject Matter by Seller with No Right to Sell]

Where title to the subject matter is unable to pass because the seller does not acquire the right to dispose of it, the buyer may cancel the contract and demand that the seller be liable for breach.

Where laws or administrative regulations prohibit or restrict the transfer of a subject matter, such statutes shall govern.

Article 598 [Basic Obligations of Seller]

A seller shall perform the obligation to deliver the subject matter, or hand over the documentation needed to take delivery thereof, and transfer the property in the subject matter to the buyer.

Article 599 [Seller's Obligation to Deliver Relevant Documentation and Data]

A seller shall hand over, in addition to the documents needed to take delivery of the subject matter, relevant documentation and data to the buyer per their contract or trade usage.

Article 600 [Ownership of Intellectual Property Right]

Where a subject matter to be sold carries intellectual property rights, unless law or the parties' agreement provides otherwise, the intellectual property rights shall not pass to the buyer.

Article 601 [Time Period for Delivery of Subject Matter]

A seller shall deliver the subject matter at the time agreed in the contract. Where the contract provides for a period of time for delivery, the seller may deliver the subject matter at any time within such period.

Article 602 [Rules to Follow When Time Period for Delivery Is Unavailable or Ambiguous]

In the absence of an agreement between the parties on the period for delivery or if their agreement is ambiguous, the provisions of Article 510 and Subparagraph 4 of Article 511 of this Code shall apply.

Article 603 [Place of Delivery of Subject Matter]

A seller shall deliver the subject matter to the agreed place of delivery.

In the absence of an agreement between the parties on the place of delivery or if their agreement is ambiguous, and the place of delivery remains undeterminable in the light of the provisions of Article 510 of this Code, the following provisions shall apply:

1. Where the subject matter needs to be transported, the seller shall hand it over to the first carrier for transmission and delivery to the buyer; and

2. Where the subject matter does not need to be transported, if the seller and the buyer knew the location of the subject matter when they concluded the contract, the seller shall deliver the subject matter at such location; if the location of the subject matter was unknown, the seller shall deliver the subject matter at the place where the seller had his/her place of business at the time of the conclusion of the contract.

Article 604 [Basic Rules for Allocation of Risks of Destruction, Damage and Loss of Subject Matter]

The risk of destruction, damage, or loss of the subject matter shall be borne by the seller before the delivery and by the buyer thereafter, unless law or the parties' agreement provides otherwise.

Article 605 [Assumption of Risks for Subject Matter Delivered Beyond Time Limit]

Where a subject matter fails to be delivered within the agreed time limit due to causes attributable to the buyer, the buyer shall assume the risk of destruction, damage, or loss of the subject matter from the time when the buyer breaches the agreement.

Article 606 [Distribution of Risk for Subject Matter Sold in Transit]

Where a seller sells a subject matter in transit after having been handed over to a carrier for transport, unless the parties agree otherwise, the buyer shall assume the risk of destruction, damage, or loss of the subject matter from the time when the contract forms.

Article 607 [Distribution of Risk for Subject Matter Involving Carriage]

A buyer shall assume the risk of destruction, damage, or loss of the subject matter when the seller has transported the subject matter to a place designated by the buyer and handed it over to a carrier per the agreement.

In the absence of an agreement between the parties on the place of delivery or if their agreement is ambiguous, if the subject matter needs to be transported per Subparagraph 1 of the second paragraph of Article 603 of this Code, the buyer shall assume the risk of destruction, damage, or loss of the subject matter when the seller hands the subject matter over to the first carrier for transmission.

Article 608 [Distribution of Risk Where Buyer Breaches by Failing to Take Delivery]

Where a seller has placed the subject matter at the place of delivery per agreement or the provisions of Subparagraph 2 of the second paragraph of Article 603 of this Code, if the buyer does not take delivery thereof in breach of their agreement, the buyer shall assume the risk of destruction, damage, or loss of the subject matter from the time of the buyer's breach.

Article 609 [Failure to Deliver Documentation and Data Does Not Affect Passage of Risk]

A seller's failure to deliver the documentation and data relating to the subject matter per agreement shall not affect the passage of the risk of destruction, damage, or loss of the subject matter.

Article 610 [Distribution of Risk in The Event of Seller's Fundamental Breach of Contract]

Where a subject matter falls short of quality requirements, and the purpose of the contract is frustrated as a result, the buyer may refuse to accept the subject matter or may cancel the contract. Where the buyer refuses to accept the subject matter or cancels the contract, the seller shall assume the risk of destruction, damage, or loss of the subject matter.

Article 611 [Assumption of Risk by Buyer and Seller's Liability for Breach of Contract]

Where a seller's performance does not conform to the agreement, the assumption of the risk of destruction, damage, or loss of the subject matter by the buyer does not affect the buyer's right to demand that the seller be liable for breach.

Article 612 [Seller's Guarantee of Subject Matter Being Free from Third-Party Right or Claim]

A seller has an obligation to guarantee that the subject matter delivered is free from any right or claim of a third party unless law provides otherwise.

Article 613 [Exemption of Seller's Obligation of Right Guarantee]

Where, at the time of the conclusion of the contract, the buyer knew or ought to have known of such right or claim of a third party to the subject matter, the seller shall be relieved of the obligation provided for in the preceding article.

Article 614 [Buyer's Right to Suspension of Payment]

Where a buyer has conclusive evidence to demonstrate that a third party has a right or claim to the subject matter, the buyer may suspend payment therefor, unless the seller provides a suitable guarantee.

Article 615 [Quality Requirements of Subject Matter]

A seller shall deliver the subject matter in conformity with the quality requirements agreed by the parties. Where the seller provides quality specifications for the subject matter, the subject matter delivered shall conform to such specifications.

Article 616 [Procedure in The Event of Unclear Quality Requirements]

In the absence of an agreement between parties on the quality requirements of a subject matter or if their agreement is ambiguous, and the quality requirements still cannot be determined by reference to the provisions of Article 510 of this Code, the provisions of Subparagraph 1 of Article 511 of this Code shall apply.

Article 617 [Quality Conformity Warranty]

Where a subject matter a seller delivers falls short of quality requirements, the buyer may demand that the seller be liable for breach per the provisions of Articles 582 through 584 of this Code.

Article 618 [Exceptions to Reduction or Exemption of Seller's Liability with Respect to Defect-Free Subject Matter Warranty]

Where the parties agree to reduce or exempt the seller's liability for defects in a subject matter, if the seller does not notify the buyer of such defects either intentionally or through gross negligence, the seller shall be deprived of the right to claim a reduction or exemption of the liability.

Article 619 [Manner of Packaging Subject Matter]

A seller shall deliver a subject matter packaged in the manner as agreed in the contract. In the absence of an agreement between the parties on the packaging manner or if their agreement is ambiguous, and the packaging manner still cannot be determined by reference to the provisions of Article 510 of this Code, the subject matter shall be packaged in the manner usual for subject matter or, where there is no such manner, in a manner adequate to preserve and protect it and conducive to saving resources and protecting the ecological environment.

Article 620 [Buyer's Obligation to Inspect]

Upon receiving the subject matter, the buyer shall inspect it within the period agreed for inspection. If no period for inspection is agreed, the buyer shall conduct a prompt inspection.

Article 621 [Buyer's Obligation to Give Notice]

Where the parties have agreed on a period for inspection, the buyer shall notify the seller of any nonconformity of the subject matter with the agreed quantity or quality within such period. If the buyer neglects to give notice, the subject matter shall be deemed to conform to the agreed quantity or quality.

Where the parties have not agreed on a period for inspection, the buyer shall notify the seller of any nonconformity of the subject matter with the agreed quantity or quality within a reasonable period after the buyer discovers or ought to have discovered the nonconformity. If the buyer does not notify the seller within a reasonable period or within two years after taking delivery of the subject matter, the subject matter shall be deemed to conform to the agreed quantity or quality. However, if there is a quality warranty period for the subject matter, such warranty period shall apply instead of the two-year provision.

Where a seller knows or ought to have known that the subject matter as delivered does not conform to the agreement, the buyer shall not be subject to the time limit for notification provided for in the two preceding paragraphs.

Article 622 [Where Agreed Period for Inspection Is Excessively Short]

Where the parties agree on a period for inspection that is excessively short and the buyer, taking into account the nature of the subject matter and relevant trade usage, has difficulty in completing a comprehensive inspection within such period, such period shall be deemed only as a period within which for the buyer to object to patent defects in the subject matter.

Where an agreed period for inspection or for quality warranty is shorter than the period prescribed by applicable laws and administrative regulations, the latter shall prevail.

Article 623 [Procedure in Absence of Period for Inspection in Contract]

Where the parties do not have an agreement on an inspection period, and the buyer has signed a goods received note, confirmation note, or a similar document on which the quantity, model, and specifications of the subject matter are stated, the buyer shall be presumed to have inspected the quantity of the subject matter and the patent defects therein, unless corresponding evidence is sufficient to rebut such presumption.

Article 624 [Inspection Standard for Delivery Made to Third Party as Instructed]

Where a seller delivers a subject matter to a third party as instructed by the buyer, if the inspection standard the seller and the buyer have agreed differs from that the buyer and the third party have agreed to, the inspection standard as agreed between the seller and the buyer shall prevail.

Article 625 [Seller's Obligation to Recycle Goods Sold]

Where per the provisions of laws and administrative regulations or the parties' agreement, a subject matter must be recycled upon expiration of its effective service life, the seller has the obligation to recycle the subject matter or delegate such recycling to a third party.

Article 626 [Amount and Mode of Payment of Price by Buyer]

A buyer shall pay the agreed price via the agreed payment method. In the absence of an agreement between the parties on the price or the payment method, or if their agreement is ambiguous, the provisions of Article 510 and Subparagraphs 2 and 5 of Article 511 of this Code shall apply.

Article 627 [Place of Payment of Price by Buyer]

A buyer shall pay the price at the agreed place. In the absence of an agreement between the parties on the place of payment, or if their agreement is ambiguous, and the place still cannot be determined by reference to the provisions of Article 510 of this Code, the buyer shall make payment at the seller's place of business. However, if payment is contingent on delivery of the subject matter or handing over of documents needed to take delivery of the subject matter, payment shall be made at the place where delivery of the subject matter or handing over of the documents takes place.

Article 628 [Time for Payment of Price by Buyer]

A buyer shall pay the price at the time agreed in the contract. In the absence of an agreement between the parties on the time for payment, or if their agreement is ambiguous, and the time for payment still cannot be determined by reference to the provisions of Article 510 of this Code, the buyer must pay simultaneously with receipt of the subject matter, or of the documentation needed to take delivery thereof.

Article 629 [Procedure Where Seller Delivers in Excess of Contract]

Where the quantity of the subject matter delivered by a seller exceeds the quantity agreed, the buyer may either accept or reject the excess. If the buyer accepts the excess, s/he shall pay for it at the price agreed in the contract. If the buyer rejects the excess, the buyer shall notify the seller without delay.

Article 630 [Ownership of Fruits of Subject Matter]

Any fruits accrued from the subject matter before delivery shall belong to the seller and any fruits accrued from the subject matter after delivery shall belong to the buyer, unless the parties agree otherwise.

Article 631 [Accessorial Subject Matter and Rescission or Cancellation of Contract]

Where a contract is rescinded or canceled due to the nonconformity of the principal subject matter with the agreed requirements, the effect of the rescission or cancellation shall be extended to the accessorial subject matter. Where a contract is [partially] rescinded or canceled due to the nonconformity of an accessorial subject matter with the agreed requirements, the effect of the rescission or cancellation shall not extend to the principal subject matter.

Article 632 [Rescission or Cancellation of Contract Whose Subject Matter Comprises Several Items]

Where the subject matter of a contract comprises several items, if one of these does not conform to the requirements as agreed in the contract, the buyer may rescind or cancel the part of the contract as regards such item. However, if the separation of such item from the others will manifestly impair the value of the subject matter as a whole, the buyer may rescind or cancel the [entire] contract in respect of the several items.

Article 633 [Rescission or Cancellation of Contract Whose Subject Matter Is Delivered in Installments]

In the event of a seller's delivery of a subject matter in installments, if the seller fails to deliver any installment of the subject matter or the delivery of any installment fails to conform with the agreement, and, as a result, the purpose of the contract is frustrated with respect to such installment, the buyer may [partially] rescind or cancel the contract as regards such installment.

Where a seller fails to deliver any installment of the subject matter or the delivery of any installment fails to conform with the agreement, and, as a result, the purpose of the contract is frustrated with respect to subsequent installments, the buyer may rescind or cancel the contract with respect to such installment and subsequent installments.

Where a buyer has [partially] rescinded or canceled the contract with any installment of the subject matter, the buyer many rescind or cancel the contract in respect of deliveries already made and of future deliveries by reason of their interdependence.

Article 634 [Sales Contract with Payment in Installments]

Where a buyer making installment payments fails to pay sums due which amount to one-fifth of the total price, if the buyer still fails to pay such sums within a reasonable period after being pressed for payment, the seller may demand that the buyer pay the total price or may rescind or cancel the contract.

A seller who rescinds or cancels the contract may demand that the buyer pay a fee for the use of the subject matter.

Article 635 [Contract of Sales by Sample]

The parties to a sale by sample shall seal the sample and may formulate specifications as to its quality. The subject matter delivered by the seller shall be identical in quality to the sample and its specifications.

Article 636 [Contract of Sales by Sample with Latent Defects]

Where a buyer in a sale by sample is unaware of a sample's latent defects, even if the subject matter delivered is identical to the sample, the quality of the subject matter delivered by the seller shall still meet the usual standard for the same category of goods.

Article 637 [Trial Period for Trial Sales]

The parties to a trial sale may agree on a period for trial use of the subject matter. In the absence of an agreement on the period for trial use or if the agreement is ambiguous, and the period for trial use still cannot be determined by reference to the provisions of Article 510 of this Code, it shall be determined by the seller.

Article 638 [Effect of Trial Sale]

A buyer to a trial sale may purchase or refuse to purchase the subject matter within a period of trial use.Where, on expiration of the period of trial use, the buyer does not indicate whether the buyer will purchase the subject matter or not, the buyer shall be deemed to have purchased it.

Where a buyer to a trial sale has, within the period of the trial use, already made partial payment or has sold, leased, or created a security interest in the subject matter, the buyer shall be deemed to have agreed to purchase it.

Article 639 [Assumption of Cost of Use in Trial Sale]

In the absence of an agreement between parties to a trial sale on the fee(s) for the use of the subject matter, or if the agreement is ambiguous, the seller shall have no right to demand that the buyer pay such fee(s).

Article 640 [Allocation of Risk of Destruction, Damage and Loss of Subject Matter During Trial Period]

The risk of destruction, damage to, or loss of the subject matter shall be borne by the seller within the period of trial use.

Article 641 [Sale with Retention of Title (ROT)]

The parties may agree in a sales contract that the title to a subject matter remains vested in the seller until the buyer pays the price therefor or fulfills certain other obligations.

The title to a subject matter retained by a seller may not be asserted against a *bona fide* third party in the absence of registration of such title.

Article 642 [Seller's Right to Repossess Subject Matter]

Where parties agree that a seller retains title to the subject matter of a contract, the seller shall have the right to repossess such subject matter before transfer of such title if any of the following circumstances applies to the buyer, causing harm to the seller, unless the parties agree otherwise:

1. The buyer does not pay per the contract, and still does not pay within a reasonable period after being urged;

2. The buyer does not fulfill the specific conditions per the contract; or

3. The buyer sells, pledges, or otherwise improperly disposes of the subject matter.

The seller may negotiate with the buyer to repossess the subject matter; if such negotiations prove unavailing, the procedures for enforcement of security interests may apply *mutatis mutandis*.

Article 643 [Buyer's Right to Redemption]

After a seller's reppossession of the subject matter per the first paragraph of the preceding article, the buyer may demand redemption of the subject matter if the cause for the seller's repossession thereof ceases to exist within the period of redemption as agreed by the parties or within a reasonable period the seller has specified.

Where a buyer fails to redeem the subject matter within the redemption period, the seller may sell the subject matter to a third party at a reasonable price. After subtracting the buyer's outstanding balance and the necessary costs from the sale proceeds, the seller shall return the difference, if any, to the buyer; shortfall, if any, shall be covered by the buyer.

Article 644 [Sale by Tender]

The rights and obligations of the parties to a sale by tender and the procedures for the bidding are subject to the provisions of relevant laws and administrative regulations.

Article 645 [Auction]

The rights and obligations of parties to an auction and the procedures therefor are subject to the provisions of relevant laws and administrative regulations.

Article 646 [Mutatis Mutandis Application of Laws Governing Sales Contract to Other Onerous Contracts]

Where laws provide for other onerous contracts, their provisions shall apply. In the absence of such provisions, relevant provisions on sales contracts shall apply *mutatis mutandis*.

Article 647 [Barter Contracts]

Where parties agree to transfer title to a subject matter via a barter trade, the relevant provisions on sales contracts shall apply *mutatis mutandis*.

Chapter X Supply and Use Contracts for Electricity, Water, Gas, and Heat

Article 648 [Definition of Electricity Supply Contract and Obligation to Conclude]

A contract for the supply of electricity is one per which a supplier provides electricity to a user who pays electricity bills therefor.

A supplier providing electricity to the public may not refuse the reasonable demand of a user to conclude a contract.

Article 649 [Content of Electricity Supply Contracts]

A contract for the supply and consumption of electricity generally contains such terms as the mode, quality and time of the supply, the amount, location, and nature of the use, the measurement method, the price, the payment method for electricity bills, and the responsibility for the maintenance of the electricity supply and consumption facilities.

Article 650 [Place of Performance of Electricity Supply Contracts]

The place of performance of a contract for the supply and use of electricity shall be agreed by the parties; in the absence of an agreement or if the agreement is ambiguous, the point of division of property in the electricity supply facilities shall be the place of performance.

Article 651 [Supplier's Obligation to Safely Supply Electricity]

A supplier of electricity shall safely supply electricity per the quality standard for power supply mandated by the State and per the [parties'] agreement. Where a supplier fails to safely supply electricity per the quality standard for power supply set by the State and per the agreement, and thereby causes losses to the user, the supplier shall be liable for compensation therefor.

Article 652 [Supplier's Obligation to Give Notice of Supply Interruption]

Where an electricity supplier needs to interrupt the electricity supply for such reasons as a planned or temporary maintenance and repair of power supply facilities, restriction of power consumption based on law, or user's unlawful use, it shall notify the user in advance per relevant State regulations. If a user receives no advance notice and thereby incurs losses, [the supplier] shall be liable for compensation therefor.

Article 653 [Supplier's Obligation of Emergency Response and Repair]

Where natural disasters and similar hazards result in a power outage, the supplier shall hasten to make prompt emergency repairs per relevant provisions of the State; if it fails to do so and thereby causes losses to a user, [the supplier] shall be liable for compensation therefor.

Article 654 [User's Obligation to Pay Electricity Bills]

A user of electricity shall pay electricity bills on time per relevant State regulations and the parties' agreement. Where a user does not pay electricity bills when due, the user shall pay agreed liquidated damages. Where a user, after being urged, still does not pay the electricity bills and the liquidated damages within a reasonable period, the supplier may suspend the supply of electricity per procedures therefor as provided by the State.

When a supplier suspends the supply of electricity per the provisions of the preceding paragraph, it shall notify the user thereof in advance.

Article 655 [User's Obligation to Safely Use Electricity]

A user shall use electricity in a safe, economical and planned manner per relevant State regulations and the parties' agreement. Where a user fails to use the electricity per applicable State regulations or the parties' agreement, and thereby causes losses to the supplier, the user shall be liable for compensation therefor.

Article 656 [Mutatis Mutandis Application to Contracts for Supply of Water, Gas, and Heat]

Relevant provisions on contracts for the supply and use of electricity shall apply *mutatis mutandis* to those for the supply and use of water, gas, and heat.

Chapter XI Gift Contracts

Article 657 [Definition of Gift Contract]

A gift contract is one per which a grantor transfers his/her property to a grantee without consideration, and the grantee indicates his/her acceptance thereof.

Article 658 [Grantor's Right to Revocation at Will and Restrictions Thereon]

A grantor may revoke a gift before the transfer of the right to the gifted property.

The provisions of the preceding paragraph do not apply to notarized gift contracts, or those for public weal or with the nature of a moral obligation which, per law, may not be revoked, such as for disaster relief, poverty alleviation, and disability support.

Article 659 [Relevant Legal Formalities Relating to Gifts]

Gifted property shall undergo registration or other formalities if law so requires.

Article 660 [Grantee's Right to Claim Delivery and Grantor's Liability for Compensation]

For notarized gift contracts or gift contracts for public weal or with the nature of a moral obligation, which may not be revoked under law, such as for disaster relief, poverty alleviation and disability support, if the grantor does not deliver the gifted property, the grantee may demand such delivery.

Where the gifted property to be delivered per the preceding paragraph is destroyed, damaged or lost due to the grantor's intentional act or gross negligence, the grantor shall be liable for compensation therefor.

Article 661 [Onerous Gift Contracts]

A gift may be burdened with an obligation.

Where a gift is burdened with an obligation, the grantee shall perform the obligation per the agreement.

Article 662 [Grantor's Warranty Against Defects in Gift]

A grantor is not liable for any defect in the gifted property. Where a gift is burdened with an obligation, if the gifted property has defect(s), the grantor shall, to the extent of the obligation imposed, assume the same liability as a seller.

Where a grantor intentionally does not notify a grantee of the defect(s) in the gifted property or has warranted that the gifted property is free from defect(s), and the grantee suffers a loss as a result, the grantor shall be liable for compensation therefor.

Article 663 [Grantor's Statutory Right of Revocation and Time Limit for Exercise Thereof]

A grantor may revoke a gift if any of the following circumstances applies to the grantee:

1. Seriously harming the legal rights and interests of the grantor or any near relative thereof;

2. Failing to perform an obligation of support owed to the grantor; or

3. Failing to perform an obligation as agreed in the gift contract.

The grantor's right of revocation shall be exercised within one year from the date the grantor knows or ought to have known of the grounds therefor.

Article 664 [Right of Revocation Enjoyed by Grantor's Heir or Legal Agent]

Where a grantee's illegal act causes the grantor's death or loss of capacity to engage in civil juristic acts, the grantor's heir or legal agent may revoke the gift.

The right of revocation enjoyed by the grantor's heir or legal agent shall be exercised within six months from the date the heir or the legal agent knows or ought to have known of the grounds therefor.

Article 665 [Effect of Revocation of Gift]

On revocation of a gift, the holder of the right to revocation may demand that the grantee return the gifted property.

Article 666 [Grantor's Defense of Poverty]

Where a grantor's financial condition clearly worsens, which seriously affects the grantor's production and business operation or family life, the grantor may discontinue performance of the gift obligation.

Chapter XII Loan Contracts

Article 667 [Definition of Loan Contract]

A loan contract is one per which a borrower borrows money from a lender and repays the loan with interest when the loan falls due.

Article 668 [Form and Content of Loan Contract]

A loan contract shall be executed in writing, except for a loan between natural persons who agree otherwise.

A loan contract generally contains terms specifying the type of the loan, the currency, purpose(s) of use, amount, interest rate, term, and method of repayment.

Article 669 [Borrower's Obligation to Disclose True Information]

On concluding a loan contract, a borrower shall, upon the lender's demand, provide true information regarding his/her business activities and financial conditions relating to the loan.

Article 670 [No Deduction of Interest from Principal in Advance]

The loan interest may not be deducted from the principal in advance. Where the interest is deducted from the principal in advance, the loan shall be repaid and the interest thereon be calculated based on the actual amount of the loan provided.

Article 671 [Consequences of Lender Failing to Provide Loan as Agreed and Borrower Failing to Utilize Loan as Scheduled]

A lender who does not provide a loan according to the agreed date and amount and thereby causes a loss to the borrower shall be liable for compensation therefor.

A borrower who does not draw down the loan facility according to the agreed date and amount shall pay interest based on the agreed date and amount.

Article 672 [Lender's Right of Supervision and Inspection]

A lender may inspect and supervise the use of the loan per the [parties'] agreement. A borrower shall regularly provide relevant financial and accounting statements or other materials to the lender per their agreement.

Article 673 [Borrower's Liability for Failing to Use Loan for Purpose Agreed in Contract]

Where a borrower does not use the loan for a purpose as stipulated in the [parties'] contract, the lender may cease providing the loan, accelerate the loan before its due date, or cancel the contract.

Article 674 [Time Limit for Payment of Interest by Borrower]

A borrower shall pay interest within the agreed time limit. In the absence of agreement on the time limit for payment of interest or if their agreement is ambiguous and such time limit still cannot be determined based on the provisions of Article 510 of this Code, the interest shall be paid with the principal when it is repaid if the term of the loan is less than one year; the interest shall be paid at the end of each full year if the term of the loan is more than one year, and the interest shall be paid with the principal when it is repaid if the remaining period is less than one year.

Article 675 [Time Period for Repayment of Loan]

A borrower shall repay a loan within the time period agreed. Where parties have not agreed on the time period for repayment of the loan or their agreement is ambiguous, and such period still cannot be ascertained based on the provisions of Article 510 of this Code, the borrower may repay the loan at any time, and the lender may demand that the borrower repay the loan within a reasonable period.

Article 676 [Borrower's Liability for Delayed Loan Repayment]

A borrower who does not repay a loan within the agreed time period shall pay penalty interest[1] per agreement or relevant State regulations.

Article 677 [Prepayment of Loan by Borrower]

Where a borrower prepays a loan, unless the parties agree otherwise, the interest shall be calculated based on the actual period of the loan.

---

1 I.e. penalty APR (penalty annual percentage rate), default interest, interest for/on late payment, statutory interest for/on late payment, interest on arrears, or penal interest.

Article 678 [Extension of Loan]

A borrower may apply to the lender for an extension of the term of the loan before it falls due. The term of such loan may be extended with the lender's consent.

Article 679 [Time for Formation of Loan Agreement Between Natural Persons]

A loan contract between natural persons forms at the time when the lender extends the loan.

Article 680 [Prohibition of Usury and Determination of Interest Rates]

Usury is prohibited, and the interest rate for lending may not violate relevant State regulations.

In the absence of an agreement on payment of interest in the loan contract, the loan shall be deemed to be interest-free.

Where an agreement on the payment of interest in a loan contract is ambiguous and the parties are unable to reach a supplementary agreement, the interest shall be determined based on such factors as the mode of doing business, trade usage and the market interest rate prevailing in the local area or between the parties. If the loan is between natural persons, the loan shall be deemed to be interest-free.

Chapter XIII Guaranty Contracts

Section 1 General Rules

Article 681 [Definition of Guaranty Contract]

A guaranty contract is one in which, for the purpose of guaranteeing the satisfaction of an underlying claim, a guarantor and an obligee agree that the guarantor will perform an obligor's obligation or be liable therefor if the obligor does not perform it when it is due, or when a circumstance as agreed by the parties occurs.

Article 682 [Subordination of Guaranty Contract and Legal Consequence of Invalidity Thereof]

A guaranty contract is an accessorial contract subordinate to a principal claim-obligation contract. Where the principal contract is void, the guaranty contract also becomes void, unless law provides otherwise.

Where a guaranty contract is voided, the obligor, guarantor, and/or obligee at fault shall each assume their respective civil liability correspondingly.

Article 683 [Persons Not Permitted to Be Guarantors]

No State agency legal person may act as a guarantor, except where a State agency may, on approval of the State Council, act as a guarantor associated with re-lending a loan from a foreign government or international economic organization.

No non-profit legal person or unincorporated entity, formed for public weal purposes, may act as a guarantor.

Article 684 [Content of Guaranty Contracts]

A guaranty contract generally contains terms specifying the kind and amount of the principal claim it guarantees, the time limit for the obligor to perform the obligation, and the mode, scope, and term of the guaranty.

Article 685 [Forms of Guaranty Contracts]

A guaranty contract may be a separate contract made in writing or a guaranty clause in a principal claim-obligation contract.

A guaranty contract forms when a third party unilaterally provides a guaranty in writing to an obligee who accepts it without objection.

Article 686 [Modes of Guaranty]

The modes of guaranty include ordinary guaranty and guaranty with joint and several liability.

In the absence of an agreement in the guaranty contract on the mode of the guaranty or if the agreement is ambiguous, the guarantor shall assume the liability of an ordinary guaranty.

Article 687 [Ordinary Guarantor's Beneficium Ordinis[1]]

Where the parties to a guaranty contract agree that the guarantor shall assume guaranty liability when the obligor is unable to perform the obligation, such guaranty is an ordinary guaranty.

A guarantor in an ordinary guaranty may refuse to assume guaranty liability to an obligee before a dispute arising from the principal contract is adjudicated or arbitrated, the obligor's property is per law judicially exhausted towards the satisfaction of the obligation and the principal obligation still remains unfulfilled, unless one of the following situations arises:

1. The obligor's whereabouts are unknown, and no property is available for execution;

2. A people's court has accepted the obligor's bankruptcy petition;

3. The obligee has evidence to demonstrate that the obligor's property does not suffice to satisfy all the debt obligations, or the obligor has lost the capability to perform the obligation; or

4. The guarantor renounces the right granted by this paragraph in writing.

Article 688 [Joint and Several Liability Guaranty]

Where the parties agree in a guaranty contract that the guarantor and the obligor shall be jointly and severally liable for the obligation, such guaranty is

1 Sometimes referred to as Discussion, Right of Discussion, or Benefit of Discussion.

a joint and several liability guaranty.

Where an obligor with a joint and several liability guaranty does not perform his/her obligation due or where a circumstance agreed by the parties occurs, the obligee may demand that the obligor perform his/her obligation, or demand that the guarantor assume the guaranty liability within the scope of the guaranty.

Article 689 [Counter-Guarantee]

A guarantor may demand that an obligor provide a counter-guarantee.

Article 690 [Contract for Revolving Guaranty]

A guarantor and an obligee may, via negotiation, conclude a revolving guaranty contract providing guaranty for a specified maximum amount of balance of claims arising successively within a specified period of time.

In addition to application of the provisions of this Chapter to revolving guaranty, the relevant provisions of Book Two of this Code on revolving mortgages shall be applied *mutatis mutandis*.

Section 2 Guaranty Liability

Article 691 [Scope of Guaranty]

The scope of a guaranty includes the creditor's principal claim and interest thereon, liquidated damages, compensatory damages, and the expenses incurred in realizing the claim, unless the parties agree otherwise.

Article 692 [Guaranty Period]

The guaranty period is the time period during which the guarantor shall assume guaranty liability, and such period may not be tolled, interrupted, or extended.

An obligee and a guarantor may set the period of guaranty by agreement, but where the date on which the agreed period expires is earlier than or the same as that for the period for performance of the principal obligation, no agreement shall be deemed to exist. In the absence of an agreement or if the agreement is ambiguous, the guaranty period shall be six months from the date when the time period for performance of the principal obligation expires.

Where the obligee and the obligor have not agreed on the time period for performance of the principal obligation or their agreement is ambiguous, the guaranty period shall be calculated from the date when the grace period allowing the obligor, as demanded by the obligee, to fulfill the obligation expires.

Article 693 [Relief of Guaranty Liability]

Where an obligee in an ordinary guaranty does not bring a lawsuit or apply for arbitration against the obligor within the period of the guaranty, the guarantor shall be relieved of the guaranty liability.

Where an obligee with a joint and several liability guaranty, within the guaranty period, fails to demand that the guarantor assume the guaranty liability, the guarantor is relieved of the guaranty liability.

Article 694 [Limitation Period for Guaranty Obligations]

Where an obligee with an ordinary guaranty files a lawsuit or applies for arbitration against the obligor before the guaranty period expires, the limitation period for the guaranty obligation shall be calculated from the date when the guarantor's right to refuse to assume the guaranty liability is extinguished.

Where an obligee with a joint and several liability guaranty, before the expiration of the guaranty period, demands that the guarantor assume the guaranty liability, the limitation period for the guaranty obligation shall be calculated from the date when the obligee makes such demand.

Article 695 [Effect of Alteration of Principal Contract upon Guaranty Liability]

Where an obligee and an obligor, without the guarantor's written consent, negotiate to alter the terms of the principal claim-obligation contract, if the obligation is diminished, the guarantor shall continue to bear guaranty liability for the obligation as altered; if the obligation is augmented, the guarantor is relieved of the guaranty liability for the added part.

Where an obligee and an obligor change the time limit for performance of the principal claim-obligation contract, the guaranty period shall remain unaffected except with the guarantor's written consent.

Article 696 [Effect of Claim Transfer upon Guaranty Liability]

Where an obligee assigns his/her claim in whole or part without giving notice thereof to the guarantor, such assignment is ineffective as against the guarantor.

Where a guarantor and an obligee agree to prohibit assignment of a claim, and the obligee assigns such claim without the guarantor's written consent, the guarantor shall be relieved of the guaranty liability.

Article 697 [Effect of Obligation Delegation or Assumption upon Guaranty Liability]

Where an obligee, without the guarantor's written consent, allows the obligor to delegate the obligation in whole or part, the guarantor shall be relieved of the guaranty liability to the extent of the obligation delegated without such consent, unless the obligee and the guarantor agree otherwise.

Where a third party assumes the principal obligation in the capacity of an added and concurrent obligor, the guarantor's liability shall remain unaffected thereby.

Article 698 [Relief of Ordinary Guarantor's Guaranty Liability]

After expiration of the time limit for performance of the principal obligation, if the guarantor in an ordinary guaranty provides true information to the obligee concerning the obligor's property available for execution, but the obligee waives or neglects to exercise his/her right, and thereby renders such property no longer available for execution, the guarantor shall be relieved of the guaranty liability to the extent of the value of such property.

Article 699 [Joint Guaranty]

Where two or more guarantors guarantee the same obligation, the guarantors shall assume the guaranty liability in proportion to their share of the guaranty per the guaranty contract. In the absence of such an agreement, the obligee may demand that anyone of the guarantors assume the guaranty liability within the scope of such guarantor's guaranty.

Article 700 [Guarantor's Right of Indemnification Against Obligor]

After a guarantor has assumed guaranty liability, unless the parties agree otherwise, the guarantor shall have the right to indemnification from the obligor within the scope of guaranty liability and enjoys the obligee's rights against the obligor if this does no harm to the obligee's interests.

Article 701 [Defenses Enjoyed by Guarantor]

A guarantor may assert a defense that the obligor has against the obligee. If the obligor waives the defense, the guarantor shall still be entitled to assert such defense against the obligee.

Article 702 [Guarantor's Right to Refuse Performance]

Where an obligor has a right of offset or revocation or invalidation against an obligee, the guarantor is entitled to refuse to assume the guaranty liability to a corresponding extent.

Chapter XIV Lease Contracts

Article 703 [Definition of Lease Contract]

A lease contract is one per which a lessor delivers a leased asset to a lessee to use or to obtain benefits therefrom, while the lessee pays rent therefor.

Article 704 [Main Elements of Lease Contracts]

A lease contract generally contains terms specifying the name, number/quantity, and purpose of use of the leased asset, the lease term, rent, and the time limit and method of rent payment, and maintenance of the leased asset.

Article 705 [Maximum Term of Lease]

A lease term may not exceed 20 years. If a lease exceeds 20 years, the excess part is void.

The parties may renew a lease contract on its expiration, but the term as agreed may not exceed 20 years from the date of renewal.

Article 706 [Effect of Registration of Lease Contract upon Validity Thereof]

Where laws and administrative regulations mandate registration of a lease contract, parties' failure to do so shall not affect the validity of such contract.

Article 707 [Forms of Lease Contracts]

A lease contract with a term exceeding six months shall be executed in writing. Where parties do not adopt a written form, and the lease term cannot be determined, the lease shall be deemed indefinite.

Article 708 [Lessor's Obligation to Deliver Leased Asset and Ensure Its Conformity to Agreed Purpose]

A lessor shall deliver the leased asset to the lessee per their agreement and keep the leased asset fit for the agreed purpose of use during the lease term.

Article 709 [Lessee's Obligation to Use Leased Asset as Agreed]

A lessee shall use the leased asset in the agreed manner. In the absence of an agreement on the manner of use or if the agreement is ambiguous, and such manner still cannot be determined by reference to the provisions of Article 510 of this Code, the leased asset shall be used per its nature.

Article 710 [Exemption of Liability for Wear and Tear of Leased Asset Used by Lessee as Agreed]

Where a lessee uses a leased asset in the agreed manner or per its nature, the lessee shall not be liable for the normal wear and tear thereof.

Article 711 [Lessee's Liability for Failure to Use Leased Asset as Agreed]

Where a lessee does not use a leased asset in the agreed manner or per its nature, thereby causing damage to or loss of it, the lessor may cancel the contract and demand compensation.

Article 712 [Lessor's Obligation for Maintenance of Leased Asset]

A lessor shall fulfill the obligation of maintaining the leased asset unless the parties agree otherwise.

Article 713 [Legal Consequence of Lessor's Nonfulfillment of Maintenance Obligation]

Where a leased asset needs maintenance or repair, the lessee may demand that the lessor have it maintained or repaired within a reasonable period. If the lessor does not perform such obligation of maintenance or repair, the lessee may, at his/her discretion, have the leased asset maintained or repaired, with the costs thereby incurred to be borne by the lessor. If the maintenance or repair of the leased asset adversely affects the lessee's use of such asset, the rent shall be abated or the lease term extended accordingly.

Where a leased asset needs to be maintained or repaired as a result of the lessee's fault, the lessor shall be relieved of the obligation of maintenance or repair as provided in the preceding paragraph.

Article 714 [Lessee's Obligation of Keeping Leased Asset with Due Care]

A lessee shall keep a leased asset with due care and shall be liable for compensation therefor if it is destroyed, damaged or lost because of the lessee's failure to do so.

Article 715 [Improvements and Additions to Leased Asset by Lessee]

A lessee may, with the lessor's consent, make improvements or additions to a leased asset.

Where a lessee makes improvements or additions to a leased asset without the lessor's consent, the lessor may demand that the lessee restore the leased asset to its original state or to compensate any loss.

Article 716 [Sublease of Leased Asset by Lessee]

A lessee may sublease the leased asset to a third party with the lessor's consent thereto.The lease contract between the lessee and the lessor shall continue in force despite the lessee's sublease, and if the third party causes loss to the leased asset, the lessee shall be liable for compensation therefor.

Where a lessee subleases the leased asset without the lessor's consent, the lessor may cancel the contract.

Article 717 [Effect of Sublease with Term Longer Than Remaining Term of Original Lease]

Where a lessee subleases the leased asset to a third party with the lessor's consent, and the term of the sublease exceeds the lessee's remaining lease term, the sublease for the period that exceeds the original lease term shall not be legally binding on the lessor unless the lessor and the lessee agree otherwise.

Article 718 [Presumed Consent of Lessor to Sublease]

Where a lessor knows or ought to have known of a lessee's sublease but does not object thereto within six months, the lessor shall be deemed to have consented to the sublease.

Article 719 [Sublessee's Right of Subrogation]

Where a lessee defaults on rent payments, the sublessee may pay the rent arrears and the liquidated damages on behalf of the lessee, except where the sublease contract is not legally binding on the lessor.

The rent and liquidated damages paid by the sublessee for the lessee may be setoff against the rent payable by the sublessee to the lessee. If the payment made by the sublessee exceeds the rent payable, the sublessee shall have the right to pursue to recover such excess from the lessee.

Article 720 [Ownership of Benefits Derived from Leased Asset]

Any benefits derived from the possession or use of a leased asset during the lease term shall belong to the lessee unless the parties agree otherwise.

Article 721 [Time Period for Rent Payment]

A lessee shall pay rent per the schedule agreed therefor. In the absence of an agreement on the time limit for paying rent or if the agreement is ambiguous, and such time limit remains unable to be determined in light of the provisions of Article 510 of this Code, the rent shall be paid when the lease term expires if the lease is less than one year, or at the end of each full year if the lease is more than one year, or upon the expiration of the lease term if the remaining term is less than one year.

Article 722 [Legal Consequences of Lessee Failing to Fulfill Obligation of Rent Payment]

Where a lessee does not pay rent or delays a rent payment without just cause, the lessor may demand that the lessee pay the rent within a reasonable period, and may cancel the contract if the lessee still fails to do so within such period.

Article 723 [Lessor's Obligation of Ensuring Freedom from Right of Third Party]

Where a lessee is unable to use or to derive benefits from a leased asset because of a third-party claim, the lessee may demand an abatement of or exemption from rent.

Where a third party claims a right to the leased asset, the lessee shall promptly notify the lessor thereof.

Article 724 [Right of Rescission or Termination by Lessee Precluded from Making Normal Use of Leased Asset Due to Causes Unattributable to Lessee]

A lessee may rescind or terminate a contract under any of the following circumstances if the leased asset cannot be used due to a cause not attributable to the lessee:

1. The leased asset is seized or sequestrated by a judicial or administrative authority per law;

2. A dispute arises over title to the leased asset; or

3. The leased asset fails to meet the conditions for use as demanded by mandatory provisions of laws and administrative regulations.

Article 725 [Change of Title Does Not Break Lease]

A change in the ownership of a leased asset during the period that a lessee occupies it per a lease contract does not affect the effectiveness of the lease contract.

Article 726 [Home Lessee's Right of First Refusal]

A lessor planning to sell a leased home shall notify the lessee within a reasonable period before the sale, and the lessee shall have the right of first refusal on the home on equal terms, unless a proportional co-owner of the home exercises the right of first refusal or the lessor sells it to a near relative.

Where a lessee does not expressly convey the intention to purchase the home within 15 days after the lessor has fulfilled the notice obligation, the lessee shall be deemed to have waived such right of first refusal.

Article 727 [Lessee's Right of First Refusal in Case of Leased Home Put up for Auction]

Where a lessor authorizes an auctioneer to sell a leased home at auction, the lessor shall notify the lessee five days before the auction. The lessee shall be deemed to have waived the right of first refusal if the lessee does not participate in the auction.

Article 728 [Legal Consequences of Infringement of Lessee's Right of First Refusal]

Where a lessor does not notify the lessee or otherwise hinders the lessee from exercising the right of first refusal with respect to the purchase of a leased home, the lessee may demand that the lessor be liable for compensation. However, the validity of the contract for sale of the leased home concluded between the lessor and a third party shall remain unaffected thereby.

Article 729 [Legal Consequences of Destruction, Damage or Loss of Leased Asset Due to Causes Unattributable to Lessee]

Where a leased asset is partially or wholly destroyed, damaged, or lost due to a cause not attributable to the lessee, the lessee may demand abatement or exemption of rent; and the lessee may rescind or terminate the contract if its purpose is frustrated because of such destruction, damage, or loss.

Article 730 [Legal Consequences of Absent or Unclear Lease Term]

In the absence of an agreement between the parties on the term of a lease, or if their agreement is ambiguous, and the lease term remains unable to be determined in light of the provisions of Article 510 of this Code, the lease shall be deemed to have an indefinite term; a party may terminate the contract at any time subject to notifying the counterparty thereof within a reasonable period in advance.

Article 731 [Lessee's Right of Termination in The Event of Substandard Leased Asset]

Where a leased asset endangers a lessee's safety or health, even if the lessee was clearly aware of the substandard quality of the leased asset when concluding the contract, the lessee may nonetheless terminate the contract at any time.

Article 732 [Treatment of Lease in Case of Death of Lessee]

Where a lessee dies within the lease term of a leased home, a person who lives with or who jointly operates a business with the decedent may continue with rent of the home according to the original lease contract.

Article 733 [Return of Leased Asset by Lessee upon Expiration of Lease Term]

A lessee shall return a leased asset on expiration of the lease term. The state of the leased asset returned shall conform with the expected state after use based on the agreement or with the normal state after use based on the nature of the leased asset.

Article 734 [Lessee's Continuing Use of Leased Asset and Home Lessee's Right of Priority to Lease]

Where a lessee continues to use a leased asset after the expiration of the lease term and the lessor does not object thereto, the original lease contract shall remain in force, but the lease term shall become indefinite.

On expiration of the lease, a lessee of a home has a preferential right to continue to rent it on equal terms.

Chapter XV Finance Lease Contracts

Article 735 [Definition of Finance Lease Contract]

A finance lease contract is one per which a lessee selects a leased item and its seller, and a lessor purchases the leased item from the selected seller and provides it to the lessee to use, while the lessee pays rent.

Article 736 [Elements and Form of Finance Lease Contracts]

A finance lease contract generally contains terms specifying the name, quantity, specifications, technical performance, and method for inspection of the leased asset, the lease term, the rent structure and the time limit, method and currency for rent payment, and arrangements as to title to the leased asset on expiration of the lease term.

A finance lease contract shall be executed in writing.

Article 737 [Invalidity of Finance Lease Contract]

A finance lease contract parties conclude on a nonexistent leased asset is void.

Article 738 [Effect of Operating License for Leased Asset on Validity of Finance Lease Contract]

Where, per the provisions of laws and administrative regulations, an administrative license must be obtained for the operation or use of a leased asset, the lessor's failure to obtain such administrative license does not affect the validity of the finance lease contract.

Article 739 [Delivery of Leased Asset to Lessee]

Where a lessor concludes a sales contract based on a lessee's selection of a seller and a leased asset, the seller shall deliver the subject matter to the lessee per agreement, and the lessee shall enjoy the rights of a buyer with respect to taking delivery of such subject matter.

Article 740 [Occasions Where Lessee May Refuse to Take Delivery of Subject Matter]

Where the seller breaches the obligation of delivering the subject matter to the lessee and one of the following situations occurs, the lessee may refuse to take delivery of the subject matter delivered by the seller :

1. The subject matter fails to conform to the agreement to a severe degree; or

2. The seller does not deliver the subject matter as agreed by the parties, and still does not deliver it within a reasonable period after being urged by [either] the lessee or the lessor.

A lessee who rejects delivery of a subject matter shall promptly notify the lessor thereof.

Article 741 [Lessee's Right of Claim Against Seller]

The lessor, the seller, and the lessee may agree that, if the seller does not perform the obligations under the sales contract, the lessee shall exercise the right to claim against the seller. The lessor shall assist the lessee in exercising such right.

Article 742 [Exercise of Right to Claim by Lessee Does Not Affect Lessee's Obligation to Pay Rent]

A lessee's exercise of the right to claim against the seller shall not affect the lessee's performance of the obligation to pay rent. However, where a lessee has relied on the lessor's expertise in selecting the leased asset or the lessor has intervened in the selection thereof, the lessee may demand corresponding rent abatement.

Article 743 [Apportionment of Liability in Case of Lessee's Failure of Claim]

Where any of the following situations arises which leads to the lessee's failure in exercising the right to claim against the seller, the lessee shall have the right to demand that the lessor bear corresponding liability therefor:

1. The lessor is fully aware that the leased asset has quality defects but does not notify the lessee thereof; or

2. When the lessee exercises the right to claim, the lessor fails to promptly provide necessary aid and assistance.

Where a lessor neglects to exercise a right to claim against a seller, which is only exercisable by the lessor, thereby causing loss to the lessee, the lessee shall have the right to demand that the lessor be liable for compensation therefor.

Article 744 [No Change of Content of Sales Contract Without Lessee's Consent]

Where a lessor concludes a sales contract based on the lessee's selection of the seller and the leased asset, the lessor may not alter those terms of the contract which are related to the lessee without the latter's consent.

Article 745 [Ownership of Leased Asset]

The lessor's title to a leased asset, being unregistered, may not be asserted against a *bona fide* third party.

Article 746 [Determination of Rent Under Finance Lease Contract]

The rent under a finance lease contract shall be determined based on the major part or whole of the purchase costs of the leased asset plus reasonable profit to be made by the lessor, unless the parties agree otherwise.

Article 747 [Quality Warranty for Leased Asset]

Where a leased asset fails to conform to the agreement or be fit for its intended use, the lessor shall be relieved of any liability, unless the lessee has relied on the lessor's expertise in selecting the leased asset or the lessor has intervened in the selection of the leased asset.

Article 748 [Lessor's Obligation of Ensuring Possession and Use by Lessee]

A lessor shall ensure and guarantee the lessee's possession and use of the leased asset.

A lessee shall have the right to demand that the lessor compensate losses where any of the following situations applies with respect to the lessor:

1. The lessor retakes possession of the leased asset without just cause;

2. The lessor hinders or interferes with the lessee's possession and use of the leased asset without just cause;

3. A third party claims a right to the leased asset due to a cause attributable to the lessor; or

4. The lessor otherwise adversely affects the lessee's possession and use of the leased asset.

Article 749 [Apportionment of Liability for Personal Injury or Property Loss Caused by Leased Asset to Third Party]

Where a leased asset causes any personal injury or property loss to a third party during the period it is in the lessee's possession, the lessor shall be relieved of liability therefor.

Article 750 [Lessee's Obligation of Properly Keeping, Using and Maintaining Leased Asset]

A lessee shall keep and use a leased asset with due care.

A lessee shall be responsible for the maintenance and repair of the leased asset during the period it is in the lessee's possession.

Article 751 [Effect of Destruction, Damage or Loss of Leased Asset upon Payment of Rent]

Where a leased asset is destroyed, damaged or lost during the period it is in the lessee's possession, the lessor shall have the right to demand that the lessee continue paying rentals, unless law or the parties' agreement provides otherwise.

Article 752 [Lessee's Obligation of Rent Payment]

A lessee shall pay rentals per agreement. Where a lessee does not pay a rental within a reasonable period after being urged, the lessor may demand payment of the whole rent, or cancel the contract and take back the leased asset.

Article 753 [Cancellation of Finance Lease Contract by Lessor]

Where a lessee transfers, mortgages, pledges, contributes as capital, or otherwise disposes of a leased asset without the lessor's consent, the lessor may cancel the finance lease contract.

Article 754 [Rescission or Termination of Finance Lease Contract by Lessor or Lessee]

A lessor or lessee may rescind or terminate a finance lease contract where any of the following circumstances arises:

1. The sales contract between the lessor and the seller is canceled or discharged, nullified or rescinded, and the parties fail to conclude a new sales contract;

2. The leased asset is destroyed, damaged, or lost due to a cause not attributable to the parties, and repairing it or finding a substitute for it becomes impossible; or

3. The purpose of the finance lease contract is frustrated due to a cause attributable to the seller.

Article 755 [Lessee's Liability for Compensation]

Where a finance lease contract is rescinded or terminated because the sales contract has been canceled or discharged, nullified or rescinded, and the seller and the leased asset were selected by the lessee, the lessor shall have the right to demand that the lessee compensate corresponding losses, unless the sales contract has been canceled or discharged, nullified or rescinded due to a cause attributable to the lessor.

Where the lessor's losses have been recouped at the time of the cancellation or discharge, nullification, or rescission of the sales contract, the lessee shall be relieved of liability for corresponding compensation.

Article 756 [Accidental Destruction, Damage or Loss of Leased Asset]

Where a finance lease contract is rescinded or terminated due to a cause not attributable to the parties, such as accidental destruction, damage, or loss of the leased asset after its delivery to the lessee, the lessor may demand compensation from the lessee, but factoring in the leased asset's depreciation.

Article 757 [Ownership of Leased Asset upon Expiration of Finance Lease]

A lessor and a lessee may agree on the post-lease ownership of a leased asset. In the absence of such agreement or if the agreement is ambiguous, and the post-lease ownership remains unable to be determined in light of the provisions of Article 510 of this Code, the leased asset shall belong to the lessor.

Article 758 [Refund of Value of Leased Asset and Impossibility of Return of Leased Asset]

Where the parties agree that the lessee shall own the leased asset on expiration of the lease term, and the lessee has paid most of the rent but becomes incapable of paying the remainder and the lessor has therefore rescinded or canceled the contract and taken back the leased asset, the lessee may demand a corresponding refund if the value of the leased asset taken back exceeds the rent in arrears and other expenses.

Where the parties agree that the lessor shall own the leased item on expiration of the lease term, and the lessee is unable to return the leased asset because of its destruction, damage or loss, or because the leased asset has become affixed to or admixed with other property, the lessor shall have the right to demand reasonable compensation therefor from the lessee.

Article 759 [Ownership of Leased Asset upon Symbolic Payment of Price]

Where the parties agree that the lessee is only required to pay the lessor a symbolic price on expiration of the lease term, the leased asset shall be deemed to belong to the lessee after the lessee has completely fulfilled the obligation of rent payment per the agreement.

Article 760 [Ownership of Leased Asset in The Event of Invalidity of Finance Lease Contract]

Where a finance lease contract is void and the parties have reached an agreement on the ownership of the leased asset in such a case, the agreement shall apply. In the absence of such agreement or if the agreement is ambiguous, the leased asset shall be returned to the lessor. However, where the contract is void due to a cause attributable to the lessee, and the lessor does not demand return of the leased asset or return of the leased asset will significantly reduce its utility, the leased asset shall belong to the lessee, who shall reasonably compensate the lessor therefor.

Chapter XVI Factoring Contracts

Article 761 [Definition of Factoring Contract]

A factoring contract is one per which a creditor of accounts receivable transfers current or after-acquired accounts receivable to a factor who provides services such as financing, management or collection of accounts receivable, or a guarantee for payment by the debtor of the accounts receivable.

Article 762 [Elements and Form of Factoring Contracts]

A factoring contract generally contains such terms as the business type, scope of services, term of service, information on the contract(s) in the underlying transaction(s) and the accounts receivable, advances by the factor, commission for the factoring service, and means of payment thereof.

A factoring contract shall be executed in writing.

Article 763 [Legal Consequences of Fabrication of Accounts Receivables]

Where a creditor and a debtor fabricate an account receivable as the subject matter of an assignment and the creditor then concludes a factoring contract based on it with a factor, the debtor of the fabricated account receivable may not assert the nonexistence of the account receivable as a defense against the factor, unless the factor has been fully aware of such fabrication.

Article 764 [Factor's Obligation to Disclose True Identity]

Where a factor notifies an account receivable debtor of the assignment thereof, the factor shall disclose its identity as a factor and present necessary supporting documents.

Article 765 [Effect upon Factor of Alteration or Termination of Underlying Transaction Contract Without Just Cause]

Where, after a debtor of an account receivable receives a notice of assignment thereof, the creditor and the debtor of the account receivable agree to alter or terminate the underlying contract without just cause, and this has an adverse impact on the factor, such alteration or termination shall be ineffective against the factor.

Article 766 [Recourse Factoring]

Where the parties agree on a recourse factoring, the factor may request the creditor of the account receivable to repay the principal and interest for the funds advanced by the factor or to buy back the account receivable assigned to the factor, or, alternatively, request the debtor of the account receivable to satisfy the claim stemming from the account receivable. If a factor claims against the debtor of the account receivable, any balance after deduction of the principal and interest on the funds advanced and other relevant expenses, shall be forwarded to the creditor of the account receivable.

Article 767 [Non-Recourse Factoring]

Where the parties' agreement is for non-recourse factoring, the factor shall claim against the debtor of the account receivable, and the factor is not required to forward to the creditor of the account receivable the amount that exceeds the principal and interest of the advances and other relevant expenses incurred.

Article 768 [Priority of Collection of Accounts Receivables Sold to More Than One Factor]

Where a creditor of an account receivable concludes factoring contracts with more than one factor and as a result the factors claim their rights to the same account receivable, the account receivable shall be obtained by the factor of a registered factoring contract in preference to the factor(s) of unregistered factoring contract(s), or, where all factoring contracts are registered, by the factor(s) in a chronological order of registration; or, where none of the factoring contracts have been registered, by the factor stated in the transfer notice which has reached the debtor of the account receivable first in time, or, where none of the factoring contracts have been registered and no transfer notice has been sent, the account receivable shall be obtained by the factors in proportion to the amount of advances each has provided, or to the service commission each is entitled to.

Article 769 [Application of Provisions Governing Claim Assignments]

For matters or circumstances not provided for in this Chapter, the relevant provisions of Chapter VI of this Book on the assignment of claims shall apply.

Chapter XVII Contracts for [Hired] Work

Article 770 [Definition of Contract for (Hired) Work and Types of Subject Matter Thereof]

A contract for work is one where a contractor, per the requirements of a customer, completes the work and delivers the work result to the customer who pays remuneration therefor.

Contracted work includes processing, manufacturing to order, repair, reproduction, testing and inspection.

Article 771 [Elements of Contract for (Hired) Work]

A contract for work generally contains such terms as the subject matter, quantity and quality of the work, remuneration for the work, the mode of contracting the work, supply of materials, period of performance, and the standard for inspection and the method thereof.

Article 772 [Principal Contractor/Performer of Hired Work]

A contractor shall complete the principal part of the work with the contractor's own equipment, technology and labor force, unless the parties agree otherwise.

Where a contractor delegates the main portion of the contracted work to a third party, the contractor shall be liable to the customer for the work completed by such third party and the customer may cancel the contract if the customer has not consented thereto.

Article 773 [Contractor Subcontracting Auxiliary Part of Work]

A contractor may delegate an auxiliary portion of the contracted work to a third party. Where a contractor delegates an auxiliary portion of the contracted work to a third party, the contractor shall be liable to the customer for such third party's completed work result.

Article 774 [Obligation of Contractor Who Supplies Materials]

A contractor who supplies materials shall select and use them per agreement and submit such materials to the customer for inspection.

Article 775 [Obligations of Both Parties Where Customer Supplies Materials]

Where a customer is to supply the materials, the customer shall do so per the agreement. The contractor shall promptly inspect the materials the customer supplies, and, if discovering any lack of conformity with the agreement, the contractor shall promptly demand that the customer replace [the nonconforming materials], make good a shortage, or take other remedial measures.

The contractor may not replace the materials the customer supplies without authorization or replace components or parts not in need of repair.

Article 776 [Obligations of Both Parties Where Customer's Requirements Are Unreasonable]

A contractor shall promptly notify a customer upon discovering that drawings or technical requirements the customer has provided are unreasonable. If the contractor incurs losses from such causes as the customer's neglect in responding, the customer shall be liable for compensation therefor.

Article 777 [Legal Consequences of Customer Altering Work Requirements]

A customer who alters the requirements of contracted work underway and thereby causes a loss to the contractor shall be liable for compensation therefor.

Article 778 [Obligation of Assistance by Customer]

Where contracted work requires assistance from the customer, the customer has the obligation to provide it. If the customer does not perform such obligation, thereby rendering completion of the contracted work impossible, the contractor may demand that the customer perform the obligation within a reasonable period and may also extend the term for performance of the contracted work accordingly. If the customer still fails to fulfill the obligation within such period, the contractor may cancel the contract.

Article 779 [Supervision and Inspection by Customer]

A contractor shall submit to the customer's necessary supervision and inspection while the work is in progress. The customer may not hinder the normal work of the contractor with such supervision and inspection.

Article 780 [Contractor Delivering Work Result]

On completion of the work, the contractor shall deliver the work result to the customer and provide the customer with necessary technical materials and relevant quality certifications.The customer shall inspect the work result for acceptance.

Article 781 [Liability for Breach of Contract Where Work Result Fails to Meet Quality Requirements]

Where the work result the contractor delivers does not conform to quality requirements, the customer may hold the contractor liable for breach of contract by reasonably choosing such remedies as repair or reworking, reduction of remuneration, or compensation for loss.

Article 782 [Time Limit for Payment of Remuneration by Customer]

A customer shall pay remuneration within the time limit agreed. In the absence of such agreement or if the agreement is ambiguous, and the time limit remains unable to be determined in light of the provisions of Article 510 of this Code, the customer shall pay at the time of delivery of the work result; if [only] a portion of the work result is delivered, the customer shall pay correspondingly.

Article 783 [Contractor's Right Before Customer Performs Obligation of Payment]

Where a customer does not pay remuneration, materials costs or other expenses, the contractor shall be entitled to a lien on the work result or to refuse delivery, unless the parties agree otherwise.

Article 784 [Contractor's Obligation to Exercise Due Custodial Care]

A contractor shall keep with due care the materials supplied by the customer and the completed work result and shall be liable for compensation therefor if such materials are or the work result is destroyed, damaged or lost due to improper custody.

Article 785 [Contractor's Obligation of Confidentiality]

A contractor shall maintain confidentiality per the customer's requirements and may not retain duplicates or technical materials without the customer's permission.

Article 786 [Several and Joint Liability of Co-Contractors]

Co-contractors shall assume joint and several liability to a customer unless the parties agree otherwise.

Article 787 [Customer's Right to Terminate Contract at Will]

A customer may terminate a contract for [hired] work at any time before a contractor completes work, but shall be liable for any loss thereby caused to the contractor.

Chapter XVIII Contracts for Construction Project

Article 788 [Definition of Contract for Construction Project]

A contract for construction project is one per which a contractor carries out construction of a project and the owner pays a price therefor.

Contracts for construction project comprise those for project surveying, design, and construction.

Article 789 [Form of Contract for Construction Project]

A contract for construction project shall be executed in writing.

Article 790 [Principles for Tendering and Bidding with Respect to Construction Project]

Tendering and bidding on a construction project shall be conducted in an open, fair and impartial manner per the provisions of relevant laws.

Article 791 [Contracting out, Contracting and Subcontracting of Construction Project]

An owner may conclude a contract for construction project with a general contractor, or conclude separate contracts for surveying, design and construction/building with surveyors, designers and constructors/builders, respectively. An owner may not parcel out to several contractors a construction project that must be completed by one contractor.

A general contractor or a surveying, design or construction contractor may delegate part of the contracted work to a third party if the owner agrees. The third party shall bear joint and several liability with the general contractor or the surveying, design or construction contractor to the owner for the work result of such third party. A contractor may not delegate the entire [part of a] construction project it has contracted to a third party or parcel out the entire [part of a] construction project it has contracted to third parties in the guise of subcontracting.

A contractor is prohibited from subcontracting the contracted project to any entity without corresponding qualifications. A subcontractor is prohibited from re-subcontracting its subcontracted project. Construction of the main structure of a construction project shall be carried out by the contractor on its own.

Article 792 [Conclusion of Contracts for Important Construction Projects of the State]

Contracts for important construction projects of the State shall be concluded per the procedures set forth therefor by the State, based on such documents as investment plans and feasibility study reports approved by the State.

Article 793 [Treatment of Invalid Contract for Construction Project Having Passed Inspection for Acceptance or Failing to Pass Inspection for Acceptance]

Where a construction contract is void but the construction project has passed its acceptance inspection, the contractor may be compensated based on the project price agreed in the contract, but subject to a discount.

Where a construction contract is void and the construction project has failed its acceptance inspection, such situation shall be dealt with per the following provisions:

1. Where the construction project passes the acceptance inspection after repair, the owner may demand that the contractor bear the costs thereof; or

2. Where the construction project still does not pass the acceptance inspection after repair, the contractor shall have no right to demand compensation based on the project price agreed in the contract subject to a discount.

Where an owner is at fault for a loss caused by a construction project failing to pass acceptance inspection, such owner shall bear corresponding liability.

Article 794 [Elements of Contracts for Surveying and Design]

A surveying or design contract generally contains terms specifying the time limit for submission of relevant basic materials and such documents as cost estimate and overall budget, quality requirements, fees, and other conditions of cooperation.

Article 795 [Elements of Contracts for Construction]

A construction contract generally contains terms specifying the scope of the project, period for construction, time for commencement and completion of intermediate projects, project quality, project costs, time for delivery of technical materials, responsibility for the supply of materials and equipment, fund allocation and settlement, project inspection for acceptance on completion, quality warranty coverage and quality guarantee period, and mutual collaboration.

Article 796 [Superintendency for Construction Project]

For any construction project to which a system of superintendency applies, the owner shall conclude a retainer contract in written form with the superintendent. The rights and obligations and the liability of the owner and the superintendent are to be defined per the provisions on contract of mandate of this Book as well as the relevant provisions of other laws and administrative regulations.

Article 797 [Owner's Right to Inspect]

An owner may inspect the progress and quality of the work at any time on condition that such inspection does not hinder the contractor's normal operations.

Article 798 [Concealed Works]

Before the concealment of concealed works, the contractor shall give notice for the owner to inspect them. If the owner does not conduct an inspection in due time, the contractor may extend the period for the completion of the project accordingly and may demand compensation for losses caused by cessation of work and forced idling of workers.

Article 799 [Inspection for Acceptance of Construction Project]

On completion of a construction project, the owner shall promptly undertake the acceptance inspection per the working drawings and descriptions and the State-issued rules for inspection and acceptance of construction projects and standards for quality inspection.Where the project passes the acceptance inspection, the owner shall pay the agreed price and take over the construction project.

A construction project may be delivered and put into use only after it has passed the acceptance inspection upon completion. A construction project may not be delivered or put into use without an acceptance inspection or if it fails such inspection.

Article 800 [Obligations of Surveyor and Designer for Surveying and Design]

Where a survey or a design fails to meet the quality requirements, or, the survey or design documents are not submitted within the agreed time period, thereby inducing a project delay and causing loss to the owner, the surveyor or designer shall continue to improve the survey or design, reduce or waive the survey or design fees, and compensate any loss.

Article 801 [Civil Liability of Constructor/Builder for Quality of Construction Project]

Where the quality of a construction project does not conform to the contract due to a cause attributable to the constructor/builder, the owner shall have the right to demand that the constructor/builder repair, rework, or rectify without further charge within a reasonable period. If delivery is rendered overdue due to such repair, reworking, or rectification, the constructor/builder shall be liable for breach.

Article 802 [Contractor's Quality Warranty During Period of Reasonable Use]

Where a construction project causes personal injury or property damage due to a cause attributable to the contractor within the length of time for which it is reasonable for the project to be used, the contractor shall be liable for compensation therefor.

Article 803 [Owner's Liability for Failure to Provide Relevant Materials per Time and Requirement Specified in Contract]

Where an owner does not provide goods and materials, equipment, construction site, funds, or technical materials at the agreed time and per the agreed requirements, the contractor may extend the period of construction accordingly and shall have the right to demand compensation for losses from cessation of work and forced idling of workers.

Article 804 [Owner's Liability for Termination and Suspension of Construction Due to Causes Attributable to Owner]

Where a construction project terminates or is suspended midway due to a cause attributable to the owner, the owner shall take measures to make good or mitigate the loss and compensate the contractor for any loss caused and actual costs incurred from cessation of work and forced idling of workers, reshipments, transfers of machinery and equipment, and backlogs of materials and structural components.

Article 805 [Owner's Liability for Reworking, Suspension or Alteration of Survey or Design Due to Causes Attributable to Owner]

Where an owner changes plans, provides inaccurate information, or does not provide necessary working conditions for survey and design as scheduled, thereby necessitating the reworking or suspension of the surveying or design work, or the alteration of the design, the owner shall pay additional fees based on the actual amount of work performed by the surveyor or designer.

Article 806 [Provisions Governing Contract Cancellation and Consequences Thereof]

Where a contractor delegates or unlawfully subcontracts a construction project to others, the client may cancel the contract.

Where the main construction materials, components and fittings, and equipment provided by the owner do not conform to mandatory standards therefor, or the owner does not perform the duty to provide aid, thereby rendering the contractor unable to perform the construction work, if the owner still does not perform the corresponding obligations within a reasonable period after being urged, the contractor may cancel the contract.

Where, after the contract is canceled, the completed construction project is found to conform to the quality standard, the owner shall make corresponding payment per agreement. If the completed construction project is found to fail the quality standard, the provisions of Article 793 of this Code shall apply *mutatis mutandis*.

Article 807 [Owner's Liability for Failure to Pay for Construction Project]

Where an owner does not pay the price per the agreement, the contractor may demand that the owner make payment within a reasonable period. If the owner still fails to make payment on expiration of such period, the contractor may negotiate with the owner to take over the construction project based upon its appraised value, or may petition a people's court to sell the project at auction per law, unless the construction project is by its nature unsuitable for takeover in payment by the contractor or for auction. The price for the construction project shall be paid preferentially from the proceeds obtained from taking of the project based on appraised value or auction thereof.

Article 808 [Application of Provisions on Contract for (Hired) Work]

The relevant provisions on contracts for [hired] work shall apply to any matters or circumstances not provided for in this Chapter.

Chapter XIX Transport Contracts

Section 1 General Rules

Article 809 [Definition of Transport Contract]

A transport contract is one per which a carrier transports a passenger or goods from a point of origin to a location agreed by the parties, and the passenger, consignor or consignee pays a fare or freight charge therefor.

Article 810 [Carrier's Obligation of Compulsory Conclusion of Transport Contract]

A carrier engaged in public transport may not reject an ordinary and reasonable request for transport from a passenger or consignor.

Article 811 [Carrier's Obligation of Secure and Reliable Transport]

A carrier shall transport a passenger or goods within an agreed or a reasonable period safely to an agreed location.

Article 812 [Carrier's Obligation of Reasonable Transport]

A carrier shall transport a passenger or goods via an agreed or a usual transport route to an agreed location.

Article 813 [Payment of Fare or Freight Charge]

A passenger, consignor or consignee shall pay a fare or freight charge. If a carrier does not provide transport via an agreed or a usual route, thereby increasing the fare or the freight charge, the passenger, consignor, or consignee may refuse to pay the increased portion.

Section 2 Passenger Transport Contracts

Article 814 [Time for Formation of Passenger Transport Contracts]

A passenger transport contract forms at the time a carrier issues a ticket to a passenger unless the parties' agreement or trade usage [indicates] otherwise.

Article 815 [Common Obligations of Public Transport Passengers]

A passenger shall travel per the time, flight number or running schedule and seat number recorded on a valid ticket. Any passenger who travels without a ticket, beyond the distance paid, at a class higher than paid for, or with a discounted ticket when unqualified therefor, shall pay the fare or make up for the difference in the fare, and the carrier may impose an extra fare per relevant rules. Where a passenger refuses to pay the aforementioned fare, the carrier may refuse the transport.

Where a passenger under a real-name passenger transport contract loses his/her ticket, the passenger may demand that the carrier record the loss and re-issue a ticket, and the carrier may not re-charge for the fare or charge other unreasonable costs.

Article 816 [Procedures for Refund or Change of Travel]

A passenger unable to board at the time recorded on a ticket for reasons attributable to the passenger shall, within the agreed period, initiate the procedures for refund or change of the travel. If the passenger does not initiate such refund or change procedure within the agreed period, the carrier may refuse to refund the ticket, and shall be relieved of the obligation to provide transport.

Article 817 [Requirements for Carry-on Luggage and Checked Bags]

A passenger's carry-on baggage shall conform to the agreed quantity limit and category requirements. A passenger carrying baggage exceeding the quantity limit or violating category requirements shall have such baggage checked.

Article 818 [Prohibition of Dangerous Goods and Contraband Carried by Passengers]

A passenger may not secretly carry on his/her person or carry in his/her baggage any inflammable, explosive, toxic, corrosive or radioactive articles, any other hazardous articles that might endanger the safety of persons and property aboard, or any contraband articles.

Where a passenger violates the provisions of the preceding paragraph, the carrier may unload or destroy the dangerous or contraband articles or hand them over to relevant authorities. If a passenger insists on carrying with him/her dangerous or contraband articles or carrying them in baggage, the carrier shall refuse to provide transport.

Article 819 [Carrier's Obligation of Giving Notice and Passenger's Obligation of Rendering Assistance]

A carrier shall strictly perform the obligation of safe transport and promptly inform passengers of transport safety instructions that warrant attention. A passenger shall actively assist and cooperate with the carrier in the latter's reasonable arrangements for safe transport.

Article 820 [Carrier's Transport Obligation as Agreed and Scheduled]

A carrier shall transport a passenger per the time, flight number or running schedule and seat number recorded in a valid ticket. In situations where the carrier delays the transport or the transport is otherwise abnormal, the carrier shall notify and warn the passenger thereof without delay, take necessary measures for alternative arrangements, and, at the passenger's demand, arrange for the passenger to take another run or flight or refund the ticket. The carrier shall be liable for compensation for any loss caused thereby to the passenger, unless such loss is not attributable to the carrier.

Article 821 [Consequences of Carrier Downgrading or Upgrading Services Without Passenger's Consent]

A carrier who unilaterally downgrades its service standard shall, at a passenger's demand, refund the ticket or reduce the fare. A carrier who upgrades the service standard may not charge an extra fare therefor.

Article 822 [Carrier's Obligation to Succor]

A carrier shall make maximum effort to succor and aid a passenger who suffers a sudden illness, goes into childbirth, or is otherwise in peril during transport.

Article 823 [Liability for Injury or Death of Passenger]

A carrier shall be liable for compensation for the injury or death of a passenger during transport, unless the injury or death is a result of the passenger's own health condition, or the carrier can prove that the injury or death resulted from the passenger's own intentional or grossly negligent act.

The provisions of the preceding paragraph shall apply to any passenger exempted from fare per regulations, holding a discounted ticket, or permitted by the carrier to travel without a ticket.

Article 824 [Liability for Destruction, Damage or Loss of Luggage]

Where an article that a passenger carries on board is destroyed, damaged or lost during transport, the carrier shall be liable for compensation therefor if at fault.

Relevant provisions on freight transport shall apply where a passenger's checked-in baggage is destroyed, damaged or lost.

Section 3 Carriage of Goods Contracts

Article 825 [Consignor's Obligation to Disclose Truthfully and Fully as Requested]

A consignor, when consigning goods for shipment, shall clearly disclose to the carrier the information necessary for shipment of the freight such as the name or entity name of the consignee or the consignee to order, the name, nature, weight and quantity of the goods, and the place of delivery.

The consignor shall be liable for a false declaration or an omission of important information, which causes loss to the carrier, and shall make compensation for such loss.

Article 826 [Consignor's Obligation to Submit Relevant Documents]

Where a freight shipment is subject to such procedures as approval and inspection, the consignor shall submit to the carrier relevant documents resulting from completion of such procedures.

Article 827 [Consignor's Obligation Regarding Packaging of Goods]

A consignor shall package goods in an agreed manner. In the absence of an agreement on the packaging manner or if the agreement is ambiguous, the provisions of Article 619 of this Code shall apply.

The carrier may refuse to provide transport if a consignor violates the provisions of the preceding paragraph.

Article 828 [Carriage of Dangerous Goods]

Where a consignor ships such dangerous goods as inflammable, explosive, toxic, corrosive or radioactive articles for shipment, the consignor shall, per State regulations on the shipment of dangerous goods, suitably package the dangerous goods, affix warning signs and labels thereto, and submit to the carrier written notices indicating the name, nature and precautionary measures with regard to the dangerous goods.

Where a consignor violates the provisions of the preceding paragraph, the carrier may refuse to provide transport, or take suitable measures to prevent losses, with the costs thereby incurred to be borne by the consignor.

Article 829 [Consignor's Right to Alter or Terminate Carriage Contract]

Before a carrier delivers goods to a consignee, the consignor may ask the carrier to stop the goods in transit, return the goods, change the destination, or deliver the goods to another consignee, but the consignor shall compensate for the losses thereby caused to the carrier.

Article 830 [Taking Delivery of Goods]

Upon arrival of the shipped goods, the carrier shall promptly notify the consignee if the carrier knows the consignee's identity, and the consignee shall promptly take delivery. Where the consignee delays taking delivery of the goods, the consignee shall pay storage and other expenses to the carrier.

Article 831 [Inspection of Goods by Consignee]

Upon taking delivery of goods, a consignee shall inspect the goods within the time limit agreed therefor. In the absence of an agreement on the time limit for inspection of the goods or if the agreement is ambiguous, and such time limit remains unable to be determined in light of the provisions of Article 510 of this Code, the consignee shall inspect the goods within a reasonable period. The fact that the consignee raises no objections as to the quantity, damage or loss of the goods within the agreed time limit or within a reasonable period shall be deemed *prima facie* evidence that the carrier has delivered the goods in accordance with the transport document(s).

Article 832 [Apportionment of Liability for Destruction, Damage or Loss of Goods During Carriage]

A carrier shall be liable for compensation for any destruction, damage or loss of the goods occurring during shipment. However, the carrier shall be relieved of liability for compensation if the carrier proves that the destruction, damage or loss of the goods resulted from *force majeure*, the inherent nature of the goods, or reasonable wear and tear, or resulted from the fault of the consignor or the consignee.

Article 833 [Calculation of Compensation]

The amount of compensation for the destruction, damage or loss of goods shall be calculated per the parties' agreement; in the absence of such agreement or if such agreement is ambiguous, and the amount of compensation remains unable to be determined in light of the provisions of Article 510 of this Code, the amount of compensation shall be calculated based on the market price of the goods at the place of delivery at the time when the goods were delivered or should have been delivered. If laws or administrative regulations provide otherwise on the calculation method or the limitation of the compensation amount, such laws or administrative regulations shall apply.

Article 834 [Successive Carriage]

Where two or more carriers carry out a connected shipment of the same mode, the carrier who concludes the contract with the consignor shall be responsible for the entire shipment. If a loss occurs on one leg of the shipment, the principal carrier who concludes the contract with the consignor and the actual carrier who performs the carriage for such leg shall bear joint and several liability therefor.

Article 835 [Treatment of Freight in Case of Loss of Goods Due to Force Majeure]

Where a loss of goods occurs during shipment due to *force majeure* before collection of the freight charge, the carrier may not demand payment of a freight charge; the consignor may demand refund of the freight charge already collected. If law provides otherwise, its provisions shall apply.

Article 836 [Carrier's Lien]

Where a consignor or consignee does not pay a freight charge, storage, or other costs, the carrier shall be entitled to a lien on the corresponding goods shipped, unless the parties agree otherwise.

Article 837 [Placement of Goods in Escrow by Carrier]

Where a consignee is unknown or a consignee rejects delivery of the goods without just cause, the carrier may place the goods in escrow per law.

Section 4 Multimodal Transport Contracts

Article 838 [Multimodal Transport Operator (MTO) to Be Responsible for Performance or Coordination of Performance of Carriage Contract]

A Multimodal Transport Operator (MTO) is responsible for performing or coordinating the performance of a multimodal transport contract and enjoys the rights and assumes the obligations of a carrier throughout the entire shipment.

Article 839 [Liability System Under Multimodal Transport Contracts]

An MTO may agree with the carriers of the different legs of the multimodal shipment on their respective responsibilities in each leg under the multimodal transport contract, but such an agreement shall not affect the obligations of the MTO for the entire carriage.

Article 840 [Multimodal Transport Documents (MTDs)]

An MTO shall issue multimodal transport documents (MTDs) on receipt of the goods the consignor consigns for shipment. The MTDs may be either negotiable or non-negotiable at the consignor's request.

Article 841 [Consignor's Fault Liability]

Where losses are caused to an MTO due to the fault of a consignor at the time of consigning the goods for shipment, the consignor shall be liable for compensation therefor even if the consignor has assigned or negotiated the MTDs.

Article 842 [Application of Laws to MTO's Liability for Compensation]

Where destruction, damage or loss of goods occurs in one leg of a multimodal transport, the provisions of relevant laws regulating the mode of transport used for that leg shall apply to the MTO's liability and limitation thereof. If the shipment leg where the destruction, damage or loss of goods occurred cannot be determined, the liability for compensation shall be assumed per the provisions of this Chapter.

Chapter XX Technology Contracts

Section 1 General Rules

Article 843 [Definition of Technology Contract]

A technology contract is a contract parties conclude to clarify their rights and obligations for technology development, transfer, licensing, consulting or services.

Article 844 [Purpose of Concluding Technology Contracts]

The conclusion of a technology contract shall favor the protection of intellectual property rights and the advancement of science and technology, and shall promote the research and development, transformation, application and spread of scientific and technological achievements.

Article 845 [Major Clauses of Technology Contracts]

A technology contract generally contains clauses specifying the name of the project, the content, scope and requirements of the subject matter, the plan, place and manner of performance, the confidentiality of technical information and materials, the ownership of technological achievements and the method of distributing benefits, the criteria for and method of acceptance inspection, and the interpretation of words and terms.

Materials related to the performance of the contract, such as technical background information, feasibility studies and technical evaluation reports, project assignments and proposals, technical standards, technical norms, original design and process documents, and other technical documents may, per the parties' agreement, be incorporated into the contract.

Where a technology contract involves a patent, it shall indicate the title of the invention, its applicant and patentee, the date of application, the application number, the patent number, and the duration of the patent right.

Article 846 [Price, Remuneration and Royalties in Technology Contracts]

The method of payment of the price, remuneration or royalties in a technology contract shall be agreed by the parties and such payment may be made in a lump-sum or in installments based on a one-time charge, or made using a royalty percentages method or one based on a royalty percentages plus an upfront fee.

Where an agreement is for a payment using the royalty percentages method, the payment may be based on a set percentage of the product price, or of the increased output value, increased profits or increased product sales revenue after exploitation of the patent and utilization of the technological secrets, or based on other means of calculation per agreement. Such percentage may be a fixed percentage, or a variable one that increases or decreases each year.

Where an agreement is for payment using the royalty percentages method, the parties may agree on a method for inspecting relevant accounting ledgers.

Article 847 [Ownership of Proprietary Rights of Job-Related Technological Achievements]

Where a right to use or transfer a job-related technical achievement belongs to a legal person or an unincorporated entity, the legal person or unincorporated entity may conclude a technology contract with respect to the technical achievement. When the legal person or unincorporated entity concludes a technology contract to transfer the technical achievement, the person or persons who have accomplished the technical achievement shall have priority in acquiring it on equal terms.

A job-related technical achievement is a technological achievement accomplished through performance of a workload assigned by a legal person or unincorporated entity or accomplished mainly by using the material and technological conditions of a legal person or unincorporated entity.

Article 848 [Ownership of Proprietary Rights of Non-Work Related Technological Achievements]

The right to use or transfer a non-work related technological achievement belongs to the individuals who have accomplished such technological achievement and such individuals may conclude a technology contract for such achievement.

Article 849 [Ownership of Personal Rights of Technological Achievements]

An individual who has accomplished a technological achievement shall have the right to indicate on its relevant documentation that s/he is the creator thereof, and to receive honorary certificates and awards therefor.

Article 850 [Invalidity of Technology Contracts]

A technology contract that illegally monopolizes technologies or infringes another person's technological achievement is void.

Section 2 Technology Development Contracts

Article 851 [Definition and Form of Technology Development Contracts]

A technology development contract is concluded between parties for research and development of a new technology, product, process, variety, or material, and a system therefor.

Technology development contracts comprise commissioned development contracts and collaborative development contracts.

A technology development contract shall be executed in writing.

Relevant provisions governing technology development contracts shall be applied *mutatis mutandis* to contracts concluded between parties for the application and transformation of scientific and technological achievements of practical value.

Article 852 [Customer's Obligations Under Commissioned Technology Development Contracts]

A customer of a commissioned development contract shall pay research and development funds and remuneration per agreement, provide technical materials, make research and development requests, complete collaborative tasks, and accept the research and development results.

Article 853 [Obligations of Research and Development (R&D) Institution/Professional(s) Under Commissioned Technology Development Contracts]

The mandated research and development institution or professional(s) of a commissioned development contract shall formulate and implement a research and development plan per agreement, reasonably use research and development funds, complete the research and development work on schedule, deliver the research and development results, provide relevant technical materials and necessary technical guidance and aid the customer in fully grasping the research and development results.

Article 854 [Liability for Breach of Commissioned Technology Development Contracts]

Where a party to a commissioned development contract breaches the agreement, thereby causing the halt, delay or failure of the research and development work, such party shall be liable for such breach.

Article 855 [Key Obligations of Parties to Collaborative Development Contracts]

The parties to a collaborative development contract shall invest as agreed by the parties, including contribution of technology as an investment, participate in research and development work through performance of [assigned] tasks, and collaborate and cooperate in research and development.

Article 856 [Liability for Breach of Collaborative Development Contracts]

Where a party to a collaborative development contract breaches the agreement, thereby causing the halt, delay or failure of the research and development work, such party shall be liable for such breach.

Article 857 [Termination of Technology Development Contracts]

Where a technology which is the subject matter of a technology development contract is disclosed to the public by others, thereby rendering the performance of the contract pointless, the parties thereto may terminate their contract.

Article 858 [Apportionment of Risks Associated with Technology Development Contract and Notice Obligation]

The parties to a technology development contract shall agree on the allocation of risks of insurmountable technological difficulties arising in the performance of the contract which lead to total or partial failure of the research and development. In the absence of an agreement or if the agreement is ambiguous, and such allocation remains unable to be determined in light of the provisions of Article 510 of this Code, the risks shall be allocated reasonably between the parties.

Where a party discovers the emergence of a situation specified in the preceding paragraph which may lead to total or partial failure of the research and development, such party shall promptly notify the counterparty and take suitable measures to mitigate any loss. Where such party fails to promptly notify the counterparty and take suitable mitigating measures, and the loss increases as a result, such party shall be liable for the increased portion of the loss.

Article 859 [Ownership of Technological Achievements Under Commissioned Technology Development Contracts]

Where an invention is achieved via commissioned development, the right to apply for a patent thereto belongs to the mandated research and development institution or professional(s), unless law provides otherwise or the parties agree otherwise. If the mandated research and development institution or professional(s) have obtained the patent right, the customer may exploit the patent per law.

Where a mandated research and development institution or professional(s) transfers its/their right to apply for a patent, the customer shall have the priority to acquire the right on equal terms.

Article 860 [Ownership of Technological Achievements Under Collaborative Technology Development Contracts]

Where an invention is achieved via collaborative development, the right to apply for a patent shall be jointly enjoyed by all parties to the collaborative development. Where one party transfers its portion of the joint patent application right, the other party or parties shall have the priority to acquire the right on equal terms, unless the parties agree otherwise.

Where a party to a collaborative development declares a waiver of its portion of a patent application right, the other party or parties may, singly or jointly, submit the application, unless the parties agree otherwise. If the applicant acquires the patent right, the party who has waived its portion of the application right may exploit the patent free of charge.

Where one party to the collaborative development does not agree to apply for a patent, the counterparty or counterparties may not apply for it.

Article 861 [Ownership and Sharing of Technical Secret]

The right to use and to transfer a technical secret achieved through commissioned development or collaborative development and the method for distributing the proceeds thereof shall be agreed by the parties. In the absence of such an agreement or if the agreement is ambiguous, and such right remains unable to be determined in light of the provisions of Article 510 of this Code, all the parties shall have the right to use and transfer such technical secret before a patent right is granted for the same technological solution as such secret. However, the commissionee of a commissioned development may not transfer the result of the research and development to a third party before its delivery to the customer.

Section 3 Technology Transfer Contracts and Technology Licensing Contracts

Article 862 [Definitions of Technology Transfer Contract and Technology Licensing Contract]

A technology transfer contract is one per which a lawful right holder of a technology assigns the relevant right in respect of a specific patent, application for a patent, or technical secret to another person.

A technology licensing contract is a contract per which a lawful right holder of a technology licenses the relevant right in respect of existing specific patent(s) and technical secrets to another person to exploit and use.

The agreement in a technology transfer contract or a technology licensing contract on the provision of special equipment and raw materials for the application of a technology or on the provision of the relevant technical consultation and technical service shall form a part of the contract.

Article 863 [Types and Forms of Technology Transfer Contracts and Technology Licensing Contracts]

Technology transfer contracts include contracts for transfer of patent rights, contracts for transfer of the right to apply for a patent, and contracts for transfer of technical secrets.

Technology licensing contracts include patent exploitation licensing contracts and technical secret licensing contracts.

Technology transfer contracts and technology licensing contracts shall be executed in writing.

Article 864 [Restrictive Clauses in Technology Transfer Contracts and Technology Licensing Contracts]

Technology transfer or technology licensing contracts may specify the scope within which to exploit a patent or to use a technical secret, but may not restrain competition or technological development.

Article 865 [Restrictions on Patent License Agreements]

A patent licensing contract is valid only within the period during which the patent is effective. Where the term of a patent right expires or the patent right is invalidated, the patentee may not conclude a patent licensing contract relating to such patent with another person.

Article 866 [Key Obligations of Licensor Under Patent License Contracts]

A licensor in a patent licensing contract shall, per agreement, permit the licensee to exploit the patent, provide technical materials related to exploitation of the patent, and offer necessary technical guidance.

Article 867 [Key Obligations of Licensee Under Patent License Contracts]

A licensee in a patent exploitation licensing contract shall exploit the patent per agreement, refrain from allowing a third party not in privity of contract to exploit the patent, and pay the agreed royalties therefor.

Article 868 [Key Obligations of Technical Secrets Transferor and Technical Secrets Licensor]

A transferor in a technical secret transfer contract or a licensor in a technical secret licensing contract shall, per agreement, provide technical materials and technical guidance, guarantee the practicability and reliability of the technology, and fulfill the obligation of confidentiality.

The obligation of confidentiality provided for in the preceding paragraph shall not restrain the licensor from applying for a patent unless the parties agree otherwise.

Article 869 [Key Obligations of Technical Secrets Transferee and Technical Secrets Licensee]

A transferee in a technical secret transfer contract or a licensee in a technical secret licensing contract shall, per agreement, exploit the technology, pay the transfer fee or royalties, and fulfill the obligation of confidentiality.

Article 870 [Technology Transferor's and Technology Licensor's Warranty Obligation]

A transferor in a technology transfer contract or a licensor in a technology licensing contract shall warrant that the transferor or licensor is the lawful owner of the technology provided therein and that the technology provided is complete, error-free, effective and capable of achieving the agreed objective.

Article 871 [Technology Transferee's and Technology Licensee's Confidentiality Obligation]

A transferee in a technology transfer contract or a licensee in a technology licensing contract shall, per the agreed scope and time limit, fulfill the obligation of confidentiality with respect to the secret portion of the technology provided by the transferor or licensor which has not been made public.

Article 872 [Licensor's and Transferor's Liability for Breach of Contract]

A licensor who does not license a technology per agreement shall refund the royalties therefor in part or in full and be liable for breach. A licensor who exploits a patent or technical secret beyond the agreed scope or, without consent from the licensee, allows a third party to exploit the patent or use the technical secret in breach of the agreement, shall cease such act of breach and be liable therefor. The licensor shall be liable for breach if the licensor breaches the duty of confidentiality agreed.

The provisions of the preceding paragraph shall apply *mutatis mutandis* to a transferor who is liable for breach of contract.

Article 873 [Licensee's and Transferee's Liability for Breach of Contract]

A licensee who does not pay royalties per the agreement shall make good on the payment of royalties and pay liquidated damages. A licensee who does not do so shall cease exploiting the patent or utilizing the technical secret, return the technical materials, and be liable for breach. Where a licensee who exploits the patent or uses the technical secret beyond the agreed scope or, without the licensor's consent, allows a third party to exploit the patent or to use the technical secret, shall cease such acts of breach and be liable therefor. A licensee who violates the agreed duty of confidentiality shall be liable for breach.

The provisions of the preceding paragraph shall apply *mutatis mutandis* to a transferee who is liable for breach of contract.

Article 874 [Liability for Infringement by Transferee and Licensee]

Where a transferee or licensee, in exploiting a patent or utilizing a technical secret per agreement, infringes another person's lawful rights and interests, the liability therefor shall be borne by the transferor or licensor, unless the parties agree otherwise.

Article 875 [Ownership and Sharing of Subsequent Improvements on Licensed Technology]

Parties may, per the principle of mutual benefit, agree on the method in their contract for sharing any subsequent improvements on a licensed patent or technical secret in the course of its exploitation or utilization. In the absence of an agreement on such method or if the agreement is ambiguous, and such method remains unable to be determined in light of the provisions of Article 510 of this Code, the subsequent improvements made by one party may not be shared by any other.

Article 876 [Transfer and Licensing of Other Intellectual Property Rights]

The relevant provisions of this Section shall apply *mutatis mutandis* to the transfer and licensing of the exclusive rights to layout designs of integrated circuits, rights to new plant varieties, computer software copyrights, and other intellectual property rights.

Article 877 [Application of Relevant Laws to Technology Import and Export Contract or Contract for Patent or for Patent Application]

Relevant provisions of laws or administrative regulations that provide otherwise for contracts for technology imports and exports, or contracts for patents and patent applications, shall apply.

Section 4 Technology Consulting Contracts and Technology Services Contracts

Article 878 [Definition of Technology Consulting Contract and Technology Services Contract]

A technology consulting contract is one per which one party uses technical knowledge to supply to a counterparty feasibility studies, technological forecasts, special technological investigations, and analysis and evaluation reports with respect to a specified technology project.

A technology services contract is one per which one party uses technical knowledge to solve specified technical problems for a counterparty. Technology services contracts exclude contracts for [hired] work or construction project contracts.

Article 879 [Client's Obligations Under Technical Consulting Contracts]

A client in a technology consulting contract shall, per agreement, clarify the issues for consultation, provide technological background information and related materials, accept the work result of the consultant, and pay remuneration therefor.

Article 880 [Consultant's Obligations Under Technical Consulting Contracts]

A consultant in a technology consulting contract shall complete a consulting report or resolve issues within an agreed time limit, and the consulting report submitted shall satisfy agreed requirements.

Article 881 [Liability for Breach of Technical Consulting Contracts]

Where failure of a client in a technology consulting contract to provide the necessary materials per the agreement adversely affects the progress and quality of the consulting work, or the client does not accept the work result or delays acceptance thereof, the client may not demand a refund of remuneration already paid and shall pay any still owing.

A consultant in a technology consulting contract who does not submit a consulting report as scheduled or submits a report failing to meet the agreed requirements, shall be liable for breach in the form of reduction or nonpayment of remuneration.

Where a client in a technology consulting contract makes a decision based on the consultant's consulting report and advice which meet the agreed requirements, any loss thereby caused shall be borne by the client, unless the parties agree otherwise.

Article 882 [Client's Obligations Under Technology Services Contracts]

The client in a technology services contract shall, per the agreement, provide working conditions, accomplish collaborative tasks, accept the work result and pay remuneration therefor.

Article 883 [Consultant's Obligations Under Technology Services Contracts]

A consultant in a technology services contract shall, per the agreement, finish the service items, solve technical problems, ensure the quality of work, and impart the knowledge necessary for the solution of technical problems.

Article 884 [Liability for Breach of Technology Services Contracts]

Where failure of a client in a technology services contract to perform contractual obligations or a client's performance of contractual obligations that does not conform to the agreement adversely affects the progress and quality of work or the client does not accept the work result or delays acceptance thereof, the client may not demand refund of the remuneration paid and shall pay any still owing.

A consultant in a technology services contract who does not complete the service work per agreement shall be liable for breach in such form as renouncement of remuneration.

Article 885 [Ownership of New Technological Achievements]

New technological achievements made by a consultant during performance of a technology consulting contract or a technology services contract using technical materials and working conditions provided by the client shall belong to the consultant, and new technological achievements accomplished by the client based on the work result of the consultant shall belong to the client, unless the parties agree otherwise.

Article 886 [Apportionment of Work Expenses]

In the absence of an agreement in a technology consulting contract or technology services contract on the apportionment of the necessary costs for the consultant to carry out the routine work, or if the agreement is ambiguous, such costs shall be borne by the consultant.

Article 887 [Application of Relevant Laws to Technology Brokerage Contracts and Technical Training Contracts]

Relevant provisions of laws or administrative regulations that provide otherwise with respect to technology brokerage contracts and technology training contracts, shall apply.

Chapter XXI Deposit Contracts

Article 888 [Definition of Deposit Contract]

A deposit contract is one per which a depositary keeps an article or articles delivered by a depositor and returns such article(s).

Where a depositor engages in shopping, dining, lodging or other activities on the depositary's premises and deposits an article at a designated area, the article is deemed to be placed in the depositary's custody unless the parties agree otherwise or trade usage indicates otherwise.

Article 889 [Custody Fees]

A depositor shall pay custody fees to the depositary per their agreement.

In the absence of an agreement on custody fees or if the agreement is ambiguous, and such fees remain unable to be determined in light of the provisions of Article 510 of this Code, the custody shall be deemed free of charge.

Article 890 [Time of Formation of Deposit Contract]

A deposit contract forms on delivery of the article(s) consigned to custody, unless the parties agree otherwise.

Article 891 [Depositary's Obligation to Produce a Receipt for Custody]

Where a depositor delivers an article to a depositary to be kept in custody, the depositary shall issue a custody receipt, unless trade usage prescribes otherwise.

Article 892 [Depositary's Obligation of Keeping Articles Deposited with Due Care]

A depositary shall keep the article(s) deposited with due care.

The parties may agree on the place and method of custody. Except in case of emergency or in the interests of the depositor, the place and method of custody may not be changed without the depositor's consent.

Article 893 [Depositor's Obligation of Disclosure]

Where a depositor delivers an article to a depositary for custody which has defects or needs special safekeeping measures based on its nature, the depositor shall notify the depositary of such relevant information. If the depositor does not do so and the deposited article suffers damage as a result, the depositary shall be relieved of liability for compensation. If the depositary suffers a loss therefrom, the depositor shall be liable for compensation therefor, unless the depositary knew of or could not have been unaware of the situation but did not take remedial measures.

Article 894 [Depositary's Obligation of Keeping Articles Deposited Personally]

A depositary may not redeposit an article in his/her custody with a third party for safekeeping, unless the parties agree otherwise.

A depositary who redeposits the article in his/her custody with a third party for safekeeping in violation of the preceding paragraph and thereby causes damage to or loss of the article shall be liable for compensation therefor.

Article 895 [Depositary's Obligation of Abstaining from Use of or Disallowing Use of Articles Deposited]

A depositary may not use or permit a third party to use an article in his/her custody, unless the parties agree otherwise.

Article 896 [Depositary's Obligation of Returning Articles Deposited and/or Notifying Depositor]

Where a third party claims a right to an article in a depositary's custody, the depositary shall perform the obligation of returning the article to the depositor, unless such article becomes subject to preservation or execution measures imposed per law.

Where a third party initiates a lawsuit against the depositary or applies for distraint of the article in the depositary's custody, the depositary shall promptly notify the depositor thereof.

Article 897 [Depositary's Liability for Compensation]

Where an article deposited is destroyed, damaged or lost due to improper keeping by the depositary during the period the article is in custody, the depositary shall be liable for compensation therefor. However, a depositary who keeps the deposited article free of charge shall be relieved of liability for compensation if the depositary can prove that the destruction, damage or loss has not been caused by the depositary's intentional act or gross negligence.

Article 898 [Depositor's Obligation of Declaration of Valuables]

A depositor shall declare such to the depositary when depositing money, securities and valuable papers, or other valuable articles, and the depositary shall examine them for acceptance, or keep them in sealed storage. If the depositor does not make such a declaration, and such article is destroyed, damaged or lost, the depositary may make compensation based on a rate for ordinary articles.

Article 899 [Retrieval of Articles in Custody]

A depositor may collect the article deposited in custody at any time.

In the absence of an agreement on the period of the custody or if the agreement is ambiguous, the depositary may, at any time, demand the depositor to retrieve the article in custody. Where an agreement on the period for the custody exists, the depositary may not request the depositor to collect the article for no special reason before such period expires.

Article 900 [Return of Articles Deposited and Fruits Thereof]

On expiration of the period for custody or where the depositor collects the article deposited before the expiration of such period, the depositary shall return the article and the fruits accrued thereon to the depositor.

Article 901 [Contract for Custody of Fungible Goods[1]]

Where money is deposited, the depositary may return the money in the same currency and amount. Where other fungible goods are deposited, the depositary may return goods as agreed of the same kind, quality and quantity.

Article 902 [Time Limit for Payment of Custody Fees]

Under a contract for paid custody, the depositor shall pay the custody fees to the depositary within the agreed time limit.

In the absence of an agreement on the time limit for payment of the custody fees or if the agreement is ambiguous, and such time limit remains unable to be determined in light of the provisions of Article 510 of this Code, payment shall be made at the time when the article in custody is retrieved.

Article 903 [Depositary's Lien]

Where a depositor does not pay custody fees or other costs, the depositary shall be entitled to retain the article in custody under a lien, unless the parties agree otherwise.

Chapter XXII Warehousing Contracts

Article 904 [Definition of Warehousing Contract]

A warehousing contract is one per which a warehouser stores goods delivered by a depositor and the depositor pays a storage fee.

Article 905 [Time for Formation of Warehousing Contracts]

A warehousing contract forms when there is an expression of a meeting of

---

1 I.e. Deposit for Consumption.

the minds between a warehouser and a depositor.

Article 906 [Warehousing of Dangerous and Perishable Goods]

Where dangerous goods such as inflammable, explosive, toxic, corrosive, radioactive, or perishable articles are to be stored, the depositor shall state the nature of such goods and provide relevant information.

Where a depositor violates the provisions of the preceding paragraph, the warehouser may refuse to accept the goods for storage, or take suitable measures to avert losses, and the costs thereby incurred shall be borne by the depositor.

A warehouser that stores dangerous goods such as inflammable, explosive, toxic, corrosive and radioactive articles shall possess corresponding storage conditions.

Article 907 [Warehouser's Obligation of Examination for Acceptance and Liability for Compensation]

A warehouser shall inspect goods per agreement before accepting them. Where a warehouser, on examining the goods, finds that the goods to be stored are inconsistent with those in the agreement, the warehouser shall promptly notify the depositor thereof. A warehouser shall be liable for compensation if, after inspection for acceptance, goods stored are discovered to be inconsistent with the agreement in terms of type, quantity or quality.

Article 908 [Warehouser's Obligation to Issue Warehouse Receipt and/or Bill of Entry]

On delivery of goods for storage by a depositor, the warehouser shall issue a certificate such as a warehouse receipt or a bill of entry.

Article 909 [Warehouse Receipt]

A warehouser shall sign or stamp a warehouse receipt. A warehouse receipt shall contain the following particulars:

1. The name or entity name and domicile of the depositor;

2. The type, quantity, quality, package, the number of items, and signs on the stored goods;

3. The standard for loss or damage to the goods during storage;

4. The place of storage;

5. The storage period;

6. The storage fee;

7. The insured amount, term of insurance, and the name of the insurer in the event that the goods for storage are covered by insurance; and

8. The name of the issuer and the place and date of issue.

Article 910 [Nature and Negotiability of Warehouse Receipt]

A warehouse receipt is a certificate for collecting stored goods. Where a warehouse receipt is endorsed by the depositor or a holder thereof and signed or stamped by the warehouser, the right to collect the stored goods may be assigned.

Article 911 [Depositor or Warehouse Receipt Holder Entitled to Examine Warehoused Subject Matter or Take Samples Thereof]

A warehouser shall, on demand of a depositor or holder of a warehouse receipt, allow the depositor or the holder to examine the stored goods or to take samples thereof.

Article 912 [Warehouser's Obligation of Notification of Perils or Hazards]

Where a warehouser finds that stored goods are deteriorating or suffering other damage, the warehouser shall promptly notify the depositor or the holder of the warehouse receipt thereof.

Article 913 [Warehouser's Obligation to Warn of Hazards and Right to Deal with Them in Emergency]

Where a warehouser finds that stored goods are deteriorating or suffering other damage, which endangers the safety and/or the normal storage of other stored goods, the warehouser may demand that the depositor or holder of the warehouse receipt deal with the situation as needed. In an emergency, a warehouser may undertake necessary measures to address the problem but shall thereafter promptly notify the depositor or holder of the warehouse receipt of the situation.

Article 914 [Collection of Warehoused Goods with Ambiguous Storage Period]

In the absence of an agreement on the storage period or if the agreement is ambiguous, a depositor or holder of the warehouse receipt may collect the stored goods at any time, and the warehouser may, also at any time, demand that the depositor or warehouse receipt holder collect the stored goods, but shall grant any necessary period for preparation.

Article 915 [Collection of Warehoused Goods on Expiration of Storage Period]

On expiration of a warehousing period, a depositor or holder of the [corresponding] warehouse receipt shall collect the stored goods by presenting such certificates as the warehouse receipt or bill of entry. Where the depositor or the holder of the warehouse receipt delays collecting the stored goods, additional storage fees shall be charged; where the stored goods are collected before the expiration of the storage period, the storage fees will not be reduced.

Article 916 [Collection of Warehoused Goods Beyond Expiration of Storage Period]

Where a depositor or a holder of a warehouse receipt does not collect the stored goods on expiration of the storage period, the warehouser may urge the depositor or holder of the warehouse receipt to collect the goods within a reasonable period; if the depositor or holder still fails to collect the goods within such period, the warehouser may place the warehoused goods in escrow.

Article 917 [Warehouser's Liability for Damages]

Where within the storage period, the stored goods are destroyed, damaged or lost due to improper keeping by a warehouser, the warehouser shall be liable for compensation therefor. Where the deterioration or damage of the stored goods is due to the inherent nature of the goods, or because they are not packaged per agreement, or because they have run out of their valid storage time, the warehouser shall be relieved of liability for compensation.

Article 918 [Application of Provisions Governing Deposit Contract]

Relevant provisions governing deposit contracts shall apply to matters or circumstances not provided for in this Chapter.

Chapter XXIII Mandate Contracts

Article 919 [Definition of Mandate Contract]

A mandate contract is one per which a mandator and a mandatary agree that the mandator's affairs are to be managed by the mandatary.

Article 920 [Scope of Mandate]

A mandator may specifically entrust management of one or more affairs to a mandatary and may also in general entrust management of all the mandator's affairs.

Article 921 [Expenses Prepaid by Mandator or Advanced by Mandatary]

A mandator shall pay in advance the costs of managing the affair(s) entrusted. Where a mandatary pays for the mandator's necessary costs in managing an entrusted affair, the mandator shall reimburse such costs and pay interest.

Article 922 [Mandatary Handling Affairs as Instructed by Mandator]

A mandatary shall manage the entrusted affairs per the mandator's instructions. Where it becomes necessary to modify such instructions, the mandator's consent shall be obtained; where an emergency arises and getting into touch with the mandator becomes difficult, the mandatary shall properly manage the entrusted affair and promptly notify the mandator of the situation thereafter.

Article 923 [Mandatary Handling Affairs Personally and Sub-Mandate]

A mandatary shall manage an entrusted affair in person. A mandatary may sub-mandate to a third party with the mandator's consent. Where such sub-mandate is consented to or ratified, the mandator may directly instruct the third party to whom the affair is sub-mandated, and the mandatary shall only be liable for the selection of such third party and instructions issued thereto. If the sub-mandate is not consented to or ratified by the mandator, the mandatary shall be liable for any act by the sub-mandated third party, unless the sub-mandate is to protect the mandator's interests in the event of an emergency.

Article 924 [Mandatar's Obligation to Inform]

A mandatary shall, on the mandator's demand, report on the management of the affairs entrusted. On termination of a mandate contract, the mandatary shall report the results of the management of the affairs entrusted.

Article 925 [Mandator's Right of Intervention]

Where a mandatary, acting within the scope of authority the mandator has granted, concludes a contract with a third party in the mandatary's own name, if the third party is aware of the agency relationship between the mandatary and the madator, such contract shall directly bind the mandator and the third party, unless conclusive evidence establishes that such contract binds only the mandatary and the third party.

Article 926 [Mandator's Right Against Third Party and Third Party's Right of Choice]

Where a contract is concluded by a mandatary in the mandatary's own name with a third party who is not aware of the agency relationship between the mandatary and the mandator, if the mandatary does not perform the obligations owed to the mandator because of the third party, the mandatary shall reveal the third party to the mandator, and the mandator may then exercise the right of the mandatary against the third party, unless the third party would not have concluded the contract if s/he had been aware of the existence of the mandator at the time of concluding the contract.

Where a mandatary does not perform the obligations toward a third party due to causes attributable to the mandator, the mandatary shall reveal the mandator to the third party, and the third party may then choose either the mandatary or the mandator as a counterparty to claim rights against. However, the third party may not change the counterparty once chosen.

Where a mandator exercises the mandatary's right against the third party, the third party may assert against the mandator a defense the third party has against the mandatary. Where the third party chooses the mandator as the counterparty, the mandator may assert against such third party both a defense the mandator has against the mandatary and a defense the mandatary has against the third party.

Article 927 [Mandatary Forwarding Benefits to Mandator]

A mandatary shall forward to the mandator any property acquired in managing the affair entrusted.

Article 928 [Payment of Remuneration by Mandator]

When a mandatary has accomplished the affair(s) entrusted, the mandator shall pay remuneration to the mandatary per agreement.

Where a mandate contract is terminated or the affair entrusted cannot be accomplished due to a cause not attributable to the mandatary, the mandator shall pay corresponding remuneration to the mandatary, unless the parties agree otherwise.

Article 929 [Mandatary's Liability for Compensation]

Under a contract for paid mandate, where losses are caused to the mandator due to the mandatary's fault, the mandator may demand compensation therefor. Under a gratuitous mandate contract, where losses are caused to the mandator through the mandatary's intentional act or gross negligence, the mandator may demand compensation.

Where a mandatary acts beyond authorization and thereby causes losses to the mandator, the mandatary shall pay compensation therefor.

Article 930 [Mandator's Liability for Compensation]

Where a mandatary suffers a loss in managing an entrusted affair due to a cause not attributable to the mandatary, s/he may demand compensation from the mandator.

Article 931 [Mandator Mandating a Person Other Than Mandatary to Handle Same Affairs]

A mandator may, with the mandatary's consent, mandate a third party other than the mandatary to manage the same affair entrusted. If a loss is thereby caused to the mandatary, the mandatary may demand compensation from the mandator.

Article 932 [Co-Mandate and Co-Mandatary]

Where two or more mandataries jointly handle an entrusted affair, they shall assume joint and several liability to the mandator with respect thereto.

Article 933 [Rescission or Termination of Mandate Contract]

A mandator or a mandatary may rescind or terminate a mandate contract at any time. Where such rescission or termination of contract causes losses to the counterparty, the party rescinding or terminating a gratuitous mandate contract shall compensate the direct loss flowing from an improperly timed rescission or termination, and the party rescinding or terminating a paid mandate contract shall compensate the direct loss and the expected profit if the contract were performed, unless the loss resulted from a cause not attributable to the rescinding or terminating party.

Article 934 [Termination of Mandate Contract]

A mandate contract terminates where the mandator dies or terminates, or where the mandatary dies, loses capacity to perform civil juristic acts or terminates, unless the parties agree otherwise or terminating the contract is unsuitable based on the nature of the entrusted affair.

Article 935 [Mandatary Continuing with Entrusted Affairs]

Where the termination of a mandate contract as a result of the death, declaration of bankruptcy or dissolution of the mandator will harm the mandator's interests, the mandatary shall continue managing the entrusted affair until the mandator's heir, executor or liquidator assumes management thereof.

Article 936 [Obligations to Be Assumed by Such Persons as Mandatary's Heir, etc.]

Where a mandate contract is terminated because of the death, loss of capacity to engage in civil juristic acts, declaration of bankruptcy or dissolution of the mandatary, the mandatary's heir, executor, legal agent, or liquidator shall promptly notify the mandator thereof. Where such termination of the mandate contract will harm the interests of the mandator, the mandatary's heir, executor, legal agent, or liquidator shall take necessary measures before the mandator copes with the ensuing consequences properly.

Chapter XXIV Property Service Contracts

Article 937 [Definition of Property Service Contract]

A property service contract is a contract per which a property service provider, within a service area, supplies a property owner with property services, such as repair and maintenance of buildings and their ancillary facilities, and management and maintenance of environmental hygiene and relevant order, for which the property owner pays property service fees.

Property service providers include property service firms and other managers.

Article 938 [Elements and Forms of Property Service Contracts]

A property service contract generally contains terms specifying the items of service , quality of service, the rates and collection methods for service fees, the use of maintenance funds, the management and use of the service premises, the term of the services and the handover thereof [to a successor].

Commitments of service made publicly by a property service provider in favor of property owners shall be a constituent part of the property service contract.

A property service contract shall be executed in writing.

Article 939 [Effect of Property Service Contract]

An original property service contract concluded between a developer and a property service provider per law, or a property service contract concluded by an owners' committee and a property service provider selected and hired by the owners' assembly per law, are legally binding on the owners.

Article 940 [Conditions for Statutory Termination of Original Property Service Contract]

Where, before expiration of the service term as agreed in an original property service contract concluded per law between a developer and a property service provider, a property service contract concluded by the owners' committee or the owners and a new property service provider takes effect, the original property service contract shall terminate.

Article 941 [Conditions and Restrictions for Sub-Mandate of Property Services]

Where a property service provider mandates a specialized service entity or other third party to provide specialized services in the property service area, the property service provider shall be responsible to the owners for the specialized services.

A property service provider may not delegate the property services, which it is obligated to provide, in their entirety to a third party or parcel them out among third parties.

Article 942 [General Obligations of Property Service Provider]

A property service provider shall, per contract and the nature of the use of the property, suitably repair, maintain, clean, landscape, and manage the common spaces within the property service area which are co-owned by the owners, maintain the basic order in the property service area, and take reasonable measures to protect the owners' personal and property security.

In the event of any violation of relevant laws and regulations on public security, environmental protection and fire protection in the property service area, the property service provider shall promptly take reasonable measures to stop the violation, report it to competent authorities, and aid in its handling.

Article 943 [Property Service Provider's Obligation to Disclose Information]

A property service provider shall, in an appropriate way, regularly make public to the owners and report to the owners' assembly and owners' committee on such things as items of service, personnel in charge, quality requirements, items for which fees are charged, rate of charge for such fees, performance of its obligations, use of maintenance funds, and management of common spaces co-owned by the owners and any income therefrom.

Article 944 [Owner's Obligation to Pay Property Service Fees]

Owners shall pay property service fees to a property service provider per agreement. Where a property service provider has provided services per agreement and relevant regulations, an owner may not refuse to pay property service fees on the grounds that s/he has not received or need not receive the subject property services.

Where an owner does not pay property service fees within the agreed period in breach of the agreement, the property service provider may urge such owner to pay within a reasonable period; if such owner still fails to pay within such period, the property service provider may bring a lawsuit or apply for arbitration.

A property service provider may not resort to such means as shutting off power, water, heat or gas to pressure an owner into paying property service fees.

Article 945 [Owner's Obligation of Notification and Assistance]

Where an owner decorates or renovates a self-owned unit in a building, s/he shall notify the property service provider in advance, observe the reasonable precautions the property service provider calls attention to, and cooperate with the property service provider in necessary on-site inspections.

Where an owner transfers or leases an exclusively owned unit within a building, creates a right of habitation therein, or changes the use of the common space per law, the owner shall notify the property service provider of the relevant circumstances without delay.

Article 946 [Owner's Right to Terminate Property Service Contract at Will]

Where owners jointly decide to dismiss a property service provider per a legally prescribed procedure, the property service contract may be terminated. In such case, the property service provider shall be notified in written form 60 days in advance, unless the parties agree otherwise.

Where termination of the contract per the preceding paragraph causes a loss to the property service provider, the owners shall compensate the loss unless the loss is sustained due to a cause not attributable to the owners.

Article 947 [Renewal of Property Service Contract]

Where owners jointly decide to continue retaining a property service provider before expiration of the service term, they may renew the contract with the property service provider before the expiration of the contract.

Before expiration of the service term, where a property service provider does not agree to its continued retention, it shall notify the owners or the owners' committee in writing 90 days before the expiration of the contract, unless the parties' contract provides otherwise on such time limit for notification.

Article 948 [Indefinite Property Service Contract]

Where, on expiration of a property service term, the owners do not decide per law whether to continue the retention of the existing service provider or to hire another service provider, and the property service provider continues providing property services, the original property service contract shall continue in force, except that the service term shall become indefinite.

Either party may terminate a property service contract with an indefinite service term at any time, but the counterparty shall be notified thereof in writing 60 days in advance.

Article 949 [Property Service Provider's Obligation of Handover and Liability Therefor]

On termination of a property service contract, the original property service provider shall withdraw from the property service area within the agreed time or within a reasonable period, return the property service premises, related facilities, and relevant data and materials necessary for property services to the owners' committee, or to owners who resolve to undertake the management themselves, or to a person they designate, cooperate with the new property service provider in the handover process, and truthfully inform as to the use and management of the property.

An original property management service provider which violates the provisions of the preceding paragraph may not demand that the owners pay the property service fees accruing subsequent to the termination of the property service contract and shall be liable for compensation therefor if loss is thereby caused to the owners.

Article 950 [Post-Contractual Obligations of Property Service Providers]

After termination of a property service contract and before the handover to the new property service provider selected by the owners or the owners' assembly or to the owners who resolve to undertake management by themselves, the original property service provider shall continue handling affairs with respect to provision of property services and may demand that the owners pay property service fees for this time period.

Chapter XXV Commission Agency Contracts

Article 951 [Definition of Commission Agency Contract]

A commission agency contract is one per which a commission agent in such commission agent's own name engages in trade activities for a principal who pays remuneration therefor.

Article 952 [Commission Agent's Obligation to Pay Costs]

The costs incurred by a commission agent in handling an entrusted affair shall be borne by the commission agent, unless the parties agree otherwise.

Article 953 [Commission Agent's Obligation to Safekeep Subject Matter]

Where a commission agent possesses the subject matter consigned, the commission agent shall keep it with due care.

Article 954 [Commission Agent's Obligation to Dispose of Subject Matter]

Where the subject matter consigned has a defect at the time when delivered to a commission agent, or if it is perishable, the commission agent may dispose of the subject matter with the principal's consent; if the commission agent is unable to make timely contact with the principal, the commission agent may reasonably dispose of the subject matter.

Article 955 [Commission Agent's Obligation to Buy or Sell at Price Designated by Principal]

Where a commission agent sells at a price lower than the price the principal has specified or buys at a price higher than that the principal has specified, the commission agent shall obtain the consent of the principal; where such a transaction is made without the consent of the principal and the commission agent makes up for the price difference, such transaction shall be binding on the principal.

Where a commission agent sells at a price higher than the price the principal has specified or buys at a price lower than the price the principal has specified, the remuneration may be increased per agreement. In the absence of an agreement or if the agreement is ambiguous, and this remains unable to be determined in light of the provisions of Article 510 of this Code, the profit shall inure to the benefit of the principal.

Where a principal has issued special instructions on the price, the commission agent may not sell or buy contrary to such instructions.

Article 956 [Commission Agent's Right to Transact for Its Own Account]

Where a commission agent sells or buys a commodity at a market price, the commission agent may act as either a buyer or seller for its own account, except where the principal expresses a contrary intent.

A commission agent in the situation as provided for in the preceding paragraph may still demand payment of remuneration from the principal.

Article 957 [The Principal Accepting, Retrieving and Disposing of Subject Matter Without Delay and Commission Agent Placing Subject Matter in Escrow]

Where a commission agent buys a subject matter as mandated per agreement, the principal shall accept delivery thereof in due time. Where, after being urged by the commission agent, the principal still refuses to take delivery of the subject matter without just cause, the commission agent may place the subject matter in escrow per law.

Where a subject matter consigned cannot be sold or the principal withdraws the sale, if the principal, after being urged by the commission agent, still does not retrieve or dispose of such subject matter, the commission agent may place the subject matter consigned in escrow per law.

Article 958 [Commissioned Agent Performing Obligation Directly with Third Party]

A commission agent who concludes a contract with a third party shall directly enjoy the rights and assume the obligations under such contract.

Where a third party does not fulfill a contractual obligation, thereby causing losses to the principal, the commission agent shall be liable for compensation therefor, unless the commission agent and the principal agree otherwise.

Article 959 [Commission Agent's Right to Commission and Right of Lien]

Where a commission agent has accomplished an entrusted affair in whole or in part, the principal shall pay corresponding remuneration therefor. Where a principal does not pay remuneration as scheduled, the commission agent shall be entitled to a lien on the subject matter consigned, unless the parties agree otherwise.

Article 960 [Mutatis Mutandis Application of Provisions Governing Mandate Contracts]

The relevant provisions on mandate contracts shall apply *mutatis mutandis* to matters or circumstances not provided for in this Chapter.

Chapter XXVI Brokerage Contracts

Article 961 [Definition of Brokerage Contract]

A brokerage contract is one per which a broker reports to a client the opportunity for concluding a contract or provides brokerage services for the conclusion of a contract, for which the principal pays remuneration.

Article 962 [Broker's Obligation to Inform]

A broker shall truthfully report to the principal on matters related to the conclusion of the contract.

Where a broker intentionally conceals important facts in relation to the conclusion of the contract or provides false information thereof, and thereby harms the principal's interests, the broker may not demand remuneration and shall be liable for compensation therefor.

Article 963 [Broker's Right to Remuneration]

Where a broker facilitates and contributes to the conclusion of a contract, the principal shall pay remuneration per the agreement. In the absence of an agreement on the remuneration for the broker or if the agreement is ambiguous, and this remains unable to be determined in light of the provisions of Article 510 of this Code, the remuneration shall be reasonably determined based on the broker's services. Where the medium services for concluding a contract provided by the broker facilitate the conclusion of a contract, the parties to such contract shall pay equal shares of the remuneration to the broker.

In facilitating the conclusion of a contract, the costs incurred in the braokerage activities are to be borne by the broker.

Article 964 [Broker's Right to Reimbursement of Necessary Expenses]

Where a broker fails to facilitate the conclusion of a contract, the broker may not demand the payment of remuneration, but may, per agreement, demand that the principal pay the necessary costs incurred in the brokerage activities.

Article 965 [Consequences of Principal Concluding Contract with Third

Party in Private]

Where a principal, after accepting the broker's services, takes advantage of the trading opportunity or brokerage services provided by the broker to bypass the broker and directly concludes a contract with a third party, the principal shall pay remuneration to the broker therefor.

Article 966 [Mutatis Mutandis Application of Provisions Governing Mandate Contracts]

The relevant provisions on mandate contracts shall apply *mutatis mutandis* to matters or circumstances not provided for in this Chapter.

Chapter XXVII Partnership Contracts

Article 967 [Definition of Partnership Contract]

A partnership contract is an agreement between two or more partners to share the benefits and assume the risks of a joint undertaking.

Article 968 [Partner's Obligation to Contribute to Partnership Capital]

A partner shall fulfill the obligation to contribute capital per the agreed method, amount and time limit therefor.

Article 969 [Partnership Property]

Capital contributions made by the partners and the profits, gains and other property obtained per law as a result of the partnership business shall be partnership property.

A partner may not demand partition of the partnership property before the termination of a partnership contract.

Article 970 [Execution of Partnership Business]

Decisions by partners on the partnership business shall be subject to the unanimous consent of all the partners, unless the partnership contract provides otherwise.

The partnership business shall be jointly executed by all partners. One or more partners may be authorized to execute the partnership business per the partnership contract or the decision made by all partners; and the other partners shall cease to execute the partnership business, but they shall enjoy the right to supervise the execution of the partnership business.

Where partners execute the partnership business separately, a managing partner may raise an objection to the affair(s) executed by the other managing partner(s), in which case, the other managing partner(s) shall suspend their execution thereof.

Article 971 [Remuneration for Execution of Partnership Business]

A partner may not demand remuneration for execution of the partnership business unless the partnership contract provides otherwise.

Article 972 [Distribution of Profits and Sharing of Losses]

The distribution of a partnership's profits and allocation of its losses shall be based on the partnership contract; in the absence of an agreement in the partnership contract or if the agreement is ambiguous, the partners shall decide via negotiation. Where such negotiation proves unavailing, the partners shall share the profits and assume the losses in proportion to their paid-in capital, or equally if the proportions of their paid-in capital cannot be determined.

Article 973 [Joint Liability of Partners and Right of Recovery]

The partners shall assume joint and several liability for a partnership's obligations. A partner who has performed partnership obligations that exceed that partner's share shall have the right to recover such excess from the other partners.

Article 974 [Transfer of Partner's Share in Partnership Property]

Unless otherwise agreed in a partnership contract, a partner who transfers all or part of that partner's share of property to a person other than a partner shall obtain the unanimous consent of all other partners.

Article 975 [Obligee Not to Be Subrogated to Rights of Partner]

No creditor of a partner may subrogate and exercise any rights of a partner provided for in this Chapter and the partnership contract, except for such partner's right to claim against the partnership for distribution of benefits.

Article 976 [Duration of Partnership]

Where the partners have not agreed on the term of the partnership or if their agreement is ambiguous, and such term remains unable to be determined in light of the provisions of Article 510 of this Code, the partnership shall be deemed to be indefinite.

Where a partner continues to conduct the partnership business on expiration of the term of the partnership, and the other partners do not object thereto, the original partnership contract shall continue in force, but with an indefinite term.

A partner may terminate an indefinite partnership contract at any time, but shall notify the other partners thereof within a reasonable period in advance.

Article 977 [Termination of Partnership Contract]

Where a partner dies, loses capacity to engage in civil juristic acts, or terminates, the partnership contract is terminated, unless the partnership contract provides otherwise, or the nature of the partnership business renders such termination improper.

Article 978 [Order of Distribution of Residual Partnership Property]

Where a partnership contract terminates, after defrayment of expenses deriving from the termination and payment of the partnership debts, any residue of the partnership property is to be distributed per the provisions of Article 972 of this Code.

Part Three Quasi-Contracts

Chapter XXVIII Negotiorum Gestio

Article 979 [Definition of Negotiorum Gestio]

Where a manager who has neither a statutory nor a contractual obligation acts to manage the affairs of another person to prevent the latter from suffering a loss of interests, such manager may demand that the beneficiary reimburse the necessary costs thereby incurred. Where such manager incurs a loss while managing the other person's affairs, the manager may demand that the beneficiary pay proper compensation therefor.

Where such management is contrary to the true will of the beneficiary, the manager shall not be entitled to the rights as provided in the preceding paragraph, unless the true will of the beneficiary violates law or counters the public order or sound morals.

Article 980 [Application of Laws in Case of Beneficiary Enjoying Benefits from Management]

Where such management of another person's affairs does not fall under any of the circumstances as provided in the preceding article, but the beneficiary has enjoyed the benefits of the management, the beneficiary shall be subject to the obligations as provided in the first paragraph of the preceding article to the manager to the extent of the benefits the beneficiary has gained thereby.

Article 981 [Manager's Obligation to Properly Manage Affairs]

A manager shall manage another person's affairs in the beneficiary's best interests. Where suspension of the management is unbeneficial to the beneficiary, the management may not be suspended without just cause.

Article 982 [Manager's Obligation to Give Notice]

Where a manager manages another person's affairs, the manager shall promptly notify the beneficiary if able to do so. Where an affair is not in need of urgent management, the manager shall await the beneficiary's instructions.

Article 983 [Manager's Obligation to Report and Deliver]

On termination of the management, a manager shall report the management of the affairs to the beneficiary. The property obtained by the manager in the management of the affairs shall be forwarded to the beneficiary without delay.

Article 984 [Consequences of Beneficiary's Subsequent Ratification]

Where the management of another person's affairs by a manager is subsequently ratified by the beneficiary, the provisions on mandate contracts shall apply to the management from the commencement thereof, unless the manager expresses a contrary intention.

Chapter XXIX Unjust Enrichment

Article 985 [Definition of Unjust Enrichment]

Where a person is unjustly enriched without a legal basis therefor, the person who thereby incurs a loss is entitled to demand that the enriched person make restitution, except under any of the following circumstances:

1. The payment was made to perform a moral obligation;
2. The payment was made to satisfy an obligation not yet due; or
3. The payment was made to pay off a debt by the claimant with full

awareness of not being liable for such payment.

Article 986 [Exemption of Bona Fide Recipient's Obligation to Make Restitution]

Where the recipient enriched did not know or could not have known that the benefit gained was without a legal basis, and the benefit no longer exists, the recipient shall have no obligation to make restitution of such benefit.

Article 987 [Mala Fide Recipient's Obligation to Make Restitution]

Where the recipient enriched knew or ought to have known that the benefit was without a legal basis, the party thus deprived may demand that the enriched person make restitution of the benefit thus received and compensate any loss per law.

Article 988 [Third Party's Obligation of Restitution]

Where the person enriched has gratuitously transferred a benefit received to a third party, the deprived party may demand that the third party assume the obligation to make restitution to a corresponding degree.

Book Four Personal and Personality Rights

Chapter I General Rules

Article 989 [Regulatory Scope of This Book]

This Book regulates the civil law relations arising from the enjoyment and protection of personal and personality rights.

Article 990 [Definition of Personal and Personality Rights]

Personal and personality rights are the rights enjoyed by civil law subject-persons, such as the right to life, the right to bodily integrity, the right to health, the right to a name, the right to an entity name, the right to a likeness, the right to reputation, the right to honor, and the right to privacy.

In addition to the personal and personality rights provided for in the preceding paragraph, a natural person enjoys other personal and personality rights and interests arising from personal liberty and human dignity.

Article 991 [Personal and Personality Rights of Civil Law Subject-Persons Not to Be Infringed]

The personal and personality rights of civil law subject-persons receive legal protection, and no organization or individual may infringe them.

Article 992 [Prohibitions on Certain Disposal of Personal and Personality Rights]

Personal and personality rights may not be renounced, transferred, or inherited.

M. Wan et al., *The Civil Code of the People's Republic of China*,
https://doi.org/10.1007/978-981-19-2794-2_4

Article 993 [Licensed Use of Indicia of Personal Identity]

Others may be authorized to use the name, entity name, likeness, or the like, of civil law subject-persons, unless such authorization is not permitted either by law or because of the nature of the right.

Article 994 [Protection of Personal and Personality Rights of Decedent]

Where the name, likeness, reputation, honor, privacy, human remains, or the like, of a decedent is harmed, the spouse, child, and parents of the decedent have the right to demand that the actor bear civil liability therefor per law. Where the decedent has left behind no spouse or child, and the parents of the decedent have also died, other near relatives of the decedent have the right to demand that the actor bear civil liability therefor per law.

Article 995 [Claims Derived from Personal and Personality Rights]

A person whose personal and personality rights are infringed shall have the right to demand that the actor bear civil liability therefor per the provisions of this Code and other laws. Where such person exercises the right to demand that the actor cease an infringement, abate a nuisance, eliminate a danger or harmful effects, restore reputation, or extend formal apologies, the provisions on limitation periods shall not apply.

Article 996 [Cumulative Mental Harm Claims]

Where one party's breach of contract harms the personal and personality rights of the counterparty and the harmed counterparty thereby suffers severe mental and emotional harm, if the harmed counterparty elects to demand that the party in breach be liable for breach of contract, the harmed counterparty's claim for damages for mental and emotional harm shall not be affected thereby.

Article 997 [Injunctions Against Acts Infringing Personal and Personality Rights]

Where a civil law subject-person has evidence demonstrating that an actor is committing or is about to commit an illegal act that infringes such civil law subject-person's personal and personality rights, and that failure to prevent the act without delay will cause irreparable harm to such civil law subject-person's lawful rights and interests, such civil law subject-person shall have the right, per law, to demand that a people's court order the actor to cease and desist from such act.

Article 998 [Factors Considered in Determining Liability for Infringement of Personal and Personality Rights]

In determining the civil liability an actor shall bear for infringing another person's personal and personality rights, other than the right to life, the right to bodily integrity, or the right to health, due account shall be taken of such factors as the occupations of the actor and the harmed person, the scope of impact of the act, the degree of fault, and the purposes, methods, and consequences of the act.

Article 999 [Reasonable Use of Personality Rights]

Those engaged in such acts for public interest as news reportage and public opinion supervision may reasonably use the name, entity name, likeness, or personal information of a civil law subject-person, but shall bear civil liability therefor per law where such use unreasonably harms the personality rights of such civil law subject-person.

Article 1000 [Assumption of Liability in Such Forms as Elimination of (Adverse) Effects, Restoration of Reputation and Formal Apology, etc.]

Where an actor assumes such civil liability as elimination of [adverse] effects, restoration of reputation, or extension of formal apologies for infringing another person's personal and personality rights, such civil liability shall be proportionate to the specific manner of the act and the scope of its impact.

Where an actor refuses to assume civil liability as provided in the preceding paragraph, a people's court may resort to such measures as posting announcements or publishing final judgments via such media as newspapers, periodicals, or online websites, and any costs thereby incurred shall be covered by the actor.

Article 1001 [Laws Applicable to Right to Identity]

The relevant provisions of Book One and Book Five of this Code and other laws shall apply to the protection of a natural person's right to identity arising from marriage and other familial relations; in the absence of such provisions, the relevant provisions of this Book on the protection of personal and personality rights shall apply *mutatis mutandis* based on the nature of the specific right.

Chapter II Right to Life, Right to Bodily Integrity, and Right to Health

Article 1002 [Right to Life]

A natural person enjoys the right to life. A natural person's security of the person and dignity of life are protected by law. No organization or individual may infringe another person's right to life.

Article 1003 [Right to Body and Bodily Integrity]

A natural person enjoys the right to his/her body. A natural person's bodily integrity and freedom of movement are protected by law. No organization or individual may infringe another person's right to bodily integrity.

Article 1004 [Right to Health]

A natural person enjoys the right to health. A natural person's physical and mental health receives legal protection. No organization or individual may infringe another person's right to health.

Article 1005 [Legal Duty to Rescue and Aid]

Where a natural person's right to life, right to bodily integrity, or right to health is infringed or otherwise in peril, organizations or individuals with legally prescribed relief obligations shall provide rescue and aid without delay.

Article 1006 [Donation of Body or Organ]

A person with full capacity to engage in civil juristic acts shall have the right to voluntarily decide per law to donate cells, tissues, organs, and human remains. No organization or individual may coerce, cheat, or entice a person into such a donation.

The consent of a person with full capacity to engage in civil juristic acts to be a donor thereof per the provisions of the preceding paragraph shall be executed in written form or via a will.

Where a natural person, during his/her lifetime, has not objected to being a donor, his/her spouse, adult children and parents may jointly decide to make a donation concerning such person after his/her death, and such donation decision shall be executed in written form.

Article 1007 [Prohibited Purchase or Sale of Body or Part Thereof]

Any form of purchase or sale of human cells, tissues, organs, or remains is prohibited.

Any purchase or sale in violation of the preceding paragraph is void.

Article 1008 [Clinical Trial Involving Human Subject]

Where clinical trials are needed to develop new drugs and medical devices or new prevention and treatment methods, subject per law both to approval by relevant competent authorities and to examination and approval by an ethics committee, the participants or the guardians thereof shall be informed of such details as the purposes, methods and possible risks of the trial, and written consent thereto shall be obtained.

No clinical trial fees may be collected from participants in the course of a clinical trial.

Article 1009 [Obligations with Respect to Medical and Scientific Research Related to Human Genes and Embryos]

Medical and scientific research activities related to such [areas] as human genes and embryos shall be subject to the relevant provisions of laws, administrative regulations, and State regulations, and may not endanger human health, contravene ethics and morals, or harm the public interests.

Article 1010 [Sexual Harassment]

A person who has been sexually harassed against his/her will by another person through speech, writing, image, physical conduct, or the like, shall have the right to demand that the actor bear civil liability therefor per law.

State agencies, enterprises, schools, and other organizations shall take reasonable precautions, accept and deal with complaints, investigate and handle allegations, and take other like measures to prevent and stop sexual harassment conducted by a person taking advantage of his/her position and power or a superior-subordinate relationship.

Article 1011 [Violation of Freedom of Movement and Illegal Body Search]

Where an actor deprives another person of freedom of movement or restricts freedom of movement thereof by such means as false imprisonment, or illegally searches another person, the injured party shall be entitled to demand that the actor bear civil liability per law.

Chapter III Right to Name and Right to Entity Name

Article 1012 [Right to Name]

A natural person enjoys the right to name, and is entitled to determine, use, change, or allow others to use his/her name per law, but may not thereby offend against public order and sound morals.

Article 1013 [Right to Entity Name]

A legal person or an unincorporated entity enjoys the right to entity name, and is entitled to decide, use, change, transfer, or allow others to use its entity name per law.

Article 1014 [No Infringement of Right to Name or Right to Entity Name]

No organization or individual may infringe another person's right to name or right to entity name by such means as interference, misappropriation, or false representation.

Article 1015 [Choice of Surname for Natural Person]

A natural person shall take the surname of either his/her father or mother, but may take a surname other than that of his/her father or mother in any of the following situations:

1. Taking the surname of a senior lineal blood relative;

2. Taking the surname of a fosterer who is not a legal carer and who provides support thereto; and

3. Taking a surname based on other rightful reasons that do not contravene

public order and sound morals.

Natural persons of ethnic minorities may take surnames in compliance with their cultural traditions and local customs.

Article 1016 [Registration of Name or Entity Name and Change Thereof Do Not Affect Effect of Previous Civil Juristic Acts]

A natural person who takes or changes his/her name, or a legal person or an unincorporated entity that decides, changes or transfers its entity name, shall undergo registration procedures with relevant authorities per law, unless law provides otherwise.

Where a civil law subject-person changes a name or entity name, civil juristic acts performed before the name change shall remain legally binding upon such subject-person.

Article 1017 [Protection of Pen Name and Stage Name]

Where a pen name, stage name, screen name, translated name, trade name, or abbreviation of a name or entity name is one of a certain social renown and the use thereof by others will suffice to induce confusion among the public, the relevant provisions on protection of the right to name and the right to entity name shall apply.

Chapter IV Right to Likeness

Article 1018 [Right to Likeness]

A natural person enjoys the right to a likeness and is entitled to make, use, publicize or authorize others to use his/her image per law.

The likeness is an external image of a specific natural person contained in video recordings, sculptures, drawings, or other media by means of which the person may be identified.

Article 1019 [Negative Right to Likeness]

No organization or individual may infringe another person's right to a likeness by smearing or defiling the image thereof, or through other means, such as falsifying another person's image by utilizing information technology. Unless law provides otherwise, no one may make, use or publicize the image of a person with a right thereto without the latter's consent.

Without consent of the holder of the right to a likeness, a person with a right in a work containing the image of such right-holder may not use or publicize the image via such means as publishing, duplication, distribution, lease or exhibition thereof.

Article 1020 [Reasonable Use of Likeness]

The following acts, if done in a reasonable way, may be engaged in without the consent of the person holding the right to a likeness:

1. Using publicly available images of a likeness right holder to the extent necessary for personal study, art appreciation, classroom teaching, or scientific research;

2. Making, using, or publicizing the image of a likeness right holder, which is indispensable for news reportage;

3. Making, using, or publicizing the image of a likeness right holder to the extent necessary for a State agency to perform its duties per law;

4. Making, using, or publicizing the image of a likeness right holder, which is indispensable for displaying a specific public environment; and

5. Engaging in other acts of making, using, or publicizing the image of a likeness right holder to protect the public interest or lawful rights and interests of such right holder.

Article 1021 [Rules for Construction of Likeness Licensing Contract]

Where a dispute arises between the parties over the understanding of the terms relating to the use of an image in a contract authorizing the use thereof, such terms shall be construed in favor of the person holding the right to a likeness to his/her image.

Article 1022 [Right to Terminate Likeness Licensing Contract]

Where parties have not agreed on the duration of authorized use of an image, or if the agreement is ambiguous, either party may terminate the contract authorizing the use of the image at any time, but the counterparty shall be notified thereof within a reasonable time in advance.

Where parties have expressly agreed on the duration of authorized use of the image, the likeness right holder may terminate the contract authorizing such use with just cause, but the counterparty shall be notified thereof within a reasonable time in advance. Where such termination of the contract causes loss to the counterparty, unless the loss resulted from a cause not attributable to the right holder, compensation shall be made therefor.

Article 1023 [Mutatis Mutandis Application of This Chapter to Name Licensing Agreement and Protection of Voice]

Relevant provisions on the authorized use of another person's image shall apply *mutatis mutandis* to the authorized use of another person's name.

Relevant provisions on the protection of the right to a likeness shall apply *mutatis mutandis* to the protection of a natural person's voice.

Chapter V Right to Reputation and Right to Honor

Article 1024 [Right to Reputation]

Civil law subject-persons enjoy the right to reputation. No organization or individual may infringe another person's right to reputation via such means as insult or defamation.

Reputation is a social evaluation of [such attributes as] the moral character, prestige, talent, and credit of a civil law subject-person.

Article 1025 [Restrictions on Right to Reputation]

An actor who engages in such acts for public interest as news reportage or public opinion supervision and in so doing adversely affects another person's reputation, shall be relieved of civil liability therefor except under one of the following circumstances:

1. The actor has fabricated or distorted facts;

2. The actor has failed to fulfill the obligation of duly verifying seriously inaccurate content provided by others; or

3. The actor has used affronting words to denigrate another person's reputation.

Article 1026 [Factors Surrounding Determination of Due Verification]

To determine whether an actor has fulfilled the obligation of duly verifying the information, as provided in Subparagraph 2 of the preceding article, the following factors shall be considered:

1. The credibility of the source of the information;

2. Whether apparently controversial information has been duly investigated;

3. The time-sensitive nature of the information;

4. The relevance of the information to public order and sound morals;

5. The likelihood that the injured party's reputation would be disparaged; and

6. The ability to verify [the information] and the cost thereof.

Article 1027 [Works Infringing Right to Reputation]

Where an actor publishes a literary or artistic work depicting real people and real events or a specific person which contains insulting or defamatory content, and thereby infringes another person's right to reputation, the injured person shall have the right to demand that the actor bear civil liability therefor per law.

Where a literary or artistic work an actor publishes does not depict a specific person, and only some plot threads or subplots resemble such specific person's circumstances, the actor shall be relieved of civil liability therefor.

Article 1028 [Remedies for Infringement of Right to Reputation by Media Providing Inaccurate or False Reports]

Where a civil law subject-person adduces evidence to prove that the content of media reports published by a newspaper, periodical or online website is inaccurate or false and thereby infringes his/her reputation, s/he shall have the right to demand that such media take necessary measures, including correcting it or deleting [the offending content] without delay.

Article 1029 [Credit Evaluation]

A civil law subject-person may inquire about his/her own credit report per law and shall have the right to object and demand that correction, deletion, or other necessary measures be taken if s/he discovers that the credit report is incorrect or unjustified. The evaluators of his/her credit standing shall examine the credit report and promptly take necessary measures if [the claim of incorrectness] is verified.

Article 1030 [Application of Laws to Relations Between Civil Law Subject-Persons and Credit Data Processors]

The provisions of this Book on the protection of personal information and relevant provisions of other laws and administrative regulations shall apply to the relations between civil law subject-persons and credit information processors such as credit reporting agencies.

Article 1031 [Right to Honor]

Civil law subject-persons enjoy the right to honor. No organization or individual may unlawfully deprive another person of his/her honorary titles or defile or demean the honor thereof.

Where an honorary title awarded should have been recorded, the civil law subject-person to whom it was awarded may demand that it be so recorded. Where an honorary title awarded is incorrectly recorded, the person may demand that that such recording be rectified.

Chapter VI Right to Privacy and Protection of Personal Information

Article 1032 [Right to Privacy]

A natural person enjoys the right to privacy. No organization or individual may infringe another person's right to privacy by prying into, invading, disclosing, or publicizing another person's private life or private affairs.

Privacy is the peace and quiet of a natural person's private life plus his/her private space, private activities, and private information that s/he wishes to remain unknown to others.

Article 1033 [Acts Infringing Right to Privacy]

No organization or individual may engage in the following acts unless law provides otherwise or a right holder clearly consents thereto:

1. Invading the peace and quiet of another person's private life through phone calls, text messages, instant messaging tools, emails and leaflets, or other means;

2. Intruding into, photographing or video recording, or peeping into another person's private spaces such as a residence or hotel room;

3. Photographing or video recording, watching secretly, wiretapping, or disclosing the private activities of another person;

4. Photographing or video recording, or peeping at another person's private parts;

5. Processing another person's private information; and

6. Invading another person's privacy via other means.

Article 1034 [Definition of Personal Information]

A natural person's personal information is protected by law.

Personal information is data recorded electronically or via other means that can be used on its own or in combination with other information to identify a natural person, including the person's name, date of birth, identification number, biometric information, residential address, telephone number, email address, health information, and whereabouts.

Provisions on the right to privacy, or, in the absence thereof, provisions on the protection of personal information, shall apply to private personal information.

Article 1035 [Principles and Requirements for Treatment of Personal Information]

Personal information shall be processed in conformity with the principles of lawfulness, justification and necessity, and may not be excessively processed, while the following requirements shall be fulfilled:

1. Consent shall be obtained from the natural person or his/her guardian, unless law or administrative regulations provide otherwise;

2. The rules for processing information are made public;

3. The purpose, method, and scope of the information processing are clearly stated; and

4. [The processing] does not violate laws or administrative regulations or the two parties' agreement.

The processing of personal information includes the collection, storage, use, refinement, transmission, provision, and disclosure of such personal information.

Article 1036 [Grounds for Exemption of Liability for Treatment of Personal Information]

When processing personal information, an actor shall be relieved of civil liability under any of the following circumstances:

1. The actor reasonably performs the act within the scope the natural person or his/her guardian consents to;

2. The actor reasonably processes the information disclosed by the natural person himself or other information already lawfully disclosed, unless such natural person expressly refuses, or the processing of the information harms such person's significant interest; and

3. The actor reasonably engages in any other acts for the protection of the public interest or the natural person's legal rights and interests.

Article 1037 [Rights of Natural Persons with Respect to Personal Information]

Natural persons may check their own personal information with, or make copies thereof from, information processors per law. Where a person discovers that relevant information is incorrect, s/he shall have the right to object and demand that rectifications be made or other necessary measures be taken without delay.

Where a natural person discovers that an information processor has violated the provisions of laws or administrative regulations or breached an agreement between the two parties while processing his/her personal information, s/he shall have the right to demand that the information processor delete it without delay.

Article 1038 [Information Processor's Obligation to Ensure Security of Personal Information]

An information processor may not disclose or tamper with the personal information which it collects and stores, and may not illegally provide to others the personal information of a natural person without the latter's consent, unless such information, after being refined, becomes incapable of being used to identify any specific individual or being restored to its original state.

An information processor shall take technical and other necessary measures to ensure the security of the personal information collected and stored, and prevent the information from being leaked, tampered with, or lost. Where a person's personal information has been or is likely to be leaked, tampered with, or lost, the information processor shall take remedial measures without delay, notify the natural persons affected thereof per regulations, and report [the matter] to competent authorities.

Article 1039 [Confidentiality Obligation of State Agency, Statutory Agency Charged with Administrative Functions and Staff Thereof]

State agencies and statutory agencies charged with administrative functions and their staff shall keep confidential the privacy and the personal information of natural persons known to them in the course of performing their duties and may not disclose or illegally provide such [information] to others.

Book Five Marriage and Family

Chapter I General Rules

Article 1040 [Regulatory Scope of This Book]

This Book regulates the civil law relations arising from marriage and family.

Article 1041 [Fundamental Principles]

Marriage and family receive State protection.

A marriage system based on freedom of marriage, monogamy, and equality between men and women is implemented.

The legal rights and interests of women, minors, the elderly, and disabled persons are protected.

Article 1042 [Proscriptive Provisions Governing Marriage and Family]

Arranged marriages, mercenary marriages, and other acts interfering with the freedom of marriage are prohibited. Demanding money or other property through marriage is prohibited.

Bigamy is prohibited. No one who has a spouse may cohabit with another person.

Domestic violence is prohibited. Mistreatment or desertion of family members is prohibited.

Article 1043 [Promotional Norms for Marriage and Family]

Families should nurture good family values, promote family virtues, and cultivate family civility.

Husband and wife should be loyal to each other, respect each other, and

M. Wan et al., *The Civil Code of the People's Republic of China*,
https://doi.org/10.1007/978-981-19-2794-2_5

love and care for each other. Family members should respect the elderly, take care of the young, help each other, and maintain a marital and familial relationship of equality, harmony, and civility.

Article 1044 [Basic Principles for Adoption]

Adoption shall be carried out based on the best interest of the adoptee principle and lawful rights and interests of both the adoptee and the adopter shall be protected.

Trafficking of minors in the guise of adoption is prohibited.

Article 1045 [Relatives, Near Relatives and Family Members]

Relatives include spouses, relatives by blood, and relatives by marriage.

Spouses, parents, children, siblings, paternal and maternal grandparents, and paternal and maternal grandchildren are near relatives.

Spouses, parents, children, and other near relatives living together are family members.

Chapter II Entry Into Matrimony

Article 1046 [Right of Voluntary Marriage]

A man and a woman shall enter into matrimony freely and voluntarily. Neither party may compel the other to conclude a marriage against the latter's will, and no organization or individual may interfere with the freedom of marriage.

Article 1047 [Legal Age for Marriage]

A man shall attain the age of twenty-two, and a woman the age of twenty to enter into matrimony.

Article 1048 [Prohibited Marriages]

Persons who are lineal relatives by blood, or collateral relatives by blood within three generations are prohibited from marrying each other.

Article 1049 [Registration of Marriage]

Both the man and the woman intending to enter into matrimony shall apply for registration of the marriage in person with a marriage registry. If the marriage proposed is found to conform to the provisions of this Code, the marriage shall be registered, and a marriage certificate shall be issued. A marital relationship shall form on the completion of the marriage registration. A couple who has failed to file a marriage registration shall complete the registration.

Article 1050 [Reciprocity of Family Membership Between Husband and Wife]

After a marriage has been registered, by mutual consent, the woman may become a member of the man's family or vice versa.

Article 1051 [Nullity of Marriage]

A marriage is null and void under any of the following circumstances:

1. Bigamy;

2. The parties to the marriage are within the prohibited degrees of relationship; or

3. Either party to the marriage has not yet attained the legal marriage age.

Article 1052 [Forced Marriage]

Where a marriage was entered into through coercion, the coerced party may apply to a people's court to annul the marriage.

Such an application to annul the marriage shall be filed within one year from the date the coercive act ceases.

Where the coerced party whose personal freedom is illegally constrained intends to annul the marriage, the application to annul the marriage shall be filed within one year from the date when such party recovers his/her liberty.

Article 1053 [Voidable Marriage Due to Concealment of Disease]

Where one of the parties suffers from a serious disease, s/he shall truthfully inform the counterparty of such disease before marriage registration; where such disease was not honestly disclosed, the counterparty may apply to the people's court to annul the marriage.

The application to annul the marriage shall be made within one year from the date when the party knows or ought to have known of the cause for the annulment.

Article 1054 [Legal Consequences of Void and Annulled Marriages]

A void or annulled marriage lacks legal effect *ab initio*, and neither party to such a marriage shall have any rights or duties arising from a valid marital relationship. Property acquired during the cohabitation period shall be disposed of via mutual agreement. Where the parties fail to reach such an agreement, a people's court shall decide in adherence to the principle of favoring the no-fault party. In disposition of the property acquired during a marriage which has been voided due to bigamy, the proprietary rights and interests of the party or parties to the lawful marriage may not be harmed. The provisions of this Code on parents and children shall apply to children born to parties to a void or annulled marriage.

Where a marriage is nullified or annulled, the no-fault party shall have the right to claim damages.

Chapter III Familial Relations

Section 1 Spousal Relations

Article 1055 [Equality of Spouses]

Husband and wife are equal in marriage and family.

Article 1056 [Spouses' Right to Name]

Both spouses have the right to use their own surname and given name.

Article 1057 [Spouses' Freedom of Participation in Various Activities]

Both spouses are free to engage in production, work, study and various activities. Neither party may constrain or interfere with such freedom of the other party.

Article 1058 [Spouses' Equal Rights and Duties in Respect of Child Support, Education and Protection]

Both spouses have the equal right and joint duty to raise, educate, and protect their minor children.

Article 1059 [Spouses' Duty of Mutual Support]

Spouses owe each other support.

The party in need of support is entitled to claim payments from the other party who has failed to fulfill the duty of support.

Article 1060 [Marital Agency with Respect to Affairs of Domestic Daily Life]

A civil juristic act performed by one spouse for the daily needs of the family is binding on both spouses, unless otherwise agreed between the third party and the spouse performing the act.

Restrictions imposed by the spouses on the scope of civil juristic acts to be performed by one spouse shall not be asserted against a *bona fide* third party.

Article 1061 [Succession Right of Surviving Spouse]

A husband and wife have the right to inherit each other's estates.

Article 1062 [Married Couple's Community Property]

The following property acquired by the spouses during their marriage constitutes community property and is jointly owned by the spouses:

1. Salaries or wages, bonuses and earnings for services;

2. Income from production, business operations and investment;

3. Income from intellectual property rights;

4. Property acquired from succession or given as a gift, except as otherwise provided in Subparagraph 3 of Article 1063 of this Code; and

5. Other property that must be jointly owned by the spouses.

A husband and wife have the equal right to dispose of community property.

Article 1063 [Spouse's Separate Property]

The following property constitutes separate property of one spouse:

1. The premarital property of one spouse;

2. Damages or compensation received by one spouse for injury sustained;

3. Property that belongs to only one spouse as provided in a will or gift contract;

4. Articles exclusively used by one spouse for daily use; and

5. Other property that shall be owned by one spouse.

Article 1064 [Married Couple's Community Debts]

Debts incurred based on the common expression of intent of both spouses, such as a debt co-signed by both or signed by one and later ratified by the other, and debts for the daily needs of the family incurred by one of the spouses in his/her own name during marriage, are community debts.

A debt incurred by one spouse in his/her own name during marriage which exceeds the daily needs of the family is not a community debt, unless the creditor is able to prove that such debt was used for both spouses' living or for the spouses' joint production and operation, or incurred based on the spouses' joint expression of intent.

Article 1065 [Matrimonial Regime Based on Agreement]

A man and a woman may agree that the property to be acquired by them during their marriage and their premarital property may be owned by them separately or jointly, or partially owned separately and partially owned jointly. Their agreement shall be in written form. In the absence of an agreement or if the agreement is ambiguous, Articles 1062 and 1063 of this Code shall apply.

The agreement on property acquired during the marriage and their premarital property is legally binding on both parties.

Where the spouses agree that the property acquired during the marriage is separately owned, a debt incurred by one spouse shall be paid off with his/her separate property if an involved third party is aware of such agreement.

Article 1066 [Partition of Community Property During Marriage]

During the marriage, one spouse may apply to a people's court for partition of their community property under one of the following circumstances:

1. The other spouse commits acts involving concealment, transfer, sale, destruction, damage or squandering of community property or involving fabrication of community debt or other acts that seriously harm the spousal interests in the community property; or

2. A person towards whom one spouse has a statutory obligation of support, suffers from a serious disease and needs medical treatment, but the other spouse does not agree to pay the corresponding medical costs.

Section 2 Relations Between Parents and Children, and Relations Among Other Near Relatives

Article 1067 [Parents' Duty of Child Support and Child's Duty of Providing Maintenance to Parents]

Where parents fail to fulfill their duty of child support, a minor child or an adult child who is incapable of supporting himself/herself, shall have the right to claim such child support from the parents.

Where an adult child does not fulfill the duty to support his/her parents, the parents who lack the capacity to work or are in financial hardship, shall be entitled to claim maintenance from such adult child.

Article 1068 [Parents' Right and Obligation with Respect to Education and Protection of Child]

Parents have the right and duty to educate and protect their minor child(ren). Where a minor child causes harm to another person, his/her parents shall bear civil liability therefor per law.

Article 1069 [Child's Respect for Parents' Marriage Right]

A child shall respect his/her parents' right to marriage and may not interfere with his/her parents' divorce, remarriage, or their married life. A child's duty to support his/her parents shall not end with a change of his/her parents' marital relations.

Article 1070 [Mutual Succession Between Child(ren) and Parents]

A child has the right to inherit his/her parents' estate, and vice versa.

Article 1071 [Rights of Child(ren) Born out of Wedlock]

Children born out of wedlock have equal rights to children born in wedlock, and no organization or individual may harm or discriminate against them.

A biological parent who lacks physical custody of his/her out-of-wedlock child shall pay child support for such child who is a minor or who is an adult but incapable of self-support.

Article 1072 [Rights and Duties Between Stepparent and Stepchild]

A stepparent may not mistreat or discriminate against a stepchild, and vice versa.

Provisions of this Code governing the parent-child relationship shall apply to the rights and duties as between a stepmother or a stepfather and a stepchild who has been raised and educated by such stepfather or stepmother.

Article 1073 [Suit to Challenge Paternity or Maternity]

Where a parent challenges paternity or maternity with just cause, s/he may initiate a lawsuit before a people's court for affirmation or negation of such paternity or maternity.

Where an adult child challenges maternity or paternity with just cause, s/he may bring a lawsuit before a people's court for affirmation of such maternity or paternity.

Article 1074 [Duty of Support and Maintenance Between Grandparent(s) and Grandchild(ren)]

Paternal or maternal grandparents, if financially able, have the duty to raise their minor grandchild(ren) whose parents are deceased or are incapable of such upbringing.

Paternal or maternal grandchildren, if financially able, have the duty to support their grandparents whose children are deceased or are incapable of providing maintenance.

Article 1075 [Duty of Support Between and Among Siblings]

Elder brothers or sisters, if financially able, have the duty to raise their minor siblings whose parents are deceased or are incapable of such upbringing.

Younger brothers or sisters who have been brought up by their elder siblings and who are financially able, have the duty to support such elder siblings who lack both the capacity to work and a source of income.

Chapter IV Divorce

Article 1076 [Divorce by Agreement]

Where husband and wife both agree to divorce, they shall execute a divorce agreement in written form and file a divorce registration in person with a marriage registry.

The divorce agreement shall contain an expression of intent by both parties to divorce of their own free will and their agreed arrangement on such matters as child support, property partition and apportionment of debts.

Article 1077 [Cooling-off Period for Divorce]

Where, within thirty days after receipt of the divorce registration application by the marriage registry, either party becomes unwilling to divorce, s/he may withdraw the divorce registration application.

Within 30 days after expiration of the period provided in the preceding paragraph, both parties shall personally return to the marriage registry to apply for issuance of a divorce certificate and their failure to do so will be deemed a withdrawal of their divorce registration application.

Article 1078 [Registration of Divorce]

On finding that both parties intend to divorce of their own free will and that they have agreed on such matters as child support, property partition and allocation of debts, the marriage registry shall register the divorce and issue a divorce certificate.

Article 1079 [Suing for Divorce]

Where a husband or wife unilaterally demands a divorce, s/he may approach a relevant organization for mediation, or present a petition for divorce directly to a people's court.

The people's court shall, during the divorce proceedings, offer mediation, and grant a divorce if the relationship between the two parties has irretrievably broken down and mediation has proved unavailing.

A divorce shall be granted where one of the following circumstances occurs and mediation has proved unavailing:

1. One spouse commits bigamy or cohabitates with another person;

2. One spouse commits domestic violence or mistreats or deserts a family member;

3. One spouse habitually engages in such unreasonable behavior as gambling, drug abuse, or the like, and refuses to rectify such behavior despite repeated admonitions;

4. The spouses have lived separate and apart for no less than two full years due to marital incompatibility; or

5. Any other circumstance under which the relationship between the spouses has irretrievably broken down.

Where one spouse is declared a missing person and the other files for a divorce, a divorce shall be granted.

Where, since a people's court last ruled against divorce, the spouses have lived separate and apart for an additional year, a divorce shall be granted when one spouse files a petition again for divorce with a people's court.

Article 1080 [Time for Dissolution of Marital Relationship]

A marital relationship is dissolved on completion of registration of divorce or when a judgment granting divorce or a mediation agreement on divorce takes effect.

Article 1081 [Protection of Military Marriage]

Where the spouse of a military serviceman or servicewoman on active duty seeks a divorce, the consent of such military serviceman or servicewoman on active duty shall be obtained, unless a serious fault lies with the latter.

Article 1082 [Restrictions on Husband's Right of Suit for Divorce]

A husband may not seek a divorce during his wife's pregnancy, within one year following her parturition, or within six months after termination of her pregnancy, unless the wife seeks a divorce, or the people's court deems it absolutely necessary to hear the husband's petition for divorce.

Article 1083 [Registration of Resumption of Marital Relationship]

Where, after divorce, both the man and the woman voluntarily resume their marital relationship, they shall once again file for registration of marriage at a marriage registry.

Article 1084 [Post-Divorce Relations Between Parents and Child(ren)]

The parent-child relationship shall not be dissolved by the divorce of a child's parents. Whether such child is in the physical custody of the father or the mother, s/he shall remain the child of both parents.

After a divorce, parents shall retain the right and duty to raise, educate, and protect their children.

As a matter of principle, custody of a child below the age of two shall be awarded to the mother. Where parents fail to agree on the physical custody of their child over the age of two, the people's court shall take into account the specific situations of both parents and decide based on the best interest of the minor child principle. If the minor child has attained the age of eight, such child's true wishes shall be respected.

Article 1085 [Payment of Post-Divorce Child Support]

After a divorce, where one parent has the physical custody of the child, the other parent shall provide child support in whole or part. The amount and duration for such support shall be determined by both parents via an agreement or, failing an agreement, decided by a people's court via a judgment.

The agreement or judgment as provided in the preceding paragraph does not preclude the child, when necessary, from making a reasonable request for payment from either parent that exceeds the amount specified in the agreement or judgment.

Article 1086 [Parents' Visitation Rights]

After a divorce, a noncustodial parent shall have the right to visit the child, and the other parent is obligated to assist.

The manner and schedule for exercising the visitation rights shall be determined by both parents by agreement or, failing an agreement, decided by a people's court.

Where a noncustodial parent's visits to a child are injurious to such child's physical or mental health, such visits shall be suspended by the people's court per law, and resumed when the cause for such suspension ceases to exist.

Article 1087 [Disposition of Community Property upon Divorce]

Upon divorce, the community property shall be shall be disposed of by the spouses by agreement or, failing an agreement, decided by a people's court based on the actual status of the property and in adherence to the principle of favoring the child(ren), the wife, and the no-fault party.

The rights and interests of the husband or wife arising from household contractual land management shall be protected per law.

Article 1088 [Economic Compensation upon Divorce]

Where one spouse has been burdened with more duties of raising the child(ren), looking after the elderly, or assisting the other spouse in his/her work, such spouse shall have the right upon divorce to demand compensation from the other spouse, who shall pay due compensation. Specific arrangements for such compensation are to be determined by the spouses by agreement or, failing an agreement, decided by a people's court.

Article 1089 [Payment of Community Debts upon Divorce]

Upon divorce, a husband and wife shall jointly pay off their community debts. Where the community property does not suffice to pay off the debts, or the property is owned by the spouses separately, such debts shall be paid off by the spouses by agreement or, failing an agreement, decided by a people's court.

Article 1090 [Financial Help upon Divorce]

Where one spouse is in financial hardship upon divorce, the other, if financially able, shall provide suitable financial support. The specific arrangements are to be determined by the spouses by agreement or, failing an agreement, decided by a people's court.

Article 1091 [Payment of Damages upon Divorce]

A no-fault spouse shall have the right to claim damages where divorce resulted from one of the following acts engaged in by the other spouse:

1. Bigamy;
2. Cohabitation with another person;
3. Commission of domestic violence;
4. Mistreatment or desertion of a family member; or
5. Other serious faults.

Article 1092 [Legal Consequences of One Spouse's Fraud on Community Estate]

Where one spouse engages in concealment, transfer, sale, destruction, damage or squandering of the community property, or in fabrication of a false community debt in an attempt to misappropriate the property of the other spouse, the former may receive less or no property on partition of the community property in the event of divorce. Where one of the foregoing acts committed by one spouse is discovered after divorce, the other party may bring a lawsuit before a people's court for re-partitioning of the community property.

Chapter V Adoption

Section 1 Creation of Adoptive Relationship

Article 1093 [Who May Be Adopted]

The following minors may be adopted:

1. An orphaned minor;

2. A minor whose biological parents cannot be found ; and

3. A minor whose biological parents are incapable of raising such minor due to unusual difficulties.

Article 1094 [Who Can Place a Minor for Adoption]

The following individuals and organizations may place a minor for adoption:

1. The guardian of an orphan;

2. A child welfare institution; and

3. A minor's biological parents who are incapable of raising such minor due to unusual difficulties.

Article 1095 [Special Provisions for Guardian Placing Minor Ward for Adoption]

Where neither of a minor's parents has full capacity to engage in civil juristic acts and they may seriously harm the minor, the minor's guardian may place such minor for adoption.

Article 1096 [Special Provisions for Guardian Placing Orphaned Minor Ward for Adoption]

Where a guardian plans to place an orphan under his/her guardianship for adoption, s/he shall obtain the consent of the person(s) charged with a legal obligation to raise such orphan. Where the person(s) with such legal obligation does not consent to the adoption and the guardian is unwilling to continue with the guardianship, a successor guardian shall be appointed per the provisions of Book One of this Code.

Article 1097 [Biological Parents Placing Child for Adoption]

Where biological parents intend to place their child for adoption, they shall act in unison. Where one of the biological parents is unknown or cannot be found, the other parent may place the child for adoption alone.

Article 1098 [Requirements for Adopter]

A prospective adopter shall meet all of the following criteria:

1. Having no child or only one child;

2. Being capable of raising, educating and protecting the adoptee;

3. Being free of any disease which renders the prospective adopter medically unfit to be an adopter;

4. Having no criminal record unfavorable to the healthy growth of the adoptee; and

5. Having attained the age of thirty.

Article 1099 [Special Provisions for Adopting Child of Collateral Blood Relative of Adopter's Peer Within Three Generations]

Adoption of a child from one's collateral blood relative of the adopter's peer within three generations may be exempted from the restrictions imposed by Subparagraph 3 of Article 1093, Subparagraph 3 of Article 1094, and Article

1102 of this Code.

Adoption of a child by an overseas Chinese from his/her collateral blood relative of the adopter's peer within three generations may further be exempted from the restrictions prescribed in Subparagraph 1 of Article 1098 of this Code.

Article 1100 [Limitation on Number of Adoptees for Each Adopter]

A childless adopter may adopt two children, and an adopter with one child may adopt only one child.

Adoption of an orphaned minor, a minor with disabilities, or a minor in a child welfare institution whose biological parents cannot be found, may be exempted from the restrictions provided in the preceding paragraph and Subparagraph 1 of Article 1098 of this Code.

Article 1101 [Joint Adoption]

Where a person with a spouse plans to adopt a child, such person and his/her spouse shall adopt the child jointly.

Article 1102 [Adoption of Child of Opposite Gender by Person Without Spouse]

Where a person without a spouse intends to adopt a child of an opposite gender, the prospective adopter shall be no less than 40 years older than the adoptee.

Article 1103 [Special Provisions for Stepparent Adopting Stepchild]

A stepparent may, with the consent of the stepchild's biological parents, adopt the stepchild, and such adoption may be exempted from the restrictions provided in Subparagraph 3 of Article 1093, Subparagraph 3 of Article 1094, Article 1098, and Subparagraph 1 of Article 1100 of this Code.

Article 1104 [Voluntary Adoption and Voluntary Placement for Adoption]

Both adoption and placement for adoption shall be based on consent. Where a minor aged eight or above is being adopted, his/her consent shall be obtained.

Article 1105 [Adoption Registration, Adoption Publication, Adoption Agreement, Adoption Notarization and Adoption Assessment]

Adoption shall be registered with the civil affairs bureau of a people's government at or above the county level. The adoptive relationship is created on registration thereof.

For adoption of a minor whose parents cannot be found, the civil affairs bureau handling the registration shall post a public notice before registering the adoption.

The parties to an adoptive relationship may execute an adoption agreement if they choose to.

An adoptive relationship shall be notarized on the demand of one or both of the parties thereto.

The civil affairs bureau of a people's government at or above the county level shall make assessments of adoptions per law.

Article 1106 [Household Registration for Adoptee]

Upon formation of an adoptive relationship, the public security bureau shall facilitate household registration of the adoptee per relevant State regulations.

Article 1107 [Fosterage]

An orphan or a child whose biological parents are incapable of raising such child may be fostered by the relative(s) or friend(s) of his/her biological parents. The provisions of this Chapter shall not apply to a relationship between the fosterer and the fosteree.

Article 1108 [Priority in Fosterage]

Where one spouse is deceased and the surviving spouse intends to place his/her minor child for fosterage, the parents of the deceased spouse shall have priority in fostering the child.

Article 1109 [Adoption with Foreign Elements]

Foreigners may adopt children in the People's Republic of China per law.

A foreigner's adoption of a child in the People's Republic of China shall be subject to the review and approval of the competent authorities of the foreigner's country of residence per the laws of that country. The foreign adopter shall provide documents issued by the authorized agencies in his/her country of residence certifying such personal information as age, marital status, occupation, financial situation, health condition, and criminal record. The foreign adopter shall conclude a written agreement with the person who places the child for adoption and register the adoption in person with the civil affairs bureau of the people's government at the level of province, autonomous region, or municipality directly under the Central Government.

The certifying documents provided in the preceding paragraph shall be authenticated by the diplomatic authorities of the country in which the foreign adopter resides or by an agency authorized by such diplomatic authorities, and then authenticated by the embassy or consulate of the People's Republic of China in such country, unless the State provides otherwise.

Article 1110 [Duty of Confidentiality]

Where an adopter or a party placing a child for adoption demands that the adoption be kept confidential, other people shall respect his/her wishes and may not disclose it.

Section 2 Effect of Adoption

Article 1111 [Effect of Adoption]

On the date of the creation of an adoptive relationship, the provisions of this Code on the parent-child relationship shall apply to the rights and duties between adoptive parents and an adopted child. The provisions of this Code governing the relationship between child and the near relatives of his/her parents shall apply to the rights and duties as between the adopted child and the near relatives of his/her adoptive parents.

The rights and duties between the adoptee and his/her biological parents as well as other near relatives shall be eliminated upon the creation of an adoptive relationship.

Article 1112 [Surname of Adopted Child]

An adopted child may take the surname of his/her adoptive father or mother, or, may retain his/her original surname with the consent of all the parties to the adoption.

Article 1113 [Adoption Null and Void]

An adoption is null and void if it fits into the category of circumstances as provided in Book One of this Code which renders a civil juristic act null and void, or, if it violates the provisions of this Book.

A void adoption lacks legal effect *ab initio*.

Section 3 Reversal of Adoptive Relationship

Article 1114 [Reversal of Adoption by Agreement and Reversal of Adoption Due to Illegal Acts]

No adopter may reverse an adoptive relationship before the adoptee has reached the age of majority without an agreement for reversal between the adopter and the party who placed the child for adoption. Where an adoptee is aged eight or above, his/her own consent thereto shall be obtained.

Where an adopter does not perform the duty to raise the adoptee or commits mistreatment, desertion, or other acts that infringe lawful rights and interests of the minor adoptee, the person who has placed the child for adoption shall have the right to demand reversal of the adoptive relationship. Where an adopter and a party who has placed the child for adoption fail to agree on the reversal of the adoptive relationship, either party may bring a lawsuit before a people's court.

Article 1115 [Reversal of Adoption by Agreement Due to Deterioration of Relations]

Where the relationship between the adoptive parents and the adopted child who has become an adult deteriorates so badly that they are unable to continue living together, the adoption may be reversed by agreement. Failing an agreement, either party may bring a lawsuit before a people's court.

Article 1116 [Registration of Adoption Reversal]

Where the parties agree to reverse an adoptive relationship, they shall register the reversal with the bureau of civil affairs.

Article 1117 [Effect of Adoption Reversal on Affinity]

After the reversal of an adoptive relationship, the rights and duties as between the adoptee and the adoptive parents as well as the other near relatives shall be eliminated, and the rights and duties as between the adoptee and his/her biological parents as well as the other near relatives shall automatically revive. However, whether the rights and duties as between an adopted adult child and his/her biological parents as well as the other near relatives will revive or not may be decided via negotiation.

Article 1118 [Effect of Adoption Reversal on Proprietary Relations]

After reversal of an adoptive relationship, an adult adoptee who has been brought up by the adoptive parents shall provide living costs to the adoptive parents who lack both the capacity to work and a source of income. Where an adoptive relationship is dissolved because the adoptee, after becoming an adult, mistreats or deserts the adoptive parents, the adoptive parents may demand that the adoptee compensate them for the costs incurred in raising the adoptee during the adoption period.

Where the biological parents of the adoptee demand the reversal of an adoptive relationship, the adoptive parents may demand that the biological parents of the adoptee appropriately compensate them for the costs incurred in raising the adoptee during the adoption period, unless the adoptive relationship is reversed because the adoptive parents have mistreated or deserted the adoptee.

Book Six Succession

Chapter I General Rules

Article 1119 [Regulatory Scope of This Book]

This Book regulates the civil law relations arising from succession.

Article 1120 [Protection of Right of Succession by State]

The State protects a natural person's right of succession.

Article 1121 [Time for Commencement of Succession and Presumption of Order of Deaths]

Succession occurs at the death of the decedent.

Where two or more persons with the right to inherit each other's estate die in the same incident and determining the time of each person's death is difficult, the person with no heir shall be presumed to have predeceased those with heir(s). Where the foregoing decedents are from different generations and all have heir(s), those of the elder generation shall be presumed to have predeceased those of the younger generation, or, where the decedents are of the same generation, they shall be presumed to have died simultaneously and no succession shall occur as between them.

Article 1122 [Definition of Estate of Decedent]

An estate refers to property a natural person legally owns upon death.

Those assets of an estate which are not inheritable per the provisions of law or based on the nature of such assets may not be inherited.

M. Wan et al., *The Civil Code of the People's Republic of China*,
https://doi.org/10.1007/978-981-19-2794-2_6

Article 1123 [Effect of Intestate Succession, Testate Succession, Testamentary Gift and Agreement on Testamentary Gift for Inter Vivos Support and Funeral]

Upon commencement of a succession, the estate shall be administered according to intestate succession; if there is a will, the estate shall be succeeded to based on testate succession or testamentary donation; if there is an agreement on testamentary gift for *inter vivos* support and funeral, the estate shall be disposed of per such agreement.

Article 1124 [Adiation and Repudiation of Inheritance]

An inheritor who, upon commencement of a succession, renounces an inheritance, shall manifest his/her decision in written form before the estate is disposed of. In the absence of such a manifestation, s/he is deemed to have accepted or adiated the inheritance.

A beneficiary shall, within 60 days after s/he learns of a testamentary gift, manifest his/her decision to adiate or repudiate it. In the absence of such a manifestation within the specified period, s/he shall be deemed to have repudiated the gift.

Article 1125 [Disinheritance and Resumption of Inheritance]

An inheritor is to be disinherited if s/he has committed any of the following acts:

1. Intentional killing of the decedent;

2. Killing of any other inheritor in a contest over the estate;

3. Abandoning or mistreating the decedent with serious circumstances;

4. Forging, tampering with, concealing or destroying the will with serious circumstances; or

5. Forcing or obstructing the decedent in drafting, altering, or withdrawing the will by means of fraud or coercion with serious circumstances.

An heir who committed one of the acts enumerated in Subparagraphs 3 through 5 of the preceding paragraph shall not be disinherited if s/he truly repented and amended his/her ways and was pardoned by the decedent or thereafter was designated an inheritor in the decedent's will.

A beneficiary who has committed any of the acts enumerated in the first paragraph of this Article shall forfeit his/her right to the testamentary gift.

Chapter II Intestate Succession

Article 1126 [Men and Women Enjoying Equal Right to Inheritance]

Men and women enjoy equal rights to inheritance.

Article 1127 [Scope of Heirs and Order of Inheritance]

The estate of a decedent shall be inherited in the following order:

1. In first order: spouse, child(ren), and parents; and

2. In second order: siblings, paternal grandparents, and maternal grandparents.

When succession commences, the heir(s) in first order shall inherit to the exclusion of the heir(s) in second order. The heir(s) in second order shall inherit the estate in default of any heir in first order.

'Children' as referred to in this Book includes children born in or out of wedlock, and adopted children and stepchildren raised by the decedent.

'Parents' as referred to in this Book includes biological parents, adoptive parents and stepparents who raised the decedent.

'Siblings' as referred to in this Book includes siblings of whole blood or half blood, adopted siblings, and stepsiblings who supported or were supported by the decedent.

Article 1128 [Inheritance in Subrogation]

Where a decedent survived his/her child, the direct lineal descendants of the survived child shall inherit in subrogation.

Where a decedent survived his/her sibling, the children of the survived sibling shall inherit in subrogation.

Heirs who inherit in subrogation may generally only take a share of an estate *per stirpes*.

Article 1129 [Widowed Daughter(s)-in-Law and Widowed Son(s)-in-Law's Right to Inherit]

Widowed daughters-in-law or sons-in-law who have performed the main duty of supporting their parents-in-law shall, in relationship to their parents-in-law, be deemed heirs in first order.

Article 1130 [Principles for Distribution of Inheritance]

Heirs in the same order shall, in general, inherit equal shares.

In distributing an estate, due favourable consideration shall be afforded an heir who has special financial difficulties and lacks the ability to work.

In distributing an estate, an heir who has performed the main duty of supporting the decedent, or who has been living with the decedent, may take a larger share.

In distributing an estate, an heir who had the ability and the means to support the decedent but failed to fulfill the duty of support, shall receive nothing or a smaller share.

An estate may be distributed unequally among heirs per their negotiated agreement.

Article 1131 [Right to Discretionary Share of Inheritance]

A suitable share of an estate may be distributed to a person, other than an heir, who was a dependent of the decedent, or to a person, other than an heir, who provided relatively more support to the decedent.

Article 1132 [Manner of Administering Inheritance]

The heirs shall handle any issue of succession via negotiation and in a spirit of mutual understanding and accommodation, peace and solidarity. The time and mode for dividing an estate and the shares into which the estate is to be divided, shall be determined by the heirs via negotiation. If failing an agreement, they may apply to a people's mediation committee for mediation or institute legal proceedings in a people's court.

Chapter III Testate Succession and Testamentary Gift

Article 1133 [Disposing of Estate by Will and Testament]

A natural person may, by executing a will per the provisions of this Code, dispose of his/her estate and appoint an executor in the will.

A natural person may, by executing a will, designate one or more of his/her statutory heirs to inherit his/her estate.

A natural person may, by executing a will, donate his/her estate to the State or a collective, or an organization or individual other than his/her statutory heirs.

A natural person may, per law, create a testamentary trust.

Article 1134 [Holographic Will]

A holographic will is a will and testament which has been entirely handwritten and signed by the testator, specifying the year, month and day of its making.

Article 1135 [Will Drafted by Witness on Behalf of Testator]

A will drafted on behalf of the testator shall be attested by two or more physically present witnesses, drafted by one of the attesting witnesses, and signed by the testator, the drafter and the other attesting witness(es) with a clear indication of the year, month, and day of its making.

Article 1136 [Will in Printed Form]

A will in printed form shall be attested by two or more physically present witnesses.The testator and the witnesses shall sign on each page and specify the year, month, and day of its making.

Article 1137 [Audio Will and Video Will]

A will made in the form of an audio or video recording shall be attested by two or more physically present witnesses. The testator and the witnesses shall record their names or likenesses in the recording and specify the year, month, and day of its making.

Article 1138 [Nuncupative Will]

A testator may, in case of emergency, execute a nuncupative will. A nuncupative will shall be attested by two or more physically present witnesses. When the emergency is no longer present and the testator is able to execute a will in written form or in the form of an audio or video recording, the nuncupative will shall become invalid.

Article 1139 [Notarial Will]

A notarial will is one executed by a testator through a notary.

Article 1140 [Restrictions on Qualification of Will Witness]

None of the following persons shall act as a witness to a will:

1. A person who lacks or has limited capacity to engage in civil juristic acts, or a person otherwise incompetent to attest a will;

2. An heir or a beneficiary; or

3. A person with a common interest with or in a conflict of interests with an heir or a beneficiary.

Article 1141 [Compulsory Portion]

A compulsory portion of an estate shall be reserved for an heir who has neither the ability to work nor a source of income.

Article 1142 [Revocation and Amendment of a Will and Effect of Conflicting Wills]

A testator may revoke or amend a will s/he has made.

After executing a will, a testator's civil juristic acts in contrary to the terms thereof shall be deemed revocation of the pertinent part of the will.

Where several wills have been made and their terms are in conflict, the will executed last in time shall prevail.

Article 1143 [Substantive Requirements for Wills]

A will executed by a person with no or limited capacity to engage in civil juristic acts is void.

A will shall express the genuine intention of the testator, and a will that the testator was fraudulently induced or compelled to have made shall be void.

A forged will shall be void.

Where a will has been tampered with, the part of the will thereby affected shall be void.

Article 1144 [Conditional Wills and Conditional Testamentary Gifts]

Where a testate succession or testamentary gift is conditional on performance of an obligation, the inheritor or beneficiary shall perform the obligation. Where such inheritor or beneficiary does not perform such obligation without just cause, the people's court may, on demand by an interested party or relevant organization, deprive such inheritor or beneficiary of the right to that portion of the estate to which performance of the obligation is attached.

Chapter IV Disposition of Estate

Article 1145 [Selection of Estate Administrator]

Upon commencement of succession, the executor of the will shall be the administrator of the estate; if no executor is appointed in the will, the inheritors shall elect an administrator without delay. Where the inheritors fail to do so, all inheritors become co-administrators. In the absence of an inheritor or if all the inheritors renounce the inheritance, the bureau of civil affairs or the villagers' committee in the place where the decedent was domiciled at the time of his/her death shall serve as the administrator.

Article 1146 [Designation of Estate Administrator]

Where a dispute arises over the determination of an administrator of the estate, any interested person may demand that the people's court designate an administrator.

Article 1147 [Responsibilities of Estate Administrator]

An estate administrator shall perform the following duties:

1. Verifying and inventorying the estate;
2. Reporting to the inheritors about the estate;
3. Taking necessary measures to prevent the estate from being destroyed, damaged, or lost;
4. Dealing with the decedent's claims and debts;
5. Dividing the estate per the will or per law; and
6. Engaging in any other act for administration of the estate.

Article 1148 [Estate Administrator's Civil Liability for Failing to Perform Properly]

An estate administrator shall perform his/her duties per law, and shall assume civil liability if any inheritor, beneficiary, or obligee of the decedent suffers harm from his/her intentional act or gross negligence.

Article 1149 [Remuneration for Estate Administrator]

An estate administrator may receive remuneration per law or per agreement.

Article 1150 [Giving Notice upon Commencement of Succession]

Upon commencement of a succession, an inheritor who knows of the death of the decedent shall notify the other inheritors and the executor of the will thereof without delay. Where none of the inheritors knows of the death of the decedent or can make the notification on learning of the death of the decedent, the organization by which the decedent was employed at the time of his/her death, or the urban residents' committee or the villagers' committee in the place where the decedent was domiciled at the time of his/her death, shall make the notification.

Article 1151 [Taking Care of Estate]

Anyone who has in his/her possession property of a decedent shall keep such property with due care, and no organization or individual may misappropriate or scramble for it.

Article 1152 [Sub-Succession/Redirection of Inheritance]

Where, upon commencement of a succession, an inheritor who has not repudiated the inheritance dies before the estate is distributed, the share of the estate that s/he is entitled to shall be inherited by his/her heirs, unless the will provides otherwise.

Article 1153 [Determination of Estate]

When dividing an estate, if the community property of husband and wife is involved, unless otherwise agreed, half of the community property shall be severed for the surviving spouse as separate property, with the remainder to go to the decedent's estate.

When dividing an estate, if the decedent's estate is a part of common property of the family, the part of the property belonging to the other family members shall first be separated.

Article 1154 [Scope of Intestate Succession]

Under any of the following circumstances, the part of the estate affected shall be disposed of via intestate succession:

1. Where a testamentary inheritor or beneficiary repudiates the inheritance or the gift;

2. Where a testamentary inheritor or beneficiary is disinherited;

3. Where a testamentary inheritor predeceases the testator, or a beneficiary predeceases the testator or terminates before the decedent's death;

4. The part of an estate affected correspondingly by a nullified part of a will; or

5. Any part of the estate which is not covered by the will.

Article 1155 [Portion Reserved for Fetus]

On dividing an estate, a share shall be reserved for a fetus. In case of a fetal stillbirth, the reserved share shall be disposed of via intestate succession.

Article 1156 [Principles and Methods for Division of Estate]

A decedent's estate shall be partitioned in a way favorable to production and livelihoods and without impairing its utility.

Where an estate or an asset of estate is unsuitable for partition, it may be disposed of by such means as taking of it based on appraised value, proper compensation, or co-ownership.

Article 1157 [Right to Disposition of Inheritance upon Remarriage]

A surviving spouse who remarries has the right to dispose of the property s/he has inherited, free from interference by any organization or individual.

Article 1158 [Agreement on Testamentary Gift for Inter Vivos Support and Funeral]

A natural person may execute an agreement on testamentary gift for *inter vivos* support and funeral with an organization or individual other than an heir. Such organization or individual assumes, per agreement, a duty to support such person during his/her lifetime and attends to his/her funeral and burial after death in return for the right to receive the testamentary gift under the agreement.

Article 1159 [Obligations upon Division of Estate]

On dividing an estate, the taxes and debts legally payable by the decedent shall be paid out of the estate, but a necessary part of the estate shall be reserved for any heir who has neither the ability to work nor a source of income.

Article 1160 [Escheat of Estate Without Will or Heir]

An estate without an heir or a beneficiary shall escheat to the State to be used for public weal purposes. If the decedent was a member of a collective before death, the estate shall escheat to such collective.

Article 1161 [Rules for Payment of Decedent's Taxes and Debts]

An heir shall pay the taxes and debts legally payable by the decedent to the extent of the actual value of the portion of the estate s/he inherits, unless the heir voluntarily pays the excess.

An heir who repudiates an inheritance is relieved of any liability for the payment of taxes and debts legally payable by the decedent.

Article 1162 [Precedence of Payment of Decedent's Taxes and Debts over Execution of Testamentary Gift]

The execution of a testamentary gift may not obstruct the payment of taxes and debts legally payable by the testator.

Article 1163 [Payment of Decedent's Taxes and Debts in the Event of Concurrence of Intestate Succession, Testate Succession and Testamentary Gift]

Where intestate succession, testate succession, and testamentary gift concurrently exist, the taxes and debts legally payable by the decedent shall be paid by the intestate heir(s); such taxes and debts that exceed the actual value of the portion of the estate inherited by the intestate heir(s) shall be paid by the testamentary inheritor(s) and the beneficiary(ies) in proportion to the share of the estate each has received.

Book Seven Tort Liability

Chapter I General Rules

Article 1164 [Regulatory Scope of This Book]

This Book regulates the civil law relations arising from harming civil rights and interests.

Article 1165 [Principle of Fault Liability]

An actor who through his/her fault harms another person's civil rights and interests shall be liable in tort therefor.

Where an actor is presumed to be at fault per the provisions of law and is unable to prove that s/he is not at fault, such actor shall be liable in tort.

Article 1166 [Principle of No-Fault Liability]

Where an actor harms the civil rights and interests of another person, if law provides that tort liability shall lie regardless of whether the actor is at fault, such provisions shall apply.

Article 1167 [Forms of Liability for Endangering Another's Person and Property]

Where a tortious act endangers another person's person or property, the injured party shall have the right to demand that the tortfeasor be liable in tort for cessation of harm, abatement of nuisance, or elimination of danger.

Article 1168 [Joint Tort]

Where two or more persons jointly commit a tortious act that causes harm to another person, they shall assume joint and several liability therefor.

M. Wan et al., *The Civil Code of the People's Republic of China*,
https://doi.org/10.1007/978-981-19-2794-2_7

Article 1169 [Aiding and Abetting Tortious Act]

A person who aids or abets an actor in the commission of a tortious act shall bear joint and several liability with the actor therefor.

A person who aids or abets an actor, who has no capacity to engage in civil juristic acts or only has limited capacity, in the commission of a tortious act shall be liable in tort therefor. The guardian of such actor shall bear corresponding liability where s/he does not fully fulfill the duties of a guardian.

Article 1170 [Joint Tortious Act Causing Harm]

Where two or more persons commit an act that endangers another's person or property and the harm is caused by one or several of them, if the specific tortfeasor(s) can be identified, they shall be liable; if the specific tortfeasor(s) cannot be identified, the actors shall all be jointly and severally liable therefor.

Article 1171 [Separate Tortious Acts Leading to Joint Liability]

Where the tortious acts committed separately by two or more persons cause the same harm to an injured party, where each act is sufficient to cause the entire harm on its own, the actors shall be jointly and severally liable therefor.

Article 1172 [Separate Tortious Acts Leading to Proportional Liability]

Where the tortious acts committed separately by two or more persons cause the same harm to an injured party, each shall be liable for their respective share of the harm if such share is able to be determined, or be liable equally if such share is difficult to determine.

Article 1173 [Comparative Negligence]

Where the injured party is also at fault for the occurrence or aggravation of the harm, the liability of the tortfeasor may be reduced.

Article 1174 [Intentional Act by Injured Party]

An actor shall be relieved of liability for any harm intentionally caused by the injured party.

Article 1175 [Fault of Third Party]

Where a harm results from a third party, the third party shall be liable in tort therefor.

Article 1176 [Assumption of Risk]

Where a person voluntarily participates in a recreational or sports activity with certain inherent risks and thereby suffers injury due to another participant's act, s/he may not demand that the other participant be liable in tort, unless the injury results from the latter's intentional act or gross negligence.

The provisions of Articles 1198 through 1201 of this Code shall apply to the liability of an organizer of such activity.

Article 1177 [Self-Help]

Where a person's lawful rights and interests are harmed, the situation is urgent and no protection from State agencies is immediately forthcoming, and s/he may suffer irreparable damage if action is not immediately taken, s/he may take reasonable measures such as seizing the property of the tortfeasor to the extent necessary to protect his/her lawful rights and interests, but s/he shall immediately thereafter request a relevant State agency to deal with the matter.

An injured party who has taken an inappropriate measure and caused harm thereby to another person shall be liable in tort therefor.

Article 1178 [Preferential Application of Special Provisions]

Where this Code or other laws provide otherwise for circumstances under which an actor's liability is exempted or reduced, such provisions shall apply.

Chapter II Damages

Article 1179 [Scope of Damages for Physical Injury]

Where an actor harms another person and causes personal injury to the latter as a result, damages shall be paid for such reasonable costs for treatment and rehabilitation as medical, nursing, transport and nutritional costs, and food allowances for hospitalization, as well as earnings lost due to missed work. Where disability results, damages shall include the costs of auxiliary equipment and disability compensation; if death results, damages shall include funeral and burial costs and compensation for wrongful death.

Article 1180 [Same Amount of Wrongful Death Damages for Each Victim of Same Tortious Act]

Where the same tortious act causes multiple deaths, the same amount of damages for wrongful death may apply to each.

Article 1181 [Determination of Claimant in Case of Death of Injured Party]

Where an injured party dies, his/her near relatives have the right to demand that the tortfeasor be liable in tort. Where the injured party is an organization and the organization thereafter splits into or merges with other organization(s), the organization succeeding to the rights thereof is entitled to demand that the tortfeasor be liable in tort.

Where the injured party dies, a person who has paid medical, funeral, burial and other reasonable costs for such injured party shall have the right to demand that the tortfeasor compensate these costs, except for those the tortfeasor has already paid.

Article 1182 [Determination of Damages for Economic Loss as a Result of Harm to Personal and Personality Rights and Interests]

Where an actor harms the personal and personality rights and interests of another person and causes economic loss thereto, damages shall be paid based on the loss incurred by the injured party or on the benefits thereby gained by the tortfeasor. Where difficulty arises in determining the loss incurred by the injured party and the benefits gained by the tortfeasor, and the injured party and the tortfeasor are unable to reach an agreement on the amount of damages, the injured party may bring a lawsuit before a people's court, which shall determine the amount of damages according to the actual circumstances.

Article 1183 [Damages for Mental and Emotional Harm]

Where an actor harms the personal and personality rights and interests of another person and thereby inflicts serious mental and emotional suffering thereon, the injured party shall be entitled to claim damages for such harm.

Where an actor, through intentional act or gross negligence, damages an object of personal significance unique to a natural person, and thereby causes serious mental and emotional harm to an injured party, such injured party shall have the right to demand damages for such harm.

Article 1184 [Method of Calculation of Loss or Damage to Property]

Where damage or loss is caused to another person's property, such damage or loss shall be calculated according to the market price at the time the damage or loss occurs or calculated by other reasonable means.

Article 1185 [Punitive Damages for Intellectual Property Infringement]

Where an actor intentionally infringes another person's intellectual property right and the circumstances are grievous, the infringed party shall have the right to demand corresponding punitive damages.

Article 1186 [Principle of Equitable Liability]

Where neither an injured party nor an actor is at fault for the occurrence of a harm, resultant losses shall be apportioned between both parties per the provisions of law.

Article 1187 [Mode of Payment of Damages]

Where harm has occurred, the parties may negotiate a mode for payment of damages. If they fail to agree, damages shall be paid in a lump sum, or paid in installments where it is truly difficult for the tortfeasor to make a lump-sum payment, but the injured party shall have the right to demand that the tortfeasor provide a corresponding guarantee.

Chapter III Special Provisions on Persons Held Liable

Article 1188 [Guardian's Liability]

Where a person with no or limited capacity to engage in civil juristic acts causes harm to an injured party, the guardian of such person shall be liable in tort therefor. The guardian's tort liability may be reduced if the guardian has fulfilled his/her duty of guardianship.

Where a person with no or limited capacity to engage in civil juristic acts has assets and causes harm to an injured party, compensation shall be paid out of such assets; where these do not suffice, the shortfall shall be covered by the guardian.

Article 1189 [Liability in Case of Delegated Guardianship]

Where a person with no or limited capacity to engage in civil juristic acts causes harm to an injured party and his/her guardian has delegated the functions and duties of guardianship to another person, the guardian shall be liable in tort, and if the person to whom the guardianship has been delegated is at fault, such person shall bear corresponding liability therefor.

Article 1190 [Tort Liability in Case of Loss of Consciousness]

Where a person with full capacity to engage in civil juristic acts is at fault in causing harm to an injured party due to a temporary loss of consciousness or loss of control, s/he shall be liable in tort therefor. Where s/he is not at fault, s/he shall properly compensate the party injured based on his/her financial strength.

Where a person with full capacity to engage in civil juristic acts causes harm to an injured party due to a temporary loss of consciousness or loss of control as a result of intoxication or abuse of narcotic or psychotropic drugs, s/he shall be liable in tort therefor.

Article 1191 [Responeat Superior / Vicarious Liability of Employer, Labor Dispatch Agency, and Enterprise Using Dispatched Labor]

Where an employee causes harm to an injured party in connection with the performance of his/her work, his/her employer shall be liable in tort therefor. The employer may, after assuming the tort liability, assert claims for indemnification against the employee who caused such harm through an intentional act or gross negligence.

Where, during the period of labor dispatch, the employee dispatched causes harm to an injured party in connection with the performance of his/her work, the employer using the dispatched labor shall be liable in tort therefor. The labor dispatch agency at fault shall [also] bear corresponding liability.

Article 1192 [Tort Liability in Labor Service Relations Between Individuals]

Where, in a labor service relationship formed between individuals, the party providing labor services causes harm to an injured party in connection with the labor services, the party receiving the labor services shall be liable in tort therefor. The party receiving the labor services may, after assuming the tort liability, assert claims for indemnification against the party providing labor services who caused the harm through an intentional act or gross negligence. Where the party providing labor services suffers harm in connection with the labor services, both parties shall bear corresponding liability based on their respective degree of fault.

Where the act of a third party causes harm to the party providing labor services while such services are being provided, the party providing services shall have the right to demand that the third party be liable in tort, or to demand that the party receiving services pay compensation. The party receiving labor services may, after paying compensation, assert claims for indemnification against the third party.

Article 1193 [Tort Liability with Respect to Contracting for Work]

Where a contractor causes harm to a third party or to him/herself while completing a contracted work, the customer shall be relieved of tort liability. However, if the customer is at fault in placing the order, issuing instructions, or selecting the contractor, such customer shall bear corresponding liability .

Article 1194 [Liability for Cyber Torts]

Network users and network service providers who, via a network, violate the civil law rights and interests of another person, shall be liable in tort therefor. If law provides otherwise, its provisions shall apply.

Article 1195 [Remedies Available to Internet Service Provider for Cyber Torts and Apportionment of Liability]

Where a network user commits a tortious act via use of a network service, an injured right holder is entitled to notify the network service provider that the latter should take such necessary measures as deletion, blocking, or disconnection. The notification shall include preliminary evidence establishing the tort and the actual information as to the identity of the injured right holder.

After receiving the notification, the network service provider shall promptly forward the notification to the subject network user and take necessary measures based on the preliminary evidence establishing the tort and the type of service complained of. A provider that fails to take necessary measures in time shall be jointly and severally liable for the aggravated portion of the harm along with the network user.

A right holder who causes harm to a network user or network service provider due to an erroneous notification, shall be liable in tort therefor. If law provides otherwise, its provisions shall apply.

Article 1196 [Declaration of Non-Infringement]

Upon receiving the forwarded notification, the network user may submit a declaration of non-infringement to the network service provider, which shall include the preliminary evidence of non-infringement and the actual identity information of the network user.

Upon receiving the declaration, the network service provider shall forward it to the right holder who issued the notification and inform the right holder of his/her right to file a complaint with the relevant authorities or bring a lawsuit before a people's court. The network service provider shall promptly terminate its measures taken if, within a reasonable period after the forwarded declaration reaches the right holder, it has not received notice that the right holder has lodged a complaint or brought a lawsuit.

Article 1197 [Joint Liability of Internet Service Provider]

A network service provider, who knows or ought to have known that a network user has infringed the civil law rights and interests of a victim by using its network services but fails to take necessary measures, shall be jointly and severally liable along with the network user.

Article 1198 [Liability of Persons Obligated to Ensure Security]

The operators or managers of business premises and public places such as hotels, shopping malls, banks, bus or train stations, airports, stadiums, and places of entertainment, or the organizers of mass activities, shall be liable in tort if they fail to fulfill their duty to ensure safety and thereby cause injury to a person.

Where the injury to a person results from a third party, the third party shall be liable in tort therefor, and the operator, manager, or organizer who fails to fulfill the duty of ensuring safety shall bear corresponding supplementary liability. After assuming such supplementary liability, the operator, manager, or organizer may assert claims for indemnification against the third party.

Article 1199 [Presumed Fault of Educational Institutions]

Where a person with no capacity to engage in civil juristic acts suffers personal injury while studying or living in a kindergarten, school, or other educational institution, such kindergarten, school, or educational institution shall be liable in tort therefor; however, such institution shall be relieved of tort liability if it can prove that it has performed its educational and administration duties.

Article 1200 [Fault Liability of Educational Institutions]

Where a person with limited capacity to engage in civil juristic acts suffers personal injury while studying or living in a school or other educational institution, such school or educational institution shall be liable in tort therefor if it fails to perform its educational and administration duties.

Article 1201 [Apportionment of Liability for Tortious Act by Third Party Inside Educational Institutions]

Where a person with no or limited capacity to engage in civil juristic acts studying or living in a kindergarten, school, or other educational institution, suffers personal injury caused by a third party other than the kindergarten, school, or educational institution, the third party shall be liable in tort therefor, and such institution shall bear corresponding supplementary liability if it fails to perform its administration duties. After assuming such supplementary liability, such kindergarten, school, or other educational institution may assert claims for indemnification against the third party.

Chapter IV Product Liability

Article 1202 [Product Manufacturer's Liability]

Where an existing defect in a product causes injury to an injured party, the manufacturer shall be liable in tort therefor.

Article 1203 [Avenues for the Injured to Seek Damages and Right of Indemnification Enjoyed by Person Initially Paying Damages]

Where an existing defect in a product causes injury to an injured party, the party injured may claim damages against the manufacturer or the seller thereof.

Where a defect results from a manufacturer, a seller who has paid damages shall have the right to indemnification against the manufacturer. Where a product defect resulted from the fault of a seller, a manufacturer who has paid damages shall have the right to indemnification against the seller.

Article 1204 [Manufacturer's and Seller's Right of Indemnification Against Third Party at Fault]

Where a defect in a product resulted from the fault of a third party, such as a transporter or warehouser, the manufacturer or seller of the product shall, after paying damages, have the right to indemnification against such third party.

Article 1205 [Forms of Liability for Endangering Person or Property]

Where a defect in a product endangers the person or property of another person, such person injured shall have the right to demand that the manufacturer or seller be liable in tort therefor in such forms as cessation of injury, abatement of nuisance, or elimination of danger.

Article 1206 [Remedies for Defective Products in Circulation and Liability for Injury Thereby Caused]

Where a defect in a product is discovered after the product is put into circulation, the manufacturer or seller shall, without delay, take such remedial measures as stopping sales, issuing warnings or recalling the product. Where the manufacturer or seller fails to take remedial measures promptly or takes ineffective measures and as a result the injury is aggravated, such manufacturer or seller shall also be liable for the aggravated portion of the injury.

Where a product is recalled per the preceding paragraph, the manufacturer or seller shall bear the necessary costs incurred by the injured party therefrom.

Article 1207 [Punitive Damages for Product Liability]

Where a manufacturer or seller manufactures or sells a product while knowing that the product is defective, or fails to take remedial measures per the provisions of the preceding article, and as a result, death or serious physical injury is caused to an injured party, the party injured shall have the right to demand award of corresponding punitive damages.

Chapter V Liability for Motor Vehicle Accidents (MVAs)

Article 1208 [Laws Applicable to Liability for Motor Vehicle Accidents]

Where a motor vehicle is involved in a traffic accident which results in harm or injury, the liability for damages shall be borne per relevant provisions of laws on road traffic safety and this Code.

Article 1209 [Tort Liability Where Owner, Manager and User of Vehicle Are Not the Same Person]

Where the owner, manager, or user of a motor vehicle are not the same person because of rental, leasing or borrowing, and a traffic accident occurs and inflicts harm or injury, the motor vehicle user shall be liable for damages therefor where the liability is attributed to the motor vehicle [driver], and the owner or manager of the vehicle, if at fault, shall bear corresponding liability for damages.

Article 1210 [Tort Liability Where Vehicle Has Been Transferred and Delivered but Not Yet Registered]

Where a party has transferred and delivered a motor vehicle via a sale or other means but has not filed for registration thereof, the transferee of the motor vehicle shall be liable for damages therefor where harm or injury is caused due to a traffic accident and the liability is attributed to the motor vehicle [driver].

Article 1211 [Tort Liability of Vehicle Affiliated to Licensed Transportation Entity]

Where a person uses a motor vehicle affiliated with a licensed transportation entity to engage in the business of road transport, if harm or injury results from a traffic accident and the liability is attributed to the motor vehicle [driver], the user and the entity shall be jointly and severally liable for damages.

Article 1212 [Tort Liability Where Vehicle Is Used Without Consent from Owner or Manager]

Where a person drives/uses another person's motor vehicle without permission, the user of the motor vehicle shall be liable for damages therefor if harm or injury is caused due to a traffic accident and the liability is attributed to the motor vehicle [driver]; the owner or manager of the motor vehicle shall, if at fault, be liable for corresponding damages, unless this Chapter provides otherwise.

Article 1213 [Order of Compensation by Persons Liable for Traffic Accident Injury]

Where harm or injury is caused to another person due to a traffic accident and the liability is attributed to the motor vehicle [driver], the insurer that underwrites the compulsory motor vehicle insurance shall pay damages within the limit of the liability insured. Shortfall, if any, shall be paid by the insurer that underwrites the commercial motor vehicle insurance per the provisions of the insurance contract. Where the motor vehicle is not covered or not sufficiently covered by commercial motor vehicle insurance, the remaining shortfall shall be paid by the tortfeasor.

Article 1214 [Tort Liability with Illegally Assembled Vehicles or Vehicles Beyond End of Useful Life]

Where a motor vehicle illegally assembled or beyond the end of its useful life is transferred via a sale or other means and such vehicle causes harm or injury involving a traffic accident, the transferor and the transferee shall be jointly and severally liable therefor.

Article 1215 [Tort Liability with Stolen, Hijacked or Carjacked Vehicle]

Where harm or injury is caused due to a traffic accident involving a motor vehicle which has been stolen, hijacked or carjacked, the thief, hijacker, or carjacker shall be liable for damages therefor. Where such motor vehicle is used by a person other than the thief, hijacker, or carjacker and causes harm or injury in a traffic accident, if the liability is attributed to the motor vehicle [driver], the thief, hijacker, or carjacker shall bear jointly and severally liable along with the user.

Where an insurer advances rescue costs within the limits of its compulsory insurance liability for the motor vehicle, it shall have the right to indemnification against the person(s) held liable for the traffic accident.

Article 1216 [Liability with Respect to Hit and Run and Aid to the Injured]

Where a driver of a motor vehicle flees after a traffic accident, if the motor vehicle is insured by a compulsory insurance scheme, damages shall be paid by the insurer within the limit of the liability insured. Where such motor vehicle cannot be traced, or is not covered by compulsory insurance, or the rescue costs exceed the limit of liability of the compulsory motor vehicle insurance, and payment needs to be made for the rescue, funeral, burial and other costs incurred due to the death or bodily injury of the injured party, such payment shall be paid in advance out of the Social Assistance Fund for Road Traffic Accidents. After the Social Assistance Fund for Road Traffic Accidents makes the advance payment, its executive body shall have the right to indemnification against the person(s) held liable for the traffic accident.

Article 1217 [Liability to Person Taking Free of Charge Road Trip in Non-Commercial Vehicle]

Where a non-commercial motor vehicle causes harm or injury in a traffic accident to a passenger traveling free of charge, if the responsibility is attributed to the motor vehicle [driver], the liability of the user of such motor vehicle for damages shall be reduced unless s/he acted intentionally or with gross negligence.

Chapter VI Liability for Medical Malpractice

Article 1218 [Principle for Apportionment of Liability for Medical Malpractice and Persons Held Liable]

Where a patient suffers injury during diagnosis and treatment, and the medical institution or its medical staff is at fault, the medical institution shall be liable for damages therefor.

Article 1219 [Obligation of Medical Staff to Inform and Patient's Right to Give Informed Consent]

Medical staff shall, in the course of diagnosis and treatment, explain medical conditions and treatment measures to a patient. If surgery, a special examination or special treatment is needed, medical staff shall explain to the patient the medical risks, alternative treatment plans and other items without delay and obtain his/her express consent thereto. Where to do so is impossible or inappropriate, the medical staff shall explain the situation to the patient's near relatives and obtain their express consent thereto.

Where the medical staff fail to fulfill their obligations as provided in the preceding paragraph and thereby cause injury to the patient, the medical institution shall be liable for damages therefor.

Article 1220 [Special Provisions Concerning Emergency Treatment Without Obtaining Informed Consent]

Where the consent of a patient or his/her near relative(s) is not available in the event of rescuing a dying patient or in a similar emergency, with the approval of the person in charge of the medical institution or an authorized person in charge, corresponding medical measures may be implemented immediately.

Article 1221 [Determination of Fault on the Part of Medical Staff in Diagnosis and Treatment]

Where the medical staff fail to meet the then current medical level in performing their duty of diagnosis and treatment, and thereby cause injury to the patient, the medical institution shall be liable for damages therefor.

Article 1222 [Where Fault on the Part of Medical Institution Is Presumed]

Under any of the following circumstances, a medical institution shall be presumed to be at fault where injury is inflicted on a patient in the course of diagnosis and treatment:

1. Violation of the provisions of laws, administrative regulations, rules, or other relevant bylaws and guidelines for diagnosis and treatment;
2. Concealment of medical records relevant to a dispute or refusal to produce them; or
3. Loss, forgery, falsification or illegal destruction of the medical records.

Article 1223 [Tort Liability for Defective Drugs, Disinfectants and Medical Instruments or Tort Liability for Transfusion of Substandard Blood]

Where injury is caused to a patient due to a defect in a drug, disinfectant, or medical instrument, or due to the transfusion of substandard blood, the patient may claim damages against the drug marketing authorization holder (MAH), the manufacturer of the drug, the blood supply institution, or the medical institution. Where the patient claims damages against a medical institution, the medical institution shall, after payment of the damages, have the right to indemnification against the responsible MAH, the manufacturer of the drug, or the blood supplier.

Article 1224 [Occasions for Exempting Liability of Medical Institution]

A medical institution shall be relieved of liability for damages for any injury caused to a patient in the course of diagnosis and treatment under any of the following circumstances:

1. The patient or his/her near relatives do not cooperate with the medical institution in diagnosis and treatment which accords with the guidelines therefor;

2. The medical staff have fulfilled their duty to provide reasonable diagnosis and treatment in an emergency, such as succoring a dying patient; or

3. Diagnosis and treatment of the patient is difficult due to the restrictions of the medical level at the time.

Under the circumstances specified in Subparagraph 1 of the preceding paragraph, if the medical institution or its medical staff are also at fault, corresponding liability for damages shall be assumed.

Article 1225 [Duty of Medical Institution with Medical Records and Patient's Right to Medical Records]

Medical institutions and their medical staff shall, per bylaws and regulations, properly enter and keep medical records such as hospital records, medical orders and prescriptions, test results, surgical and anesthesia history, pathological data, and nursing records, etc.

Where a patient demands to examine or make copies of his/her medical records as provided in the preceding paragraph, the medical institution shall provide such records without delay.

Article 1226 [Protection of Patient's Privacy and Personal Information]

Medical institutions and their medical staff shall keep confidential their patients' privacy and personal information. Anyone who divulges such privacy or personal information of a patient or discloses his/her medical records without the patient's consent shall be liable in tort therefor.

Article 1227 [Prohibition of Excessive Examination in Violation of Medical Bylaws and Guidelines]

Medical institutions and their medical staff may not conduct unnecessary examinations on their patients in violation of bylaws and guidelines for diagnosis and treatment.

Article 1228 [Protection of Lawful Rights and Interests of Medical Institution and Medical Staff]

The legal rights and interests of a medical institution and its medical staff are protected by law.

Anyone, who interferes with the order of a medical institution, obstructs the work or life of the medical staff, or violates their lawful rights and interests, shall be liable therefor per law.

Chapter VII Liability for Environmental Pollution and Ecological Damage

Article 1229 [Tort Liability for Environmental Pollution and Ecological Damage]

A tortfeasor who has polluted the environment or damaged the ecological system and thereby causes harm to others shall be liable in tort therefor.

Article 1230 [Onus Probandi Concerning Environmental Pollution and Ecological Damage]

Where any dispute arises from environmental pollution or ecological damage, the burden of proof of non-liability or reduced liability and lack of causation between the act and the damage shall rest on the actor per law.

Article 1231 [Determination of Respective Liability in The Event of More Than Two Tortfeasors]

Where two or more tortfeasors cause environmental pollution or ecological damage, the proportion of liability of each tortfeasor shall be determined according to such factors as the type, concentration and discharged quantity of the pollutants, as well as the manner, scope, and degree of ecological damage, and the respective contribution of their acts to the consequences of the harm.

Article 1232 [Punitive Damages for Environmental Pollution and Ecological Damage]

Where a tortfeasor intentionally pollutes the environment or damages the ecological system in violation of provisions of laws, resulting in grievous consequences, an injured party shall have the right to demand corresponding punitive damages.

Article 1233 [Tort Liability for Environmental Pollution and Ecological Damage Due to Third Party's Fault]

Where environmental pollution or ecological damage caused is due to the fault of a third party, the injured party may claim damages against either the tortfeasor or the third party. After paying damages, the tortfeasor shall have the right to indemnification against the third party.

Article 1234 [Liability for Remediation of Ecological Environment]

Where a tortfeasor causes damage to the ecological environment in violation of State regulations and remediation is possible, the State authorized agencies or organizations authorized by law shall have the right to demand that the tortfeasor be liable for remediation within a reasonable period. Where the tortfeasor fails to remediate within the time limit, the State authorized agencies or organizations authorized by law may carry out the remediation on their own or delegate it to others, but any costs incurred thereby shall be borne by the tortfeasor.

Article 1235 [Scope of Damages for Public Interest Litigation (PIL)]

Where ecological damage is caused in violation of State regulations, State authorized agencies or organizations authorized by law shall have the right to demand that the tortfeasor compensate the following losses and costs:

1. Losses caused by failure of the functioning of ecosystem services from the time the ecological environment is damaged to the time the remediation is complete;

2. Losses caused by permanent damage to ecological functions;

3. Costs of investigation, appraisal, and assessment of the damage to the ecological environment;

4. Costs of cleanup of the pollution and remediation of the ecological environment; and

5. Other reasonable costs incurred to prevent the occurrence or spread of the damage.

Chapter VIII Liability for Ultra-Hazardous Activities

Article 1236 [General Rule for Ultra-Hazardous Activity Liability]

A person who engages in ultra-hazardous operations and thereby causes harm to another person shall be liable in tort therefor.

Article 1237 [Liability for Harm Caused by Civil Nuclear Facilities or Materials]

Where a nuclear accident involving a civil nuclear facility or nuclear materials being transported into or out of such facility causes harm to another person, the operator of such facility shall be liable in tort therefor. However, the operator shall be relieved of such liability if able to prove that the harm resulted from such circumstances as war, armed conflict or riot, or that the injured party intentionally caused the harm.

Article 1238 [Liability for Harm Caused by Civil Aircraft]

Where a civil aircraft causes harm to another person, the operator of the aircraft shall be liable in tort therefor, but the operator shall be relieved of liability if able to prove that the injured party intentionally caused the harm.

Article 1239 [Liability for Harm Connected with Possession or Use of Ultra-Hazardous Materials]

Where the possession or use of flammable, explosive, highly toxic, highly radioactive, strongly corrosive or highly pathogenic materials, or other ultra-hazardous materials causes harm to another person, the possessor or user thereof shall be liable in tort therefor, but such a possessor or user shall be relieved of any liability if able to prove the injured party intentionally caused the harm or that the harm resulted from *force majeure*. Where the injured party is grossly negligent as to the occurrence of the harm, the liability of the possessor or user may be reduced.

Article 1240 [Liability for Damage Caused by Such Ultra-Hazardous Activities as Working at Height, Working at High Voltage, Working with High Pressure Equipment, Underground Excavation, or Use of High-Speed Rail (HSR)]

Where harm is caused to another person due to work at height, work at high voltage, work with high pressure equipment, or underground excavation activities, or use of high-speed rail transport vehicles, the operator shall be liable in tort therefor, but the operator shall be relieved of any liability if able to prove that the injured party intentionally caused the harm or that the harm resulted from *force majeure*. Where the injured party is grossly negligent as to the occurrence of the harm, the liability of the operator may be reduced.

Article 1241 [Liability for Damage Caused by Lost or Abandoned Ultra-Hazardous Materials]

Where harm is caused to another person by an ultra-hazardous material lost or abandoned, the owner shall be liable in tort therefor. Where the owner has delivered the ultra-hazardous material to another person for management, the tort liability therefor shall be borne by the manager, but the owner, if at fault, shall assume joint and several liability along with the manager.

Article 1242 [Liability for Damage Connected with Illegal Possession of Ultra-Hazardous Materials]

Where harm is caused to another person by an illegally possessed ultra-hazardous material, the illegal possessor shall be liable in tort therefor. The owner or manager of the material, if unable to prove fulfillment of a high duty of care to prevent the illegal possession, shall bear joint and several liability along with the illegal possessor .

Article 1243 [Liability for Failure to Ensure Security of Ultra-Hazardous Locations]

Where a person, without authorization, enters an area where ultra-hazardous activities are conducted or ultra-hazardous materials are stored and is injured thereby, the manager may be relieved of liability or only assume reduced liability if able to prove that adequate security measures have been taken and that the duty of adequate warning has been fulfilled.

Article 1244 [Limitation of Liability for Ultra-Hazardous Activities]

Provisions of laws that limit damages for liability incurred due to an ultra-hazardous activity shall apply, unless the actor causes harm intentionally or through gross negligence.

Chapter IX Liability for Harm Caused by Domestic Animals

Article 1245 [General Rules for Liability for Harm Caused by Domesticated Animals]

Where a domesticated animal causes harm to a person, the keeper/owner or person in charge of the animal shall be liable in tort therefor, but may be relieved of liability or bear reduced liability if able to prove that the injured party caused the harm intentionally or through gross negligence .

Article 1246 [Liability for Failure to Take Security Measures Against Animal Causing Harm]

A keeper or person in charge of an animal who, in violation of the rules of administration, does not take safety measures with respect to the animal and thereby causes harm to another person, shall be liable in tort therefor, but may have the liability reduced if able to prove that the injured party intentionally caused the harm.

Article 1247 [Liability for Harm Caused by Banned Dangerous Animal]

Where harm is caused to a person by banned dangerous animals such as a savage dog, the keeper or person in charge of the animal shall be liable in tort therefor.

Article 1248 [Liability for Harm Caused by Zoo Animals]

Where a zoo animal causes harm to a person, the zoo shall be liable in tort therefor, unless it can prove that it has fulfilled its management duties.

Article 1249 [Liability for Harm Caused by Animal Abandoned or Escaped]

Where an abandoned or escaped animal causes harm to a person during the period of abandonment or escape, the original keeper or person in charge of the animal shall be liable in tort therefor.

Article 1250 [Liability for Harm Caused by Animal Due to Third Party's Fault]

Where an animal causes harm to a person due to a third party's fault, the injured party may claim damages against the keeper or person in charge of the animal, or against the third party. A keeper or person in charge of the animal who has paid damages shall have the right to indemnification against the third party.

Article 1251 [Obligations Associated with Keeping of Animals]

Anyone who keeps an animal shall comply with laws and regulations, respect social virtues, and may not obstruct the lives of others.

Chapter X Liability for Harm Caused by Buildings and Objects

Article 1252 [Liability for Harm Caused by Collapse or Subsidence of Buildings, Structures or Other Facilities]

Where a building, structure, or other type of facility collapses or subsides and thus causes harm to a person, the project owner and the constructor shall be jointly and severally liable, unless they can prove the absence of defects in quality. Where another person should be held liable for the harm, the project owner or constructor who has paid damages shall have the right to indemnification against such person liable.

Where, due to the fault of the owner, manager, user or a third party, a building, structure or other facility collapses or subsides and thereby causes harm to another person, such owner, manager, user or third party shall be liable in tort therefor.

Article 1253 [Liability for Harm Caused by Dropping or Falling off of Buildings, Structures or Other Facilities and Objects Placed Thereupon or Hanging Thereto]

Where a building, structure, or other facility, or any object placed thereon or hanging thereto breaks loose, falls off or drops and thereby causes harm to a person, the owner, manager or user shall be liable in tort therefor if unable to prove absence of fault. Where another person should be held liable for the harm, the owner, manager or user who has paid damages shall have the right to indemnification against such person liable.

Article 1254 [Liability for Harm Caused by Object of Unknown Origin Thrown from Inside Building or Dropped from Building]

Throwing objects from inside a building is prohibited. Where an object thrown from inside a building or falling off a building causes harm to a person, the tortfeasor shall be liable in tort therefor per law. Where identifying a specific tortfeasor through investigation becomes difficult, any user of the building who may have caused the harm shall pay compensation, unless able to prove his/her innocence. After payment of compensation by the user or users of the building who may have caused the harm, such user or users shall have the right to indemnification against the tortfeasor.

The manager of a building, such as a property service firm, shall take necessary security measures to prevent the occurrence of such incidents as specified in the preceding paragraph; if no necessary security measures are in place, the manager of the building shall be liable in tort therefor per law for failure to perform the obligation of providing security measures.

Where an incident as specified in the first paragraph of this Article occurs, relevant authorities, such as a public security department, shall conduct a timely investigation per law and trace the person(s) responsible.

Article 1255 [Liability for Harm Caused by Stacked Objects Collapsing, Rolling over or Sliding]

Where a pile or stack of objects collapse, roll over or slide, and thereby cause harm to a person, the piler or stacker shall be liable in tort therefor if unable to prove an absence of fault.

Article 1256 [Liability for Harm Caused by Obstructions Placed, Dumped, Spilled or Dropped on Public Road]

Where a person causes harm to another person by piling up, dumping, spilling or dropping an object or a thing on a public road, and this obstructs passage, the actor shall be liable in tort therefor. A public road manager shall bear corresponding liability if unable to prove its fulfillment of duties, such as the duty of clean-up, protection and warning.

Article 1257 [Liability for Harm Caused by Broken or Fallen Trees or Fallen Fruits]

Where a broken or fallen tree or a fallen fruit causes harm to a person, the owner or manager of the tree shall be liable in tort therefor if unable to prove an absence of fault.

Article 1258 [Liability for Harm Caused by Construction Works in Public Place, Roadworks or by Such Underground Facilities as Manholes]

Where excavation of the ground or, repair or installation of underground facilities is conducted in a public place or on a public road, which causes harm to a person, the constructor shall be liable in tort therefor if unable to prove that an obvious warning sign has been posted and safety measures taken.

Where underground facilities, such as a utility access pit, cause harm to a person, the manager shall be liable in tort therefor if unable to prove its fulfillment of management responsibilities.

Supplementary Provisions

Article 1259 [Meanings of Legal Terms]

In the civil law, the terms 'above/or more/more than/no less than', 'not more than', 'within' and 'expiration/expire on' include the given figure; the terms 'less than/below', 'exceeding' and 'beyond' do not include the given figure.

Article 1260 [Date of Entry into Force and Entire Repeal of Old Laws]

This Code shall come into effect as of January 1, 2021. The Marriage Law of the People's Republic of China, the Succession Law of the People's Republic of China, the General Principles of the Civil Law of the People's Republic of China, the Adoption Law of the People's Republic of China, the Guarantee Law of the People's Republic of China, the Contract Law of the People's Republic of China, the Property Law of the People's Republic of China, the Tort Liability Law of the People's Republic of China, and the General Provisions of Civil Law of the People's Republic of China shall be simultaneously and entirely repealed.

M. Wan et al., *The Civil Code of the People's Republic of China*,
https://doi.org/10.1007/978-981-19-2794-2

Bibliography

1. 全国人大常委会法制工作委员会审定：《中华人民共和国民法典》（汉英双语版），法律出版社 2021 年版。

2.《中华人民共和国民法典》(大字条旨版)，法律出版社 2020 年版。

3. Georges Rouhette, Anne Rouhette-Berton, *French Civil Code*, 2006.

4. The Langenscheidt Translation Service, *German Civil Code*, juris GmbH, Saarbrücken, 2009.

M. Wan et al., *The Civil Code of the People's Republic of China*,
https://doi.org/10.1007/978-981-19-2794-2